GACE Middle Grades
012 Reading
Teacher Certification Exam

By: Sharon Wynne, M.S.

XAMonline, Inc.
Boston

To obtain permission(s) to use the material from this work for any purpose including workshops or seminars, please submit a written request to:

XAMonline, Inc.
25 First Street, Suite 106
Cambridge, MA 02141
Toll Free: 1-800-509-4128
Email: info@xamonline.com
Web www.xamonline.com
Fax: 1-617-583-5552

Library of Congress Cataloging-in-Publication Data

Wynne, Sharon A.
    GACE Middle Grades Reading 012: Teacher Certification / Sharon A. Wynne. 2nd ed.
    ISBN 978-1-58197-535-2
    1. GACE Middle Grades Reading 012.   2. Study Guides.   3. GACE
    4. Teachers' Certification and Licensure.   5. Careers

Disclaimer:
The opinions expressed in this publication are the sole works of XAMonline and were created independently from the National Education Association, Educational Testing Service, or any State Department of Education, National Evaluation Systems or other testing affiliates.

Between the time of publication and printing, state specific standards as well as testing formats and website information may change that is not included in part or in whole within this product. Sample test questions are developed by XAMonline and reflect similar content as on real tests; however, they are not former tests. XAMonline assembles content that aligns with state standards but makes no claims nor guarantees teacher candidates a passing score. Numerical scores are determined by testing companies such as NES or ETS and then are compared with individual state standards. A passing score varies from state to state.

Printed in the United States of America   œ-1

GACE: Middle Grades Reading 012
ISBN: 978-1-58197-535-2

Table of Contents

Great Study and Testing Tips!

What to study in order to prepare for the subject assessments is the focus of this study guide but equally important is *how* you study.

You can increase your chances of truly mastering the information by taking some simple, but effective steps.

Study Tips:

1. Some foods aid the learning process. Foods such as milk, nuts, seeds, rice, and oats help your study efforts by releasing natural memory enhancers called CCKs (*cholecystokinin*) composed of *tryptophan*, *choline*, and *phenylalanine*. All of these chemicals enhance the neurotransmitters associated with memory. Before studying, try a light, protein-rich meal that includes eggs, turkey, or fish. These foods release memory-enhancing chemicals. The better the connections, the more you comprehend.

Likewise, before you take a test, stick to a light snack of energy boosting and relaxing foods. A glass of milk, a piece of fruit, or some peanuts all release various memory-boosting chemicals and help you to relax and focus on the subject at hand.

2. Learn to take great notes. A by-product of our modern culture is that we have grown accustomed to getting our information in short doses (i.e. TV news sound bites or USA Today style newspaper articles.)

Consequently, we've subconsciously trained ourselves to assimilate information better in *neat little packages.* If your notes are scrawled all over the paper, it fragments the flow of the information. Strive for clarity. Newspapers use a standard format to achieve clarity. Your notes can be much clearer through use of proper formatting. A very effective format is called the *"Cornell Method."*

> Take a sheet of loose-leaf lined notebook paper and draw a line all the way down the paper about 1 inch to 2 inches from the left-hand edge.

> Draw another line across the width of the paper about 1 inch to 2 inches up from the bottom. Repeat this process on the reverse side of the page.

Look at the highly effective result. You have ample room for notes, a left hand margin for special emphasis items or inserting supplementary data from the textbook, a large area at the bottom for a brief summary, and a little rectangular space for just about anything you want.

3. Get the concept, then the details. Too often we focus on the details and don't gather an understanding of the concept. However, if you simply memorize only dates, places, or names, you may well miss the whole point of the subject.

A key way to understand things is to put them in your own words. If you are working from a textbook, automatically summarize each paragraph in your mind. If you are outlining text, don't simply copy the author's words.

Rephrase them in your own words. You remember your own thoughts and words much better than someone else's and subconsciously tend to associate the important details to the core concepts.

4. Ask *Why?* Pull apart written material paragraph by paragraph and don't forget the captions under the illustrations.

Example: If the heading is "Stream Erosion," flip it around to read "Why do streams erode?" Then answer the question.

If you train your mind to think in a series of questions and answers, not only will you learn more, but it also helps to lessen test anxiety because you are used to answering questions.

5. Read for reinforcement and future needs. Even if you only have 10 minutes, grab your notes and book. Your mind is a super computer; you have to input data in order to have it processed. *By rereading passages, you are creating neural connections for future retrieval.* The more times you read something, the more you reinforce the learning of ideas.

Even if you don't fully understand something on the first pass, *your mind stores much of the material for later recall.*

6. Relax to learn—Go into exile. Our bodies respond to an inner clock called biorhythms. Burning the midnight oil works well for some people, but not everyone.

If possible, set aside a particular place to study that is free of distractions. Shut off the television, cell phone, and pager and exile your friends and family during your study period.

If you really are bothered by silence, try background music. Light classical music at a low volume has been shown to aid in concentration over other types of music. Music that evokes pleasant emotions without lyrics is highly suggested. Try just about anything by Mozart. It relaxes you.

7. <u>**Use arrows not highlighters.**</u> At best, it's difficult to read a page full of yellow, pink, blue, and green streaks. Try staring at a neon sign for a while and you'll soon see that the horde of colors obscures the message.

A quick note, a brief dash of color, an underline, and an arrow pointing to a particular passage is much clearer than a horde of highlighted words.

8. <u>**Budget your study time.**</u> Although you shouldn't ignore any of the material, *allocate your available study time in the same ratio that topics may appear on the test.*

Testing Tips:

1. Get smart, play dumb. *Don't read anything into the question.* Don't make an assumption that the test writer is looking for something else than what is asked. Stick to the question as written and don't read extra things into it.

2. Read the question and all the choices *twice* before answering the question. You may miss something by not carefully reading, and then rereading, both the question and the answers.

If you really don't have a clue as to the right answer, leave it blank on the first time through. Go on to the other questions, as they may provide a clue as to how to answer the skipped questions.

If later on, you still can't answer the skipped ones . . . *Guess!* The only penalty for guessing is that you *might* get it wrong. Only one thing is certain; if you don't put anything down, you will get it wrong!

3. Turn the question into a statement. Look at the way the questions are worded. The syntax of the question usually provides a clue. Does it seem more familiar as a statement rather than as a question? Does it sound strange?

By turning a question into a statement, you may be able to spot if an answer sounds right, and it may also trigger memories of material you have read.

4. Look for hidden clues. It's actually very difficult to compose multiple-foil (choice) questions without giving away part of the answer in the options presented.

In most multiple-choice questions you can often readily eliminate one or two of the potential answers. This leaves you with only two real possibilities and automatically your odds go to fifty-fifty for very little work.

5. Trust your instincts. For every fact that you have read, you subconsciously retain at least some portion of that knowledge. On questions that you aren't really certain about, go with your basic instincts. *Your first impression on how to answer a question is usually correct.*

6. Mark your answers directly on the test booklet. Don't bother trying to fill in the optical scan sheet on the first pass through the test. *Just be very careful not to miss-mark your answers when you eventually transcribe them to the scan sheet.*

7. Watch the clock! You have a set amount of time to answer the questions. Don't get bogged down trying to answer a single question at the expense of 10 questions you can more readily answer.

DOMAIN I.   READING AND LITERATURE

COMPETENCY 1.0   UNDERSTAND LANGUAGE ACQUISITION, READING PROCESSES, AND THEORIES OF READING DEVELOPMENT

Skill 1.1   Demonstrate knowledge of fundamental processes of first- and second-language acquisition that relate to reading development

Children from families where English is not spoken may lack a solid understanding of its syntactic and visual structure. Therefore, as they are being recorded for progress using the oral running record, they may need additional support from their teacher and from an English Language reading specialist in examining the structure and meaning of English. Children from a non-native English Language speaking background may often pronounce words that make no sense to them and just go on reading. They have to learn to stop to construct meaning and may have to be prompted to self-correct.

Children from non-native English Language speaking backgrounds can benefit from independent reading opportunities to listen to a familiar story on tape and read along. This also gives them practice in listening to standard English oral reading. Often these children can begin to internalize the language structures by listening to the book on tape several times.

Highly proficient readers can sometimes support early readers through a partner relationship. Some children, particularly the emergent and beginning early readers, benefit from reading books with partners. The partners sit side by side and each one takes turns reading the entire text.

Audio books and author web resources provides special needs learners—those with visual or auditory handicapping conditions—with immediate contact with authors and direct sharing in the joy of storytelling. In addition to the accessibility of the keyboard, their responses to literature can be shared with a broad network of other readers, including close peers and distant peers. Technology literally enfranchises special needs learners into the circle of connected readers and writers.

In the classroom, there are numerous ways to determine which students are in need of additional assistance. The most effective methods include examining classroom performance, reviewing assessment data available, and working individually with the student.

When classroom teachers have concerns about the reading competency of students with whom they are working, they may seek out help from a reading specialist for additional strategies and support to help increase the students reading skills. It is important that the specialist be able to determine what difficulties require additional assistance, and in which specific areas of reading, in order to provide that assistance.

As previously discussed, running records are of tremendous value in helping in this area. This is a fast and efficient way to examine the type and number of errors the students are making. Also, the levels at which the students are able to read can be a warning flag. If a student is struggling with material several grade levels below their current grade it is important to determine the cause.

Once a general warning flag appears, it may be necessary for the specialist to administer additional skill-specific assessments or examine the data present in a more in-depth manner. In general, it's good to keep in mind the five larger areas of reading as a method of narrowing down the problem. These include: phonemic awareness, phonics, fluency, comprehension, and vocabulary.

Identifying which of these areas is causing the problems helps both the teacher and the specialist to determine an appropriate plan of action to address the skill deficits. Many children will demonstrate deficits in more than one area so it is critical to follow the appropriate skill sequence to move the students forward in the most efficient manner possible.

Even knowing the broad area of difficulty may not be enough in itself. Sometimes intensive skill-specific assessment or identification will need to occur before the instruction can begin. Other times, a more global approach would be prudent. For example, a global approach might be more beneficial with a student who has all of the phonics skills in isolation but has difficulty applying them in text. In this case, spending more time reteaching the phonics skills will not benefit the child. Rather, spending the time helping the child to use other cueing systems beyond phonics through reading many passages and texts would be more effective.

See also Skill 15.5.

Skill 1.2   Recognize the relationship between reading development and language development and between reading development and learning

Reading, writing, listening, and speaking are the four main components of language arts at any grade level. They are interrelated and they complement each other. By ensuring that all four of these strands are woven into your language arts classes, you can ensure that you provide a balance of experiences to give students the instruction and support they need. With such a balance, the students are able to integrate all of the English language processes and build on their prior knowledge and experiences.

Speaking and listening may be viewed as separate from reading and writing, but all four form the main communication system of the English language. They are *interdependent.* All other forms of communication depend on the ability to speak and listen. They are also the foundation for many other language skills, which is why teachers should provide ample opportunities for students to speak and listen in class as part of the daily routine. Classrooms are places where talk flows freely. By taking advantage of this talk to find out where students are in their thinking about topics, themes, and responses to literature, teachers can easily assess this component of language arts. When students can express ideas in their own words, it helps them to make meaning of their experiences with reading.

Although students don't have a lot of problems with speaking in class, listening often must be nurtured and taught. Good listeners will respond emotionally, imaginatively, and intellectually to what they hear. Students need to be taught how to respond to presentations by their classmates in ways that are not harmful or derogatory in any way. There are also different types of listening that the teacher can develop in the students:

- Appreciative listening to enjoy an experience

- Attentive listening to gain knowledge

- Critical listening to evaluate arguments and ideas

Within the classroom setting, many opportunities will present themselves for students to speak and listen for various purposes and often these may be spontaneous. Activities for speaking and listening should be integrated throughout the language arts program, but there should also be times when speaking and listening are the focus of the instruction. By incorporating speaking and listening into the language arts program, students will begin to see the connection between the two and thus improve their reading skills more efficiently.

Some of the ways that speaking and listening can be integrated include:

- Conversations
- Small group discussions
- Brainstorming
- Interviewing
- Oral reading
- Readers' theater
- Choral speaking
- Storytelling
- Role playing
- Book talks
- Oral reports
- Class debates
- Listening to guest speakers

Reading and writing are two interrelated aspects of language development. Students will read print and then realize that they can convey similar messages by using written language. The connections to the generally more formal language in reading and the same type of language the students will be asked to produce in writing are plentiful. Students can begin to draw phrases from text and the conventions of written language from reading before they are able to apply those same strategies in writing. By combining the two, and explicitly showing students these connections, teachers can develop both skills more rapidly.

Strategies for Promoting Awareness of the Relationship between Spoken and Written Language

- The teacher writes down what the children are saying on a chart.

- Highlight and celebrate the meanings, uses, and print products found in the classroom. These products include: posters, labels, yellow sticky pad notes, labels on shelves and lockers, calendars, rule signs, and directions.

- The intentional reading of big-print and oversized books to teach print conventions such as directionality.

- Practice exercises in reading to others (for grades K, 1, and 2) where young children practice how to handle a book, how to turn pages, how to find tops and bottoms of pages, and how to tell the difference between the front and back covers of a book.

- Have children match oral words to printed words by forming an echo chorus as the teacher reads the story aloud. They echo the reading. Often this works best with poetry or rhymes.

- Have the children combine, manipulate, switch, and move letters to change words and spelling patterns.

- Work with letter cards to create messages and respond to the messages that they create.

Search and discuss adventures in word awareness and close observation where children are challenged to identify and talk about the length, appearance, and boundaries of specific words.

Developing the writing skills of students is a complex process. As with any other aspect of teaching, it's important to provide as many realistic opportunities as possible. When students read for an authentic purpose, the reading becomes more important and there is an increased interest in completing the task. The same is true of writing.

In writing, teachers often spend time having the students complete journals, write stories, or complete other assignments. While all of these types of writing provide skill development and can be important to complete with students, it is when you can find ways to incorporate authentic and relevant writing that students can find the same increased interest and understand the importance of writing.

Sometimes in schools these realistic reasons to write automatically present themselves. There will be times when the students are dissatisfied with a rule or decision that has been made within the school. During such a situation, the students could expand upon their persuasive writing skills to attempt to change the rule with which they disagree.

In other cases, students may keep pen pal letters with children in another state or country. This type of correspondence, even if accomplished via email, develops letter-writing skills in a more realistic setting than asking the students to write a fictitious letter for the teacher.

Similarly, students could write and add their own books to the library or even write books to share with younger students. Writing contests would provide another more realistic reason for students to write.

In the end, it is not the type of writing to be completed or the reason for which it is completed that is important. It is the understanding that children take away from the process that writing has a purpose in society, that writing is a relevant skill that needs to be developed.

Using these authentic methods, children will begin to see the relevance in their own lives. They will then be able to come up with their own ideas and reasons to write. This takes the skill to the next level, that of application. Bringing students to the application level is the goal of education.

Skill 1.3   Demonstrate knowledge of major theories and current research relating to the reading process and reading instruction and current trends and issues in reading education

Decoding

In the late 1960s and early 1970s, many reading specialists, most prominently the linguist Charles C. Fries (1962), believed that successful decoding resulted in reading comprehension. This meant that if children could sound out the words, they would then automatically be able to comprehend the words. Many teachers of reading and many reading texts still subscribe to this theory.

Asking questions

Another theory or approach to the teaching of reading that gained currency in the late sixties and the early seventies was the importance of asking inferential and critical thinking questions of the reader which would challenge and engage the children in the text. This approach to reading went beyond the literal level of what was stated in the text to an inferential level of using text clues to make predictions and to a critical level of involving the child in evaluating the text. While asking engaging and thought-provoking questions is still viewed as part of the teaching of reading, it is only viewed currently as a component of the teaching of reading.

Comprehension "Skills"

As various reading theories, practices, and approaches percolated during the 1970s and 1980s, many educators and researchers in the field came to believe that the teacher of reading had to teach a set of discrete "Comprehension Skills" (Otto et al., 1977). Therefore, the reading teacher became the teacher of each individual comprehension skill. Children in such classrooms came away with: main idea, sequence, cause and effect, and other concepts that were supposed to make them better comprehenders. However, did it make them lifelong readers?

Transactional Approach

During the late 1970s and early 1980s, researchers in the field of education, psychology, and linguistics, began to examine how the reader comprehends. Among them was Louise Rosenblatt who posited that reading is a transaction between the reader and the text. It is Rosenblatt (1978) who explained successful reading as the reader constructing a meaning from the text that reflected both the reader and the text. She differentiates two separate modes in the experience of reading: *efferent* and *aesthetic*. They each have a distinct purpose. Efferent reading is looking for and remembering information to use functionally. Examples would be filling out a job application, reading a story in preparation for a test, or reading a newspaper article to find out who won the state basketball championship. Aesthetic reading is done to connect one's own life to the text, to be swept away by the beauty of a poem, or to respond emotionally to a book such as *Bridge to Terabithia.*

These differing purposes call for somewhat different reading strategies. For example, one might skim a newspaper article for basketball information but read a poem closely ten times and create mental images of different passages. Lastly, when children are asked to read all fiction differently (What's the setting? What's the main conflict in the plot? There will be a test on this on Thursday!), it can thwart a child's joy in the written word and work against the student's desire to be a lifelong reader.

Bottom-up, Top-down, Interactional Theories of Reading

Bottom-up theories of reading assume that children learn from part-to-whole starting with the smallest segments possible. Instruction begins with a strong phonics approach, learning letter–sound relationships and often using basal readers or *decodable books*. Decodable books are vocabulary controlled using language from word families with high predictability. Thus we get sentences like "Nan has a tan fan." Reading is seen as skills based, and the skills are taught one at a time.

Top-down theories of reading suggest that reading begins with the reader's knowledge, not the print. Children are seen as having a drive to construct meaning. This stance views reading as moving from the whole to the parts. An early top-down theory was the *whole word* approach. Children memorized high-frequency words to assist them in reading the *Dick and Jane* books of the 1930s.

Then teachers helped children discover letter–sound correspondences in what they read. A more recent top-down theory is the *whole language* approach. This approach was influenced by research on how young children learned language. It was thought that children could learn to read as naturally as they learned to talk. Children were surrounded by print in their classrooms, using quality literature often printed in Big Books. They were viewed as writers from the start. Advocates of whole language viewed the "skill 'em—drill 'em—kill 'em" approach based on bottom-up theories as a deadly dull introduction to the world of reading.

Interactive theories of reading combine the strengths of both bottom-up and top-down approaches. Right from students' earliest days in school, teachers must teach decoding, vocabulary, and comprehension skills that support children's drive for meaning and promote a stimulating exchange with high-quality literary texts. Strategies include shared, guided, and independent reading, Big Books, reading and writing workshops, and the like. Today this approach is called the *Balanced Literacy Approach.* It is considered to be a synthesis of the best from bottom-up and top-down methods.

Literacy and Literacy Learning

To be literate in the 21st century means more than being able to read and write. To live well and happily in today's society, one must be able to read not only newspapers and books, but e-mails, blogs, directions for cell phone use, and the like. There is a "disconnect" between the isolated reading comprehension skills the schools were teaching and the literacy skills including listening and speaking that are crucial for employment and personal and academic success. Thornburg (1992, 2003) has also noted that technology capacities and the ability to communicate online are now integral parts of our sense of literacy.

Cooper (2004) views literacy as reading, writing, thinking, listening, viewing, and discussing. These are not viewed as separate activities or components of instruction, but rather as developing and being nurtured simultaneously and interactively. Children learn these abilities by engaging in authentic explorations, readings, projects and experiences.

Just as the child learning to ride a bike goes through various approximations before learning how to actually ride, the reader uses the scaffold (support) of the teacher to go through various approximations before developing his/her own independent literacy skills and capacities..

Emergent Literacy. This concept states that young children are emerging into reading and writing with no real beginning or ending point. Children are introduced into the word of print as soon as their parents read board books to them at the age of one or two. When children scribble write or use invented spelling during their preschool years, they reveal themselves as detectives of the written word, having watched parents and teachers make lists, write thank-you notes, or leave messages. This view of the reader assumes that all children have a drive to make meaning out of print and will begin doing it almost on their own if surrounded by a print-rich environment.

Reading Readiness. In contrast to emergent literacy, this approach assumes that all children must have mastered a sequence of reading skills *before* they can begin to read.

Language Acquisition. This is continuous and never-ending. From the perspective of this theory and research, all children come to school with a language base upon which the school must build. Since oral language and reading are connected, it is important that schools build literacy experiences around the language the child brings to the school.

Prior Knowledge, Schemata, Background, and Comprehension

Schemata are structures that represent generic concepts stored in our memory (Rumelhart 1980). Young children develop their schemata through experiences.

Prior knowledge and the lack of experiences in some cases influence comprehension. The more closely the reader's experiences and schemata approximate those of the writer, the more likely the reader is to comprehend the text. Schemata deficits among children from other-language backgrounds or struggling socio-economic family structures indicate the need for intense teacher support as these children become emergent and early readers.

Often the teacher will have to model and scaffold for the child the steps to form a schemata from the information provided in a text.

Comprehension

Cooper defines comprehension as "a strategic process by which readers construct or assign meaning to a text by using the clues in the text and their own prior knowledge." We view comprehension as a process where the reader transacts with the text to construct or assign meaning. Reading and writing are both interconnected and mutually supportive. Comprehension is a strategic process in which readers adjust their reading to suit their reading purpose and the type or genre of text they are reading. Narrative and expository texts require different reading approaches because of their different text structures.

Strategic readers also call into play their metacognitive capacities as they analyze texts so that they are aware of the skills needed to construct meaning from the text structure.

The Role of Literature in Developing Literacy

The Balanced Literacy Approach advocates the use of "real literature"—recognized works from the best children's fiction and non-fiction trade books and winners of such awards as the Newbery and Caldecott medals for helping children develop literacy.

Balanced literacy advocates argue that:

- Real literature engages young readers and assures that they will become lifelong readers.

- Real literature also offers readers a language base that can help them expand their expressiveness as readers and as writers.

- Real literature is easier to read and understand than grade-leveled texts

There are districts in the United States where the phonics-only approach is heavily embedded. However, the majority of school districts would describe their approach to reading as the Balanced Literacy Approach which includes phonics work as well as the use of real literature texts. To contrast the phonics and Balanced Literacy Approaches as opposite is inaccurate, since a balanced approach includes both.

It is important to go online and to visit the key resources of the National Council of Teachers of English (NCTE) and the International Reading Association (IRA) to keep abreast of the latest research in the field.

Skill 1.4 Recognize interrelationships among reading, writing, listening, speaking, viewing, and visually representing

Reading for enjoyment makes it possible to mentally go to places in the world we may never be able to physically visit. Additionally, once we learn, through reading, about the enchantments of a particular place, we might set a goal of going there someday. When *Under the Tuscan Sun* by Frances Mayes was published, it became a best seller. It also increased tourism to Italy. Many of the readers of that book visited Italy for the first time in their lives.

In fiction, we can live through experiences that we may never encounter. We delve into feelings that are similar to our own or are so far removed from our own that we are filled with wonder and curiosity. In fact, we read because we're curious—curious to visit, experience, and know new and different things. The reader lives with a crowd of people and a vast landscape. Life is constantly being enriched by the reading, and the mind is constantly being expanded. To read is to grow.

Sometimes the experience of reading a particular book or story is so delicious that we go back and read it again and again, such as the works of Jane Austen. We keep track of what is truly happening in the world when we read current best-sellers because they not only reflect current interests, they can influence trends. We can know in depth what television news cannot cram in by reading publications like *Time* and *Newsweek,* either printed or online.

How do we model this wonderful gift for our students? We can bring those interesting stories into our classrooms and share the excitement we feel when we discover them. We can relate things that make us laugh so students may see the humor and laugh with us. We can vary the established curriculum to include something we are reading that we want to share. The tendency of students nowadays is to receive all of their information from television or the internet. It's important for the teacher to help students understand that television and the internet are not substitutes for reading. They should be an accessory, an extension, and a springboard for reading.

Another thing teachers can do to inspire students to become readers is to assign a book they have never read before and read along with them, chapter by chapter. Run a contest in which the winner gets to pick a book that teacher and students will read chapter by chapter. If the teacher is excited about it and is experiencing satisfaction from the reading, that excitement will be contagious. Be sure that the discussion sessions allow for students to relate what they are thinking and feeling about what they are reading. Lively discussions and the opportunity to express feelings will lead to more spontaneous reading.

The teacher can also hand out a reading list of his/her favorite books and spend some time telling the students what he/she liked about each. Make sure the list is diverse. It's good to include nonfiction along with fiction. Don't forget that a good biography or autobiography may encourage students to read beyond thrillers and detective stories.

When the class is discussing the latest movie, whether formally as a part of the curriculum or informally, if the movie is based on a book, this is a good opportunity to demonstrate how much more can be derived from the reading than from watching. The teacher can also point out that the two experiences combined make the story more satisfying and worthwhile. Share with students the excitement you have for reading. Successful writers are usually good readers. The two go hand-in-hand.

To discover multiple layers of meaning in a literary work, the first step is a thorough analysis, examining such things as setting, characters and characterization, plot (focusing particularly on conflicts and pattern of action), theme, tone, figures of speech, and symbolism. It is useful, in looking for underlying themes, to consider the author's biography, particularly with regard to setting and theme, and the date and time of the writing, paying particular attention to literary undercurrents at the time as well as political and social milieu.

Once the analysis is complete and data accumulated on the historical background, determine the overt meaning. What does the story say about the characters and their conflicts, where does the climax occur, and is there a denouement? Once the forthright, overt meaning is determined, then begin to look for undercurrents, sub-themes that are related to the author's life and to what is going on in the literary, political, and social background at the time of writing.

In organizing the presentation, it's usually best to begin with an explanation of the overt meaning and then follow up with the other messages that emerge from the text.

To *interpret* means essentially to read with understanding and appreciation. It is not as daunting as it is made out to be. Simple techniques for interpreting literature are as follows:

- **Context:** This includes the author's feelings, beliefs, past experiences, goals, needs, and physical environment. Incorporate an understanding of how these elements may have affected the writing to enrich an interpretation of it.

- **Symbols:** Also referred to as a sign, a symbol designates something which stands for something else. In most cases, it represents something that has a deeper meaning than its literal denotation. Symbols can have personal, cultural, or universal associations. Use an understanding of symbols to unearth a meaning the author might have intended but not expressed, or even something the author never intended at all.

- **Questions:** Asking questions, such as "How would I react in this situation?" may shed further light on how students feel about the work.

A common fallacy in reasoning is the *post hoc ergo propter hoc* ("after this, therefore because of this") or the false-cause fallacy. This occurs in cause/effect reasoning, which may either go from cause to effect or effect to cause. It happens when an inadequate cause is offered for a particular effect, when the possibility of more than one cause is ignored, and when a connection between a particular cause and a particular effect is not made. An example of a *post hoc*: "Our sales shot up 35 percent after we ran that television campaign; therefore, the campaign caused the increase in sales." It might have been a cause, of course, but more evidence is needed to prove it.

COMPETENCY 2.0   UNDERSTAND THE CHARACTERISTICS OF A VARIETY OF GENRES AND TYPES OF LITERATURE AND INFORMATIONAL TEXTS

Skill 2.1   Identify the characteristics of major literary genres including poetry, drama, and prose (e.g., short story, novel, historical fiction, and science fiction)

Authors use various methods to tell a story while employing various literary techniques. If teachers want students to understand the technique, they need to teach them the characteristics of each narrative genre. It may be necessary to draw the students' attention to the elements and structure of narratives as well to the strategies they can use for reading each of the genres. Before students actually read a selection, the teacher can prepare students by addressing relevant literary techniques, writing forms, and vocabulary in mini-lessons to provide the students with knowledge about what they will be reading. This helps students to become more engaged with the text and to have an idea of what they should think about as they are reading.

Narrative Genres

Prose Fiction. This is literature about imaginary people, places, and events. The purpose of this narrative genre is to stimulate the students' imaginations and to present the author's view of the world. This genre includes novels, short stories, and plays, each of which has its own distinctive characteristics. They all have a setting, conflict, plot, climax, and resolution, to varying degrees.

Short Story. This narrative usually has only one focus and a smaller world view. The students do have to determine whether the person telling the story is a narrator or is a character within the story. They do have to take note of the central conflict and determine why the characters act as they do. As a response to the story, they can decide how they feel about the characters and their actions and ask questions about the message the author is trying to convey in the story.

Novel. A novel is a longer version of the short story, often with sub-plots. During the reading the students have to be able to keep the subplots separated and understand their relationship to the main plot of the novel. They must be aware of the motives of the various characters and of their reactions to the characters' actions.

Prose Non-fiction. This is literature that is about real events, times, and places. It includes essays, journals, articles, letters, biographies, and autobiographies. Much of contemporary nonfiction reads like fiction with suspense, expression, and ingenuity of style. Because it is vivid and personal, it can provide the students with a model for their own writing. When students are reading for information, they need to keep this purpose in mind and may need time and instruction to help them summarize or restate the main ideas.

Poetry. In this form of literature, the author communicates ideas and feelings through composition written in verse. Poetry can be used to capture a mood, tell a story, or explore different ideas. There are various literary techniques authors use in writing poetry which the teacher can discuss with the class through mini-lessons.

Plays. These can be read for the purpose of performance or for literary effect. Students pay attention to the literary devices that the author uses. When reading a play, students can work on putting expression into their reading so that they can bring the characters to life.

Types of Text

There are six different types of texts that are usually used in a school setting. Each type of text has a specific use within the classroom depending on the purpose for reading set forth by the teacher. The *types* of texts vary from the *genres* of reading and should not be confused.

Wordless Books. Wordless picture books are generally used to increase discussion and develop vocabulary. These books are good for generating ideas for writing or discussions among students. They provide pictures filled with details to serve as a springboard to oral language development or increasing the quality of description in writing.

Predictable Texts. Predictable texts allow the beginning reader to feel rapid success with the process of reading.. They provide the same words or phrases repeated over and over so that students can participate in the act of reading. They are also generally very much enjoyed by students due to the natural rhythm that develops by the repetitions. However, this type of text should be moved through rapidly so that children begin to attend to the words in reading and not rely on their auditory memory alone for what comes next.

Controlled Vocabulary Texts. Texts of this nature are usually used to increase student vocabulary with the use of high-frequency words. This sight word reading vocabulary is critical to later success with more advanced reading tasks. This type of book generally has a very slim plot or story line and is more beneficial for word recall than for building comprehension.

Decodable Texts. Decodable texts are comprised of specific phonics skills. There is usually a range of these books spanning a great many different phonics skills. The stories are usually progressive as the skills learned in earlier books are reinforced in later books. As with controlled vocabulary texts, these books rarely have well developed story lines and are not well suited to comprehension development. They do, however, have a significant place in helping students unlock the code to reading.

Authentic Literature. This is the type of reading that most people are familiar with and is the typical goal of all reading. All children should have the experience of reading authentic literature and real stories. These can be fiction or nonfiction but provide numerous details and allow for the development of comprehension skills. They range in difficulty and length, but are at the core of reading.

Created, Easy-to-Read Texts. This last text type would encompass teacher-created reading passages or books to fill a specific purpose within the curriculum for all or a group of students.

Students should be aware of the purpose for reading so they know what thinking is expected of them. When reading any text, students need to employ certain strategies. Therefore teachers need to engage the students in the reading process and model the appropriate strategies of:

- Connecting
- Making meaning
- Questioning
- Predicting
- Inferring
- Reflecting
- Evaluating

Skill 2.2   Recognize the elements of fiction (e.g., plot, character, setting, and theme)

In fiction, writers use various elements to gain reader interest. The elements a fiction author uses in developing the narrative include:

- Plot
- Character
- Setting
- Theme

When readers understand these elements, they will have a greater understanding and appreciation for the fictional text. These elements help readers to segment the story and blend the story into a whole. The knowledge of these elements is necessary for readers to be able to discuss and respond to the text.

Plot. Plot is an attribute shared by novels, short stories, and plays. Plot is *not* the same thing as *story*. *Story* is merely a synopsis of the temporal order of what happens in a narrative, while *plot* is the events and actions in the narrative performed by its character. Usually, the plot develops from the conflicts in the story. There are several different types of conflict that can be found within a work of fiction including

- Person versus person—external conflict that develops among two or more characters

- Person versus self—internal conflict in which a character is torn with regards to his/her feelings, actions, beliefs, or emotions

- Person versus nature—external conflict in which a character battles the forces of nature

The plot develops as the character makes choices and decisions affecting the outcome of the story. Complications can also develop in the plot which are the twists and turns that keep the readers captivated. Other elements of plot include:

- Rising action—the series of events leading up to the turning point of the story

- Climax—the turning point where the conflict is just about to be resolved

- Falling action—the way the conflicts are resolved bringing the story to a close.

Character. The characters in a story are an integral part of the plot. It is through the author's words that the reader comes to know the characters, their thoughts, feelings, and the reasons they act the way they do. The reader can also learn what the characters looks like because the author offers a description through the words of the text.

There are various types of characters in any fictional text. There is usually a protagonist who is the main character, and an antagonist who is in conflict with the protagonist. Characters can also be round or flat. A round character is one that is fully developed in the story and is often prone to change. A flat character is usually a one-dimensional character not central to the story line.

The author reveals the characters by showing their thoughts and actions through words and by telling what others think and say about them.

Setting. The setting is where the story takes place. There can be several different settings in one story. The author describes the setting of the story by using imagery and colorful words in order to give the reader a visual representation of the area. The setting can also be a time period which is important to understanding why and how the characters act the way they do.

Theme. The theme of a story is the central message the author wished to convey. Sometimes the theme may be directly stated and at other times, it may be inferred through the thoughts and actions of the character(s). It can be a revelation into the insight of people in general, or an opinion on a way of life. It is not, however, the moral of the story. There are certain requirements for an idea to be the central theme of a text:

1. It must be related to all the elements of the story.
2. It cannot be contradicted by any details presented in the story.
3. It has to be supported by evidence from the text.

Skill 2.3   Analyze how literary devices (e.g., imagery, simile, metaphor, foreshadowing, hyperbole, and refrain) contribute to an author's purpose, meaning, and style

Instruction in the meaning of literary elements and how to recognize them in a work of fiction leads the reader to greater understanding into the author's purpose, meaning, and style. When students read several works by the same author, they can see how the author tends to use the same types of literary devices to accomplish his/her mission in writing.

Literary Devices Used in Fiction

Imagery.   Imagery is the language that authors use to describe something in detail. It includes the setting of a story or a description of a character. The words used are intended to create visual representations in the reader's mind; they include sensory words as well as those describing sound. Imagery is more than simple description; it activates all five senses in readers.

Simile. A simile is a phrase used to directly compare two things that are not alike in most ways but are similar in one important way. It is used to help the reader understand what something looks, feels, smells, tastes, or sounds like. The words *like* or *as* must be present for the phrase to be considered a simile. For example, "The sky was like a ball of fire" tells the reader the sky was red. The two things being compared are the sky and fire--two unrelated objects and the word *like* makes the comparison.

Metaphor. A metaphor is an indirect comparison between two objects that are not alike but, unlike a simile, it doesn't involve the use of the words *like* or *as*. It says that one object is another, such as saying "Education is a gateway to success."

Foreshadowing. In some fictional texts, there are clues throughout the story telling the reader something is about to happen. Future events and sometimes the outcome of the story are foretold by the author so that the readers can expect certain things to happen. There are many different ways in which an author can accomplish foreshadowing. Foreshadowing can be direct or subtle.

Hyperbole. This is the use of exaggeration, through which the author strives to make a point or to convey a description to the reader. In hyperbole the exaggeration is extreme, and usually conveys positive or negative images.

Refrain. A refrain is a repetition in the story. In books for early readers, there is usually a phrase repeated at regular intervals so that when the reader reaches that point, he/she already knows the words and can read along.

Skill 2.4 **Identify the characteristics of major nonfiction genres (e.g., essay, biography, autobiography, memoir, and editorial) and types of informational texts (e.g., textbook and news article) including common textual features (e.g., paragraphs, topic sentences, concluding sentences, and glossary) and graphic features (e.g., maps, charts, diagrams, and illustrations) of nonfiction and informational texts**

Nonfiction Genres

Essay. An essay is a short work of nonfiction giving the author's opinion on a specific topic. While nonfiction essays are expository, they also tend to be subjective and can include narrative. Essays can also be literary criticism, political manifestos, arguments, observations, or even personal reflections. Quite often the first exposure students have to an essay is the five paragraph essay, which consists of an introductory paragraph, three paragraphs about the topic and a concluding paragraph. There are also different types of academic essays:

- Descriptive—provides a vivid picture of a location, person, object, event, or debate

- Narrative—tells a story as a way of presenting a point of view or opinion on a topic

- Compare and contrast —develops the relationship between two or more objects

- Persuasive—attempts to persuade the reader to accept or agree with an idea or a point of view

- Argumentative—argues one side of an issue, giving supporting evidence

Biography. A biography is a written account of a person's life. It usually highlights specific aspects of personality, gives insight into events in the person's life, and often includes intimate details that are not widely known. A biography is written about a person by a different author and, because of this, is written from the third person point of view.

Autobiography. An autobiography is an account of a person's life written by that person. When one is telling about one's life, the opinions expressed may be biased as the author is telling about his/her own life. Therefore events may be exaggerated or events may be omitted. It is written from the first person point of view.

Memoir. A memoir is a type of autobiography, but usually deals with only one or two aspects of the author's life. It is not as structured as an autobiography because it is usually about only one portion of the author's life rather than the entire life. Like the autobiography, a memoir is usually written from the first person point of view.

Editorial. An editorial is a statement or a news article written by a news organization. It expresses the opinion of the editor, editorial board, or the publisher on topics of interest to the readers. They often address current events or public controversies. Such writing is usually short, and is always labeled an editorial. There is no byline, but it does say that the information contained in the piece is the opinion of the writer and does not reflect that of the organization as a whole.

Textbook. A textbook presents information for the formal study of a subject area and includes many different topics. The book is divided into chapters, each one focusing on a specific topic. There are many features in a textbook, such as a table of contents, index, and glossary, along with photos, charts, maps, and diagrams.

News Article. A news article presents factual information usually about recent events or happenings or on an item of interest to the readers. Fundamental to these writing is answering the Five Ws (*Who? What? When? Where?* and *Why?*) and *How?* News articles may be accompanied by photos or illustrations.

Textual Features. To make the most of their reading experiences, students need to know the various features of texts that can help them understand the material. These include:

- **Paragraphs**—Ideas are arranged into paragraphs with each paragraph centered around one main idea. There is a beginning sentence, three or four supporting sentences and a concluding sentence. The *topic sentence* is usually the first sentence, but it can be anywhere in the paragraph. All the other sentences are designed to provide more information about the topic sentence. They give details, reasons, and examples to support the topic. The *concluding sentence* brings closure to the paragraph and restates the main point of the paragraph.

- **Glossary**—This section of a text provides definitions for words in the text. Throughout the text, words included in the glossary are written in bold type so that they are easily identified.

- **Graphic Features**—Some of the graphic features included in texts are maps, charts, diagrams, and illustrations designed to elaborate on information presented in the text.

Skill 2.5 **Identify common organizational structures (e.g., chronological order, logical order, and cause and effect) of informational texts**

Common organizational structures of informational texts include such things as:

- **Chronological Order** —a listing of events as they happen from beginning to end.

- **Logical Order**—the physical order of the text; differs according to topic. In some informational texts the information can be arranged in alphabetical order or in order of importance.

- **Cause and Effect**—a type of informational text discussing the topic in terms of what causes it or what it causes and the effect this has on other objects or people

COMPETENCY 3.0   UNDERSTAND LITERARY TEXTS FROM VARIOUS GENRES, CULTURES, AND TIME PERIODS AND HOW TO USE EVIDENCE AND MAIN IDEAS AS THE BASIS FOR INTERPRETATION

Skill 3.1   Analyze language, character development, setting, theme, mood, tone, point of view, foreshadowing, irony, and other elements in literary texts

See Competency 2.0.

Skill 3.2   Analyze figurative language in literary texts (e.g., rhyme, alliteration, personification, metaphor, and simile)

Metaphor and simile are covered in Skill 2.3.

Rhyme—The repetition of a sound, rhyme is most often used in poetry so the ends of the lines match each other in sound. Examples include rhyming couplets, ballads, and nursery rhymes.

Alliteration—A literary device in which all the words in a list or a sentence begin with the same letter. When used in poetry, it gives the text a musical quality; when used in prose, it can add humor to the text.

Personification—Giving life to inanimate objects. In prose and poetry it tends to infer that inanimate objects perform human actions, such as in the statement "The tree branches waved in the wind."

Skill 3.3   Demonstrate knowledge of inference and interpretation skills applied to literary texts and how to support inferences (e.g., about setting, characters, and events) with convincing evidence from text

Teaching children to make inferences must begin at the word level and then can be broadened to more complex concepts. From a very young age, students can evaluate the textual and picture information provided within the stories to make appropriate inferences.

It is important to remember that the process of making an inference about anything related to a story requires the reader to utilize their prior knowledge and information presented within the story to draw a conclusion. These conclusions may be unique to each student because each person's prior knowledge will be different. Therefore, it is important children understand the components of making an inference.

These components include:

- Looking back at the words/pictures

- Paying close attention to the words

- Using what they already know

- Thinking about what makes sense with what they know, see, and have read

It is important to provide children with structured opportunities to practice confirming their inferences/predictions. If they can find confirmation or contradictions, within the text, it helps them to use the information to become more strategic readers. Inferences will need to be made when students are reading and come to unknown items. It is an important skill to develop.

Skill 3.4 Analyze the ways in which a literary work reflects the traditions, perspectives, and culture of a particular group of people or time period

There are many different types of literature available throughout our world. See Skill 3.5 for listing of different types of literature and some examples of ways they incorporate traditions, perspectives, and cultures into the genres.

Many authors use their work to reflect a culture, show a perspective or share a message. For some books, this can become an issue at a later date and time. Some things, which are an accepted part of the culture at the time of the work's publication, later become unacceptable. This has resulted in these books becoming the subject of controversy. An example of this would be some of the works by Mark Twain. Language used by authors is another example of a way in which literature can be used to reflect a particular group of people. The book *The Outsiders* uses gang slang terms, which were common when the book was written. However, today's youth may not recognize or relate to the terms. This is the unique effect literature has in our society. The ability to freeze time and make it available to generations yet to come, or in some other cases to predict the future, is a legacy literature has to offer.

Skill 3.5   Compare and contrast traditional literature with mythology, folktales, and legends from different cultures

Traditional literature is that which is defined as being handed down through the generations. Although it does include mythology and folktales, it also includes jokes, riddles, superstitions, proverbs, moral tales, fables, and parables.

Mythology is related to religious and cultural literature and is made up of a group of stories about the official beliefs of a culture or religion. For example, myths attempt to explain the origin of the world, why various phenomena occur in nature, the origin of civilizations, the end of the world, and the relationship between gods and ordinary people. There are certain characteristics of myths that show how they are different from traditional literature. Once they are written down they do not change and they retain their original features. In mythology, animals usually portray human characteristics.

Folktales, while they are a form of traditional literature, do change according to the region in which they originated. The same folktale from different regions can have different characters and problems that are unique to those regions. There are several different types of folktales:

- Fairy tales

- Nonsensical stories

- Explanatory tales

- Talking animal tales

- Realistic tales

- Religious tales

- Formula tales that follow a pattern, such as the Gingerbread Boy

Legends are stories of human heroes and, although there may be gods in the stories, the main characters are human. In the legends of old, the main characters are almost always men, although there are a few legends with women heroines. The tales of the Greek heroes fall into the legends category as do the Norse sagas. Through reading legends, teachers can help students understand various cultures and their beliefs.

COMPETENCY 4.0 UNDERSTAND METHODS FOR PROMOTING LITERACY AS A LIFELONG SKILL

Skill 4.1 Identify factors in the classroom that influence students' reading (e.g., language-rich and print-rich classroom environments, grouping procedures, types of reading tasks, and high-interest reading choices)

The creation of the meeting area and the reading chair (sometimes a rocking chair) with throw pillows around it promotes a love of reading. Beyond that, some classrooms have adopted an author's hat, decorated with the pictures of famous authors and book characters which children wear when they read from their own works.

Many classrooms also have children's storyboards, artwork, story maps, pop-up books, and "in the style of" writing inspired by specific authors. Some teachers buy calendars for the daily schedule which celebrate children's authors or types of literature. Children are also encouraged to bring in public library books and special books from their home libraries. The teacher can model this habit of sharing beautiful books and inviting stories from his/her home library.

In addition, news stories about children's authors, series books, television versions of books, theatrical film versions of books, stuffed toy book character decorations and other memorabilia related to books can be used to decorate the room

Various chain book stores including Barnes and Nobles and Borders give out free book marks and promotional display materials related to children's books which can be available in the room for children to use as they read independently or in their guided groups. They might even use these artistic models to inspire their own book themed artifacts.

Skill 4.2 **Identify ways to cultivate students' enthusiasm for reading (e.g., book clubs, discussion groups, reading incentives, author studies, plays, reader's theater, and literature circles) and their interest in exploring a variety of reading materials**

In choosing materials, teachers should also keep in mind that not only do students learn at different rates, they bring a variety of cognitive styles to the learning process. Prior experiences influence the individual's cognitive style, or method of accepting, processing, and retaining information. According to Marshall Rosenberg, students can be categorized as:

a) rigid-inhibited

b) undisciplined

c) acceptance-anxious

d) creative

"The creative learner is an independent thinker, one who maximizes his/her abilities, can work by his/herself, enjoys learning, and is self-critical." This last category constitutes the ideal, but teachers should make every effort to use materials that will stimulate and hold the attention of learners of all types.

Aside from textbooks, there is a wide variety of materials available to today's teachers. Personal computers with high-speed connections are becoming more commonplace in school classrooms and libraries, and teachers can bring alive the content of a reference book in text, motion, and sound. Videocassettes (VCRs) and digital video discs (DVDs) are common and permit the use of home-produced or commercially produced materials. Textbook publishers often provide films, recordings, and software to accompany the text, as well as maps, graphics, overhead transparencies, and colorful posters to help students visualize what is being taught. To stay current in the field, teachers can usually scan the educational publishers' brochures that arrive at their principal's or department head's office on a frequent basis. Another way to stay current is by attending workshops or conferences. Teachers will be enthusiastically welcomed on those occasions when educational publishers are asked to display their latest products and revised editions of materials.

In addition, yesterday's libraries are today's media centers. Teachers can usually have opaque projectors delivered to the classroom to project print or pictorial images (including student work) onto a screen for classroom viewing. Some teachers have chosen to replace chalkboards with projectors that reproduce the print or images present on the plastic sheets known as transparencies, which the teacher can write on during a presentation or have machine-printed in advance. In either case, the transparency can easily be stored for later use. In an art or photography class, or any class in which it is helpful to display visual materials, slides can easily be projected onto a wall or a screen. Some teachers are using their computers to create their own electronic presentations using programs like Microsoft PowerPoint or Adobe Acrobat.

Cameras are inexpensive enough to enable students to photograph and display their own work, as well as keep a record of their achievements in teacher files or student portfolios.

Studies have shown that students learn best when what is taught in lecture and textbook reading is presented more than once in various formats. In some instances, students themselves may be asked to reinforce what they have learned by completing some original production—for example, by writing a monologue or dialogue to express what some historical figure might have said on some occasion or by acting out (and perhaps filming) episodes from a classroom reading selection. Students usually enjoy having their work displayed or presented to an audience of peers. Thus, their productions may supplement and personalize the learning experiences the teacher has planned for them.

Skill 4.3   Identify strategies for learning about and using students' personal interests to motivate and enhance their independent reading

Asking students to complete an interest survey will give the teacher clues as to what themes or topics he/she can use when looking for age- and grade-appropriate literature for the classroom. Reading conferences are another way teachers can find out what students like to read. Teachers can compile a class list of favorite books and display it in the classroom. One activity that doubles as a literacy response and an enhancement for other students is to have the students rate a book and recommend it for others to read.

Skill 4.4 **Recognize the value of inquiry and demonstrate knowledge of strategies for helping students use reading to set and pursue their own research goals, select resources, investigate topics, organize and interpret data, and present their conclusions**

Although there may be times when teachers do not want students to read certain books texts, it is important to respect their choices when selecting reading material. Good readers often choose to read easy material simply because they do not want to be challenged. On the other hand, students who have difficulty in reading at grade level may be reluctant to read lower level books because it reinforces the knowledge that they cannot read as well as their peers. When they are unable to read material at grade level, it sets up a cycle of failure.

Teachers should try to have adequate reading material in the classroom library to meet the needs of the varying reading levels in the class. There should be a variety of reading material matching the themes and topics. By letting students know what their reading level is and pointing them in the right direction, it will help them experience success and therefore keep them reading.

The most important thing is that students are reading. Comic books in the classroom are perfectly acceptable as long as students are reading.

There are many ways teachers can encourage reading for pleasure in their classrooms. One of the best ways is to read aloud from a novel each day. Author studies in all grades will encourage students to seek out books by that author and read them on their own.

Even within the content areas, there is a wealth of fiction that relates to the theme at hand and provides students with background information that will help them with their studies. For example, when studying Colonial America in Social Studies, there are many illustrated books teachers can use as introductions for the lessons. Using part of the class to read aloud from a novel about that period in history will help students to develop an interest in reading about the themes and help them understand how much enjoyment reading can bring.

Monthly book clubs are also an excellent way of getting age-appropriate reading material into students' hands. Since these book clubs offer the books at fairly inexpensive prices, parents realize they can get more value for their money when they order each month. Book fairs at school provide students the chance to win books for themselves and their classrooms.

Read-a-thons encourage reading because the students realize that they are helping a cause by reading. Some of these offers include prizes for students. The teacher or school could initiate this kind of motivation.

Responding to literature is one of the most important parts of reading. By the responses students give to what they have read, teachers can determine the level of comprehension. It takes practice for students to be able to respond critically to a text because they have the idea that all published authors are perfect and they should not criticize what they write.

Some of the strategies teachers can use to provide opportunities for students to give creative and personal responses to their reading include:

1. Reading Conferences—Ask a student to read a section of the text and then explain to you why he/she chose that section. Teachers can also ask students why they are reading a certain book or ask about their favorite author.

2. Reading Surveys—Teachers can devise a list of questions to find out what students are reading, how they decide what books to read, and how students feel about the topics or language used in the book.

3. Daily Reading Time—This could be a set time when everyone in the class, including the teacher, is reading, or it could be a center activity for a small group of children.

4. Literature Circles—Using the role sheets developed by Harvey Daniels in Voice and Choice in a Student-Centered Classroom, students take on different roles each day. They discuss the chapter or book, find new vocabulary words, illustrate a scene or pose questions for the group.

5. Reader's Theatre—Students adapt part of the book or story and make it into a choral reading with expression that shows how they felt about what they have read.

Responding to literature does not always take the form of written responses. In a Reader's Workshop, students can choose to respond to what they read by using art, painting, song, dance or any number of ways that serve as an interpretation of the reading. Interviewing the author or asking students to change a scene so the result is different are other examples of how students can give a personal response to reading.

Students who have a hard time coming up with a response would benefit from a sheet listing ideas for ways they can respond. These ideas usually take the form of open-ended sentences such as:

1. The character I liked the best was _____.

2. The character that is most like me is _____.

3. If I were _____, I would have _____.

<u>DOMAIN II.</u>   <u>READING ACROSS THE CURRICULUM</u>

COMPETENCY 5.0   **UNDERSTAND THE STRATEGIES FOR PROMOTING CONTENT-AREA KNOWLEDGE THROUGH READING AND FOR IMPROVING RESEARCH HABITS AND STUDY SKILLS**

Skill 5.1   **Demonstrate knowledge of various methods for improving students' comprehension of content-area texts (e.g., analyzing text structure or format, summarizing, semantic mapping, and creating graphic organizers)**

Reading comprehension is the ultimate goal of any reading activity. As students progress through the grades, it becomes increasingly important that they be able to read factual information in the content areas, like science and social studies, with as much efficiency and solid comprehension. So much learning and teaching occurs through the use of texts that students need to be taught specific methods to gain comprehension from these books.

Typically, content-area texts are nonfiction in nature. Therefore, students can use specific strategies to help gain more insight. First, students can begin by analyzing the text itself. Looking at the organization and layout of the text can provide:

1. Cues students may use to filter out their need to read nonpertinent information.

2. Pointers to the specific places in the text where the answers sought may be located

3. Additional ways to connect information to prior knowledge, thus making the content more meaningful.

This analysis of text structure is a critical skill for students to achieve.

Additionally, the texts generally will have large amounts of information to convey. This can be overwhelming to students. Students will need some sort of organizational tool to absorb the necessary information. Using *summarizing skills,* the students can break the information and into smaller, more manageable pieces.

Another beneficial tool for students is *semantic mapping.* In semantic mapping, students begin to make the connections between the information they already know about the topic and the new information they are learning. It is typically a more graphic representation of the information, but it is built upon words and ideas. Mapping generally increases knowledge and improves vocabulary development.

Other types of graphic organizers can also help students acquire information from content area texts. Mind mapping, for example, is a strategy that combines pictures and words to convey the underlying concepts of what was read. There are many different types of graphic organizers from which a teacher can draw to support students. However, students need to be able to apply these skills on their own. In other words, they need to be able to create their own graphic organizer to meet the needs of the task before them. A personally created organizer can become the most efficient and most meaningful strategy of all.

Skill 5.2 **Demonstrate knowledge of strategies for promoting students' use of common textual features (e.g., paragraphs, topic sentences, concluding sentences, glossary, and index) and graphic features (e.g., charts, graphs, maps, diagrams, captions, and photos) to locate, analyze, organize, and recall information**

When reading, students need to utilize as many different strategies as possible to increase their comprehension. With good comprehension being the end goal of all reading, teachers can help their students use specific features of texts to clarify or enhance their understanding of what has been read.

Specific textual features can facilitate the location of important information in the text, which allows students to create their own schema. Using this schema, students can analyze and organize the information in a manner that is tied directly to their own personal experience and prior knowledge. Once such connections are made, it is easier for the students to recall and utilize the information when needed.

Most texts provide brief introductions. These introductions can be used by the reader to determine if the information they are seeking is located within the passage to be read. By reading a short passage, the student can quickly ascertain whether he/she needs to do a complete reading or a quick skim will suffice.

As we teach students to write, we often spend a lot of time focusing on writing paragraphs with topic sentences and concluding sentences. However, we also need to focus on how these same features—topic and concluding sentences— may be used to better understand the text. These parallels can help students better understand what they are reading and also help them develop their writing skills. Understanding that topic sentences tell the main idea of the paragraph, and that concluding sentences restate that idea, can help students' comprehension as well.

When searching for information, students can become much more efficient if they learn to use a glossary and index. Students can find the necessary facts in a more rapid manner and also clarify information that was difficult to understand the first time.

Additionally, charts, graphs, maps, diagrams, captions, and photos in text can work in the same way as looking up unknown words in the glossary. They can provide more insight and clarify the concepts and ideas the author is conveying.

Skill 5.3 Demonstrate knowledge of strategies for promoting various study skills (e.g., highlighting, outlining, mapping, note-taking, and test-taking skills)

Content area subjects often have texts with a great deal of information. Typically, more information is included than is necessary for students to know at one time. In such cases, it is necessary for the students to develop specific study skills to help them take in the important information while weeding out the less important.

Highlighting is a difficult strategy for students to master. Even at the college level it seems students have a hard time determining what is important and necessary. Key ideas or vocabulary are a good place to start with highlighting. Teaching students to highlight less information, rather than more is also important. It is not a good study skill if a student highlights an entire page of information.

Outlining is a skill many teachers use to help students understand the important facts. Sometimes the teacher can provide the outline to the students to use as a guide when taking their own notes. In this way, the students know the important parts to focus upon when reading. Developing outlines can be very difficult for some students. For those students, mapping might be a more appropriate study aid.

Mapping involves using graphics, pictures, and words to represent the information in the text. The students can personalize and use colors and pictures which have meaning to them. This provides the natural bridge to prior knowledge and frames the information in a more personal way.

Note-taking skills also are something that requires direct instruction. Sometimes, in fact, too often, teachers assume students understand how to take notes based on a lecture format, when in fact the majority of students are trying to write down as much as they hear. Teachers can help in this process by taking the time to specifically teach and highlight the key factors. Students sometimes lag in skill development in test taking. Teaching students to eliminate automatic wrong answers first, then narrowing down the choices is a start. In open-ended questions, students need to be able to restate the question in their answer and understand they need to answer all parts of the question being asked. Combining all of these approaches will allow students the opportunity to read, take in new information and use that information to respond appropriately.

Note taking is also are something that requires direct instruction. Too often teachers assume students understand how to take notes based on a lecture format when, in fact, the majority of students are trying to write down as much as they hear. Teachers can help in this process by taking the time to specifically teach and highlight the key factors.

Test-taking skills are another area where students sometimes lag in skill development. Teaching students to eliminate obvious wrong answers first to then narrow down the choices is a start. In open-ended questions, students need to be able to restate the question in their answer and also answer all parts of the question being asked.

Combining all of these approaches will allow the students the opportunity to read, take in new information, and use that information to respond appropriately.

Skills 5.4   Demonstrate knowledge of strategies for relating students' prior knowledge and experiences to subject-area content

As previously discussed, one of the most important thing to improve reading comprehension is to help students understand how the new information relates to information they have already. Using prior knowledge and experiences can make the difference between what is remembered and what is forgotten.

Making learning as real as possible with real-life practical applications is one strategy to increase students' use of prior knowledge. If the students are learning about adding money and discounts, try relating that information to shopping for clothes that are "cool". This real-life application automatically engages the student in recalling prior knowledge while staying interested in the current lesson in the classroom.

Another strategy for helping students tap prior knowledge is to use *Know, Wonder, Learn* (KWL). Students typically already have some information about topics being discussed in class. When the students share that prior knowledge, either as individuals or in a group, the teacher is able to point out specific connections. Although there are many different forms of the KWL chart, the one below is the simplest.

Know	Wonder	Learn
In this box, the teacher or students list the information they already know about the topic to be discussed	In this box, the teacher or students list the questions they have about the topic, which may be answered through research or the activities already planned to be completed	In this box, the teacher or students list what information has been learned at the *end* of the teaching process. This becomes a nice reflective piece for both students and teachers, and can even be used as a quick assessment for the teacher to whether ascertain all predetermined objectives were met

Skill 5.5 **Demonstrate knowledge of strategies for promoting students' ability to analyze how certain words and concepts relate to multiple subject areas**

See Skill 5.3 and Skill 5.4

COMPETENCY 6.0   UNDERSTAND THE USE OF WORD-IDENTIFICATION STRATEGIES AND VARIOUS METHODS FOR PROMOTING AND EXPANDING VOCABULARY DEVELOPMENT

Skill 6.1   Demonstrate knowledge of word-analysis strategies and skills used to gain meaning from unfamiliar words (e.g., decoding and structural analysis)

Development of Word-Analysis Skills and Strategies, Including Structural Analysis

The explicit teaching of **word analysis** requires that the teacher preselect words from a given text for vocabulary learning. These words should be chosen based on the storyline and main ideas of the text. The educator may even want to create a story map for a narrative text or develop a graphic organizer for an expository text. Once the story mapping and/or graphic organizing have been done, the educator can compile a list of words which relate to the storyline and/or main ideas.

The number of words that require explicit teaching should only be two or three. If the number is higher than that, the children need guided reading and the text needs to be broken down into smaller sections for teaching. When broken down into smaller sections, each text section should only have two to three words which need explicit teaching.

Some researchers, including Tierney and Cunningham, believe that a few words should be taught as a means of improving comprehension.

It is up to the educator whether the vocabulary selected for teaching needs review before reading, during reading, or after reading.

Introduce vocabulary BEFORE READING if. . .

- Children are having difficulty constructing meaning on their own. Children themselves have previewed the text and indicated words they want to know.
- The teacher has seen that there are words within the text which are definitely keys necessary for reading comprehension
- The text itself, in the judgment of the teacher, contains difficult concepts for the children to grasp.

Introduce vocabulary DURING READING if . . .

- Children are already doing guided reading.
- The text has words which are crucial to its comprehension and the children will have trouble comprehending it, if they are not helped with the text.

Introduce vocabulary AFTER READING if. . .

- The children themselves have shared words which they found difficult or interesting
- The children need to expand their vocabulary
- The text itself is one that is particularly suited for vocabulary building.

Strategies to support word analysis and enhance reading comprehension include:

- Use of a graphic organizer such as a word map
- Semantic mapping
- Semantic feature analysis
- Hierarchical and linear arrays
- Preview in context
- Contextual redefinition
- Vocabulary self-collection
- (Note that these terms are in the Glossary.)

Structural analysis is a process of examining the words in the text for meaningful word units (affixes, base words, and inflected endings). There are six word types that are formed and therefore can be analyzed using structural analysis strategies. They include:

1. Common prefixes or suffixes added to a known word ending with a consonant
2. Adding the suffix –ed to words that end with consonants
3. Compound words
4. Adding endings to words that end with the letter e
5. Adding endings to words that end with the letter y
6. Adding affixes to multisyllabic words

When teaching and using structural analysis procedures in the primary grades, teachers should remember to make sound decisions on which to introduce and teach. Keeping in mind the number of primary words in which each affix appears and how similar they are will help the teacher make the instructional process smoother and more valuable to the students.

Adding affixes to words can be started when students are able to read a list of one-syllable words by sight at a rate of approximately 20 words correct per minute. At the primary level, there is a recommended sequence for introducing affixes. The steps in this process are:

- Start by introducing the affix in the letter-sound correspondence format

- Practice the affix in isolation for a few days.

- Provide words for practice which contain the affix (word lists/flash card).

- Move from word lists to passage reading, which includes words with the affix (and some from the word lists/flash cards).

Structural Analysis Activities

Word Study Group. This involves the teacher taking time to meet with children from grades 3–6 in a small group of no more than six children for a word study session. Taberski (2000) suggests that this meeting take place next to the word wall. The children selected for this group are those who need to focus more on the relationship between spelling patterns and consonant sounds.

It is important that this not be a formalized traditional reading group that meets at a set time each week or biweekly. Rather the group should be spontaneously formed by the teacher based on the teacher's quick inventory of the selected children's needs at the start of the week. Taberski has templates in her book of *Guided Reading Planning Sheets.* These sheets are essentially targeted word and other skills sheets with her written dated observations of children who are in need of support to develop a given skill.

The teacher should try to meet with this group for at least two consecutive 20-minute periods daily. Over those two meetings, the teacher can model a *Making Words Activity*. Once the teacher has modeled making words the first day, the children would then make their own words. On the second day, the children would "sort" their words.

Other topics for a word study group within the framework of the *Balanced Literacy Approach* that Taberski advocates are: inflectional endings, prefixes and suffixes, and/or common spelling patterns. These are covered later in this chapter.

It should be noted that this activity would be classified by theorists as a structural analysis activity because the structural components (i.e. prefixes, suffixes, and spelling patterns) of the words are being studied.

Discussion Circles. J. David Cooper (2004) believes that children should not be "taught" vocabulary and structural analysis skills. Flesch and E. D. Hirsch, key theorists of the phonics approach and advocates of Cultural Literacy (a term coined and associated with E. D. Hirsch), believe that specific vocabulary words at various grade and age levels need to be mastered and must be explicitly taught in schools. As far as Cooper is concerned, all the necessary and meaningful vocabulary (for the child and ultimately adult reader) can't possibly be taught in schools. To Cooper it is far more important that the children be made aware of and become interested in learning words by themselves. Cooper feels that through the child's reading and writing, he/she develops a love for and a sense of "ownership" of words. All of Cooper's suggested structural analysis word strategies are therefore designed to foster the child's love of words and a desire to "own" more of them through reading and writing.

Discussion Circles is an activity that fits nicely into the balanced literacy lesson format. After the children conclude a particular text, Cooper suggests they respond to the book in discussion circles. Among the prompts, the teacher-coach might suggest that the children focus on words of interest they encountered in the text. These can also be words that they heard if the text was read aloud. Children can be asked to share something funny or upsetting or unusual about the words they have read. Through this focus on children's response to words as the center of the discussion circle, peers become more interested in word study.

Banking, Booking, and Filing It: Making Words Their Own. Children can realize the goal of making words their own and exploring word structures through creating concrete objects or displays that demonstrate the words they own.

Encourage children to create and maintain their own files of words they have learned or are interested in learning. Although they can categorize these files according to their own interests, they should develop files using science, history, physical education, fine arts, dance, and technology content. Newspapers and web resources approved by the teacher are excellent sources for such words. In addition to benefiting the students, this filing activity provides the teacher with the opportunity to instruct children in age-appropriate and grade-level research skills. Even children in grades 2 and 3 can begin simplified bibliographies and webliographies for their "found" words. They can learn how to annotate and note the page of a newspaper, book, or URL for a particular word.

Children can also copy down words as they appear in the text (print or electronic). If appropriate, they can place the words found for given topics or content in an actual bank of their own making or print the words on cards. This allows for differentiated word study and appeals to those children who are kinesthetic and spatial learners. Of course, children can also choose to create their own word books showcasing their specialized vocabulary and descriptions of how they identified or hunted down their words. Richard Scarry, watch out! Scarry books can be anchor books to inspire this structural analysis activity.

ELL learners can share their accounts in their native language first and then translate (with the help of the teacher) these accounts into English, posting both the native language and the English language versions for peers to view.

Write Out Your Words, Write with Your Words. Ownership of words can be demonstrated by having the children use the words in their writings. The children can author a procedural narrative (a step-by-step description) of how they went about their word searches to compile the words they found for any of the activities. If the children are in grades K–1, or if the children are struggling readers and writers, their procedural narratives can be dictated. Then they can be posted by the teacher.

ELL students can share their accounts in their native language first and then translate (with the help of the teacher) these accounts into English with both the native language and the English language versions of the word exploration posted.

Children with special needs may model a word box on a specific holiday theme, genre, or science/social studies topic with the teacher. Initially this can be done as a whole class. As the children become more confident, they can work with peers or with a paraprofessional to create their own individual or small team/pair word boxes.

Special needs children can create a storyboard with the support of a paraprofessional, their teacher, or a resource specialist. They can also narrate their story of how they all found the words, using a tape recorder.

Word Study Museum in the Classroom. This strategy has been presented in detail so it can be used by the teachers within their own classrooms. In addition, the way the activity is described and the mention at the end of the description of how the activity can address family literacy, ELL, and special needs children's talents, provides an example of other audiences a teacher should consider in curriculum design.

Almost every general education teacher and reading specialist will have to differentiate instruction to address the needs of special education and ELL learners. Family or shared literacy is a major component of all literacy instruction. Children can create a single or multiple exhibits, museum style, within their classrooms celebrating their word study. They can build actual representations of the type of study they have done including word trees (made out of cardboard or foam board), elaborate word boxes and games, word history timelines or murals, and word study maps. They can develop online animations, *Kidspiration* graphic organizers, *QuickTime* movies, digital photo essays, and PowerPoint presentations to share the words they have identified.

The classroom, gym, or cafeteria can be transformed into a gallery space. Children can author brochure descriptions for their individual, team, or class exhibits. Some children can volunteer to be tour guides or docents for the experience. Other children can work to create a banner for the *Word Study Museum*. The children can name the museum themselves and send out invitations to its opening. Invitations can be sent to parents, community, staff members, peers, and younger classes.

Depending on their age and grade level, children can also develop interactive games and quizzes focused on particular exhibits. An artist or a team of class artists can design a poster for the exhibit, while other children choose to build the exhibits. Another small group can work on signage and a catalogue or register of objects within the exhibit. Greeters who will welcome parents and peers to the exhibit can be trained and can develop their own scripts.

If the children are in grades 4–6, they can also develop their own visitor feedback forms and design word-themed souvenirs. The whole museum can be photographed, with the pictures hung later near the word walls along with a description of the event. Of course, the children can use many of their newly recognized and owned words to describe the event.

The *Word Study Museum* activity can be used with either a phonics-based or a Balanced Literacy Approach. It promotes additional writing, researching, discussing, and reading about words.

It is also an excellent family literacy strategy in that families can develop their own word exhibits at home. This activity can also support and celebrate learners with disabilities. It can be presented in dual languages by children who are ELL learners and fluent in more than a single language.

This aspect of vocabulary development is to help children look for structural elements within words which they can use independently to help them determine meaning.

Some teachers choose to directly teach structural analysis, in particular, those who teach by following the phonics-centered approach for reading. Other teachers, who follow the balanced literacy approach, introduce the structural components as part of mini lessons that are focused on the students' reading and writing.

Structural analysis of words as defined by J. David Cooper (2004) involves the study of significant word parts. This analysis can help the child with pronunciation and constructing meaning.

Definition questions—multiple choice questions which have only a single right answer—test whether the teacher candidate has memorized the appropriate terminology. They constitute no less than 15% of the multiple choice questions on the test. Therefore, by taking the time to memorize these easy definitions, scores are likely to improve. Structural analysis components are explicitly taught in schools which advocate the phonics-centered approach and are also incorporated into the word work component of the schools which advocate the balanced literacy approach for instruction. The list of terms below is generally recognized as the key structural analysis components.

Key Structural Analysis Components Definitions

Root Word. This is a word from which another word is developed. The second word can be said to have its "root" in the first, such as *vis, to see,* in visor or vision. This structural component can be illustrated by a tree with roots to display the meaning for children. Children may also want to literally construct root words using cardboard trees to create word family models.

ELL students can construct these models for their native language root-word families, as well for the English language words they are learning. ELL students in the 5th and 6th grade may even appreciate analyzing the different root structures for contrasts and similarities between their native language and English. Learners with special needs can focus in small groups or individually with a paraprofessional on building root-word models.

Base Words. These are stand-alone linguistic units which cannot be deconstructed or broken down into smaller words. For example, in the word *retell*, the base word is "tell."

Contractions. These are shortened forms of two words in which a letter or letters have been deleted. These deleted letters have been replaced by an apostrophe.

Prefixes. These are beginning units of meaning which can be added (the vocabulary word for this type of structural adding is "affixed") to a base word or root word. They cannot stand alone. They are also sometimes known as "bound morphemes" meaning that they cannot stand alone as a base word. Examples are *re-, un-,* and *mis-*.

Suffixes. These are ending units of meaning which can be "affixed" or added on to the ends of root or base words. Suffixes transform the original meanings of base and root words. Like prefixes, they are also known as "bound morphemes," because they cannot stand alone as words. Examples are *-less, -ful,* and *-tion*.

Compound Words. These occur when two or more base words are connected to form a new word. The meaning of the new word is in some way connected with that of the base word. Examples are *firefighter, newspaper*, and *pigtail*.

Inflectional Endings. These are types of suffixes that impart a new meaning to the base or root word. These endings in particular change the gender, number, tense, or form of the base or root words. Just like other suffixes, these are also termed "bound morphemes." Examples are *–s* or *-ed*.

Some of the following activities are presented in detail to help answer the constructed response problems of the test.

Knowledge of Greek and Latin Roots That Form English Words

Knowledge of Greek and Latin roots which comprise English words can measurably enhance children's reading skills and can also enrich their writing.

Word Webs. Taberski (2000) does not advocate teaching Greek and Latin derivatives in the abstract to young children. However, when she comes across (as is common and natural) specific Greek and Latin roots while reading to children, she uses that opportunity to introduce children to these rich resources.

For example, during readings on rodents (a favorite of first and second graders), Taberski draws her class's attention to the fact that beavers gnaw at things with their teeth. She then connects the root *dent* with other words with which the children are familiar. The children then volunteer *dentist, dental, denture.* Taberski begins to place these in a graphic organizer, or word web.

When she has tapped the extent of the children's prior knowledge of *dent* words, she shares with them the fact that *dens/dentis* is the Latin word for teeth. Then she introduces the word *indent,* which she has already previewed with them as part of their conventions of print study. She helps them to see that the *indenting* of the first line of a paragraph can even be related to the *teeth* Latin root in that it looks like a "print" bite was taken out of the paragraph.

Taberski displays the word web in the Word Wall Chart section of her room. The class is encouraged throughout, say, a week's time to look for other words to add to the web. Taberski stresses that for her, as an elementary teacher of reading and writing, the key element of the Greek and Latin word root web activity is the children's coming to understand that if they know what a Greek or Latin word root means, they can use that knowledge to figure out what other words mean.

She feels the key concept is to model and demonstrate for children how fun and fascinating Greek and Latin root study can be.

Greek and Latin Roots Word Webs with an Assist from the Internet. Older children in grades 3–6 can build on this initial activity by searching online for additional words with a particular Greek or Latin root which has been introduced in class.

They can easily do this in a way that authentically ties in with their own interests and experiences by reading reviews for a book which has been a read-aloud online or by just reading the summaries of the day's news and printing out those words which appear in the stories online that share the root discussed.

The children can be encouraged to circle these instances of their Latin or Greek root and also to document the exact date and URL for the citation. These can be posted as part of their own online web in the word wall section study area. If the school or class has a website or webpage, the children can post this data there as a special Greek and Latin root- word page.

Expanding the concept of the Greek and Latin word web from the printed page to the Internet nicely inculcates the child in the habits of lifelong reading combined with online researching. This beginning expository research will serve them well in intermediate level content area work and beyond.

Use of Syllabification as a Word Identification Strategy.

Strategy: Clap Hands, Count those Syllables as They Come!! (Taberski, 2000)

The objective of this activity is for children to understand that every syllable in a polysyllabic word can be studied for its spelling patterns in the same way that monosyllabic words are studied for their spelling patterns.

The easiest way for the K–3 teacher to introduce this activity to the children is to share a familiar poem from the poetry chart (or to write out a familiar poem on a large experiential chart).

First the teacher reads the poem with the children. As they are reading it aloud, the children clap the beats of the poem and the teacher uses a colored marker to place a tic (/) above each syllable.

Next, the teacher takes letter cards and selects one of the polysyllabic words from the poem which the children have already "clapped" out.

The children use letter cards to spell that word on the sentence strip holder or it can be placed on a felt board or up against a window on display. Together, the children and teacher divide the letters into syllables and place blank letter cards between the syllables. The children identify spelling patterns they know.

Finally, and as part of continued small-group syllabification study, the children identify other polysyllabic words they clapped out from the poem. They make up the letter combinations of these words. Then they separate them into syllables with blank letter cards between the syllables.

Children who require special support in syllabification can be encouraged to use many letter cards to create a large butcher paper syllabic (in letter cards with spaces) representation of the poem or at least a few lines of the poem. They can be told that this is for use as a teaching tool for others. In this way, they authenticate their study of syllabification with a real product that can actually be referenced by peers.

Techniques for Identifying Compound Words. The teaching of compound words should utilize structural analysis techniques. (See section on structural analysis). Here are some other strategies for helping students to identify and read compound words.

- Use songs and actions to help children understand the concept that compound words are two smaller words joined together to make one bigger word
- Use games like *Concentration, Memory,* and *Go Fish* for students to practice reading compound words
- Use word sorts to have students distinguish between compound words and nonexamples of compound words

Identification of Homographs. Homographs are words that are spelled the same but have different meanings. A subgroup within this area includes words that are spelled the same, have different meanings, and are pronounced differently. Some examples of homographs include:

- Lie
- Tear
- Bow
- Fair
- Bass

Teaching homographs can be interesting and fun for the students, incorporating them into passages where the students can use the context clues to decipher the different meanings of the homographs. Using games is also a good strategy to help students understand multiple meaning words. Jokes and riddles are usually based on homographs, and students love to make collections or books of these.

Semantic Feature Analysis. This technique for enhancing vocabulary skills by using semantic cues is based on the research of Johnson and Pearson (1984) and Anders and Bos (1986). It involves young children in setting up a feature analysis grid of various subject content words which is an outgrowth of their discussion about these words.

For instance, Cooper (2004) includes a sample of a Semantic Features Analysis Grid for Vegetables.

Vegetables	Green	Have Peels	Eat Raw	Seeds
Carrots	–	+	+	–
Cabbage	+	–	+	–

Note: that the use of the + for yes, – for no, and possible use for + and – if a vegetable like squash could be both green and yellow.

Teachers of children in grade one and beyond can design their own semantic analysis grids to meet their students' needs and to align with the topics the children are learning. Select a category or class of words, e.g., planets, rodent family members, winter words, or weather words.

Use the left side of the grid to list at least three if not more items that fit this category. The number of actual items listed will depend on the age and grade level of the children with three or four items fine for K–1 and up to 10–15 for grades 5 and 6. Brainstorm with the children. If better suited to the class, the teacher may list his/her own features that the items have in common. From the example excerpted from *Cooper's Literacy: Helping Children Construct Meaning (2004)*, common features that are usually easy to identify include vegetables' green color, peels, and seeds.

Show the children how to insert the notations +, –, and even ? (if they are not certain) on the grid. The teacher might also explore with the children the possibility that an item could get both a + and a –. For example, a vegetable like broccoli might be eaten cooked or raw depending on taste and squash can be green or yellow.

Whatever the length of the grid when first presented to the children (perhaps as a semantic cue lesson in and of itself tied in to a text being read in class), make certain that the grid as presented and filled out is not the end of the activity.

Children can use it as a model for developing their own semantic features grids and share them with the whole class. Child-developed grids can become part of a Word Work center in the classroom or even be published in a Word Study Games book by the class as a whole. Such a publication can be shared with parents during open school week and evening visits and with peer classes.

Skill 6.2   Demonstrate knowledge of strategies for determining and verifying the meaning of unfamiliar words or words with multiple meanings using context clues (e.g., contrast, restatement, cause and effect, and syntax)

It is inevitable in reading that students will come across words they are unable to read. When this happens, the student will need a variety of strategies to draw upon to figure out the unknown word and gather meaning from the word and text.

When they encounter unknown words, students typically begin with decoding or the application of phonics skills. If they are unable to correctly decode the word, they may use other strategies such as structural analysis and context clues.

In structural analysis, students use word patterns and parts they recognize to figure out unknown words. When decoding, students tend to look at no more than two letters together. In contrast, structural analysis allows students to look at larger portions of words.

Contextual reading is something we all do from a very young age to adult years. Sometimes, regardless of our ability to decode or apply structural analysis, we are unable to read certain words. In this case, readers can use other words in the sentence or paragraph to help decide the unknown word.

Good readers use the syntax, the manner in which the sentence is put together, to help determine meaning from context. They also find ways to put the sentence or passage in their own words or look for contrasting ideas. All of these strategies help the reader to draw meaning from what is being read. This frame of reference helps to provide more details for the reader. Contrast is also a method readers may use to build context or determine meaning.

All of these strategies together help readers develop their comprehension ability. However, some words have more than one meaning. In this case, the student may be able to identify the word but have difficulty determining meaning. In some cases, meaning can be confusing as the student only knows one meaning of the word, and when reading, it simply does not make sense.

It is in this instance that the use of context clues can be most beneficial. Students can begin to learn more than one meaning by basing their analysis on the rest of the words in the passage. In this way, they can learn the multiple meanings of words without having to rely on skill and drill vocabulary activities.

Skill 6.3 **Demonstrate knowledge of strategies for determining and verifying meanings, pronunciations, synonyms, antonyms, and parts of speech of unfamiliar words or words with multiple meanings through the use of technology and other reference materials (e.g., dictionary and thesaurus)**

When students are reading something that does not make sense, they should start with using the strategies described in detail in Skill 6.2 (context clues, syntax, decoding, and semantics). However, there are other times when it is necessary to be more specific in determining if the definition is correctly inferred. In these cases, the reader may need to look outside of the text at additional resources to ensure their accuracy. Students might begin with the glossary, if included, as it is located within the same text. However, other times, they may need to refer to some other mode of finding the meaning or pronunciation of the words. Students may use a dictionary to help with these skills.

Dictionary skills are important for students to learn and use regularly. The dictionary can provide the reader with several different meanings for the word. The student can use the different meanings provided along with the contextual information they gained from the text to determine which meaning is most appropriate. They can also use the pronunciation guide to determine how to say the word, which will help later in reading.

Sometimes, it is helpful to use synonyms or antonyms to help clarify meaning. A thesaurus is formatted similar to a dictionary in design and layout; however, instead of providing the definition and pronunciation of the words, it provides words that are synonyms and antonyms for the word given. This can help the student to put the passage in more reader friendly terms or in terms with which they are more familiar. The use of synonyms and antonyms is an excellent way to build vocabulary.

In today's society, all of these tools can be found in various technological forms. There are online dictionaries and thesauruses. Additionally, there are pocket personal electronic dictionaries with built-in thesauruses. There is also a reading pen, which teachers use to help determine unknown words. The tip of the pen is rubbed lightly across the unknown word. The computer-generated voice built into the pen speaks it orally with the correct pronunciation for the student to hear. Then it provides the definition, synonyms, and antonyms on a digital display. On some models, this information can also be repeated orally.

Skill 6.4 **Recognize criteria for selecting appropriate vocabulary words for study (e.g., key words, content-specific words, words needed to comprehend a passage, words that have roots and affixes that give clues to their meaning)**

Students completing reading activities will need to increase their vocabularies in order to build their comprehension skills. In many classrooms, vocabulary words to learn are predetermined by the teacher and assigned to the students. However, students may also need to develop strategies to identify their own set of vocabulary words to learn based on their personal reading and writing word knowledge.

Identifying vocabulary to study is an important skill no matter the reading task presented. In some cases, the student may need to find the definitions of certain words to be able to understand the passage or chapter they are reading. In this instance, the students may not need to study the word for retention at a later time, but rather need to have clarification that will help process the information and develop a proficient level of comprehension.

In content area reading, this process can be more cumbersome as there may be more content-specific words. For these words, the students need to understand the general framework of the topic being studied. In that way, they can begin to see which words are important to further development of the topic. Text publishers have made this process somewhat easier for students by including key words or important content-specific words in bold or italics.

Using this strategy, the students can take a quick glance through the required reading and quickly determine which terms are key and/or content-specific. At this point, further exploration as to the definitions and pronunciation can occur. This front-end work can help the student better understand the reading—with less rereading necessary later.

Students can also pay specific attention to affixes, both prefixes and suffixes, as well as look at root words to help them determine which vocabulary needs to be studied. Knowing the definitions of affixes can help students tremendously when reading. Words that look complex and contain many different syllables may not need further study or analysis if the student has a complete understanding of affixes and root words.

Reading vocabularies are very individual and developed based on the unique experiences and prior knowledge of the student reading. Due to this factor, the student needs to be able to determine for themselves which words require further study and which do not.

Skill 6.5   Demonstrate knowledge of instructional strategies and activities for promoting vocabulary development (e.g., word classification, etymology, semantic mapping, and applying vocabulary words in new contexts)

Developing the vocabulary of students is important to helping them become life-long learners as well as improving their understanding of many topics. There are a number of different strategies that can be used to increase the development of vocabulary skills in students. Some of these strategies are described and detailed below:

Word Classification. In this method, the students draw comparisons between different types of words. For younger children, this might begin by looking at parts of speech. Students might classify words as action, describing, nouns, etc. At older ages, the students may begin to look at classifying the words in more specific categories based on the content area or other classification system.

Etymology. Etymology is the study of the history of words. Understanding the language basis of words can help in determining the meaning and in building comprehension. It is particularly useful to know the definitions of affixes and root words; these can help determine the meaning of several other words. In science, for example, understanding Latin derivatives can be beneficial in classifying different scientific terms and understanding their meaning.

Semantic Mapping. This strategy involves the student beginning to make the connections between the information they already know about the topic and the new information they are learning. It is typically a more graphic representation of the information and is built upon words and ideas. It generally increases knowledge and improves vocabulary development.

Application of Vocabulary Words in New Situations. Students also need to be able to develop their ability to make transfers of knowledge. Understanding what a word means in one context helps the student for that one reading passage. Being able to transfer that understanding to new and varied situations helps the students become life-long learners and readers. This transfer of knowledge can be done by asking the students to think of other ways or situations where the word can be used, or by providing examples from other content areas where that same term is used.

COMPETENCY 7.0   UNDERSTAND HOW TO VARY READING STRATEGIES FOR DIFFERENT TEXTS AND PURPOSES FOR READING AND HOW TO FACILITATE STUDENTS' USE OF VARIOUS READING MATERIALS

Skill 7.1   Demonstrate knowledge of different types and functions of texts and strategies for teaching students how to vary reading strategies (e.g., skimming, scanning, rereading, and in-depth reading) for different texts and purposes for reading

Throughout their lives, students will be reading a multitude of texts for a variety of purposes. The purpose behind reading often drives the type of reading completed by the student. The type of text can also drive the type of reading strategies the students use to successfully navigate the information.

When reading for pleasure, students tend to read less carefully, and may even skim some portions of the text. Because the book is simply for pleasure, this is perfectly acceptable and should be allowed. In fact, skimming skills can be introduced and used for other types of readings. Students who are looking for vocabulary words or definitions may skim a great deal of information at a more rapid pace before finding the appropriate part of the passage. This is also a good strategy when used to look for specific pieces of information.

In addition to skimming, scanning is another technique students can use to look through a large amount of text for specific details and/or information. This can be particularly helpful for students when they are searching through different books to determine if any of the information is pertinent to meet their needs.

Teachers need to take the time to teach students when it is necessary to reread information. Typically, students understand that it is important to reread when something is not understood clearly. However, there are other times when rereading may be important. In content-heavy texts, rereading can not only provide further clarification, it can also provide additional details the reader may have missed the first time. It is easy to miss information when so much is packed into small passages. Thus, rereading can be an important factor in learning and making sure students have absorbed all of the details.

In-depth reading can be a tiring task and difficult to complete on all books students encounter. Students need to understand that reading with an eye for detail is called for mostly in nonfiction texts which are laden with information. When reading in depth, students are trying to absorb as much information as possible.

Skill 7.2   Recognize ways to select, organize, and manage instructional materials and technologies to address the reading needs and interests of groups and individuals

Reading specialists need to have a large amount of materials available to them to be able to meet the needs of the various students they encounter. Children's needs span a wide range of skills. Therefore, they may require many different materials, books (both levels and interests) and technological items. This information can be overwhelming to think about, let alone find, organize, and manage in the classroom.

In regards to organizing materials, there are various accepted methods. In most cases, the texts should be leveled according to some standards. Many people use the Fountas and Pinnell leveling system or the Developing Readers Assessment system. Either system provides teachers with lists of books and their corresponding levels. In fact, most major publishing companies provide this information for all of their materials. Knowing these levels will be helpful in efficiently meeting the instructional needs of the students.

The books can be organized by author, genre, series, topics, or in other ways that can be helpful to both teacher and student. Boxes and inexpensive crates can be purchased rather inexpensively to hold the books. Labeling each container will be helpful, though time consuming at the beginning.

Supportive materials, such as lesson plans, worksheets, and activity guides can be stored in filing cabinets labeled by book title or kept in the same storage container as the books. Keeping all materials together can be difficult to manage, but is the most efficient way to organize an overwhelming amount of information.

Selecting materials to meet the instructional needs of students is important. Assessment data, including running records, provide the basis for beginning instruction. Interest surveys are another method of gaining insight into the minds of students to assess their needs.

Technological advances allow for not only the purchase of activities and games on compact discs, but also web-based reading support programs. These sites can be bookmarked for ease of use at later times with various groups of students. Technology is often quite inspirational to students and they enjoy completing activities involving computers, tape recorders, and other devices.

Skill 7.3 **Demonstrate knowledge of a wide body of grade-level appropriate literature, texts, and other resources that reflect various subject areas and disciplines and identifying appropriate strategies for facilitating reading of given texts**

As the reading specialist, it is important to be familiar with various genres of literature, including those which specifically appeal to the students with whom the teacher is working. In addition, it is important to locate appropriate resources that can support content area learning for students. There are numerous fictional genres which can apply to students in kindergarten through twelfth grade. They include:

- Mystery
- Fantasy
- Drama
- Historical Fiction
- Fable
- Mythology
- Fairy tale
- Poetry
- Folklore
- Legends
- Realistic Fiction
- Tall Tales
- Science Fiction

When reading any genre of fiction, students need to have well-developed phonemic awareness, phonics, and fluency skills. Vocabulary and comprehension development will continue to occur throughout schooling, and should be an integral part of the reading process. Texts for teaching reading specifically, should include many of the various genres, both nonfiction and fiction, and should provide some authentic works of literature even if in a condensed format. It is imperative to expose students to various types of authentic literature.

In the nonfiction realm, it is important for students to have access to materials that will support their learning in content areas as well as books that match their interests and learning desires. Some nonfiction genres include:

- Essays
- Narrative Nonfiction
- Biography
- Speech
- Autobiographies

Understanding and using these different types of nonfiction text will provide the students with the opportunity to explore various topics or support their learning in content-specific classes. In addition to books, it may be necessary to utilize reference materials including:

- Dictionaries
- Thesauruses
- Encyclopedias
- Almanacs

Skill 7.4   Demonstrate knowledge of strategies for promoting students' ability to locate, select, and use information from a variety of print, nonprint, and technological references and resources

The information a student, or for that matter a teacher, seeks can be located, if they understand where and how to locate it. Teaching students how to find, determine the appropriateness of, and utilize information gathered is an ongoing skill.

Teaching students to find information and select the most appropriate for the purpose can be a daunting task. The amount of information available today can seem overwhelming. Whittling it down into manageable chunks is essential for success.

In these cases, it can be helpful to coordinate services and support with the school librarian/media specialist. In this way, students can become familiar with what materials are available to them through the media center, while locating and selecting suitable resources for the task presented.

It is important for students to learn to use the card catalogue system, internet search engines, indexes, and other information/organizational tools. It will allow them to be able to answer their own questions throughout the remainder of their lives. They will have the necessary tools to be successful at locating any information they need.

Once the facts have been found, it is necessary for the students to have specific strategies for determining the relevance and potential usefulness of what has been gathered. No one person can manage all of the knowledge about a topic. Students need to understand this fact and learn to weed out the irrelevant information.

Graphic organizers, like outlines, may provide students with the skills to determine the relevant information.   For example, though they may read about an interesting bug just found on the island about which they are studying, if insect life is not a topic on their study project outline, that information isn't important to completing the assigned task.

Determining and rating information on the basis of importance takes practice and guidance. Students who are successful with it will be most able to take the gathered information and use it to complete the assigned tasks. Because this is the end goal, it is important to demonstrate this process in a very explicit way for students to ensure success.

Skill 7.5   **Demonstrate knowledge of strategies for motivating students to read across the curriculum and for supporting their reading of both informational and fictional texts in a variety of genres and modes of discourse, including texts related to various subject areas**

Every reader has their favorite genres. We all tend to develop an appreciation for a specific type of book and are drawn to the same genre and/or authors over and over. In education, it is our responsibility to take the time to introduce our students to books across all genres.

Encouraging students to explore outside of their comfort zone is important in developing the appreciation of literature as a whole, and to increase the field of available resources for students.   Perhaps a student has a natural affinity for the sciences, but is never exposed to science books. Would this natural ability ever be developed?

Motivating students to read across various subjects and disciplines can be a daunting task. It is important to build an interest. If teachers can generate enthusiasm about a subject, the students will want to learn more about it. Having a reason to read can be the start down a tremendous path. This can be done through many different methods.

Using topics that come directly from students' prior knowledge is a tremendous way to increase interest and motivate students. Listening to students as they talk among themselves and drawing upon their experiences and discussions can be a way to begin. Sometimes, guest speakers, role playing or simulations can spark the interest to explore.

When topics of discourse develop in the classroom, the discussions and debates can lead the teacher to provide texts or articles supporting both sides of the issues. This can be another way to increase the desire to explore many different types of reading.

Sometimes, sharing the books the teacher is reading will incite excitement in your students to start down a different path. Knowing that the teacher is a reader as well, for pleasure and work, models for the students what teachers want for them. Sharing both pleasure books and more technical texts can provide the students with real-life examples of this skill.

DOMAIN III.   **COMPREHENSION**

**COMPETENCY 8.0   UNDERSTAND FLUENCY AND OTHER FACTORS
THAT AFFECT READING COMPREHENSION**

Skill 8.1   Recognize the role of oral reading fluency (e.g., reading rate, rhythm, flow, and prosody) in facilitating comprehension and strategies for promoting students' oral reading fluency to support comprehension

Reading fluency has been shown to have strong correlations to comprehension skills, which are the goal of any reading activity. Therefore, it is very important for students to have well developed fluency skills. For students who do not naturally develop their fluency skills, the teacher must provide strategies or activities that help develop them.

Choral Reading. Choral reading is an effective reading strategy used to increase fluency. Students can read with a group or the teacher to build their fluency. In this strategy, reading should be done at an appropriate pace and with good prosody.

Reader's Theater. This strategy helps to bring drama back into the classroom by creating, scripts with different parts for different characters. The students practice the script in small groups for a few days, and then they complete a reading with good fluent reading for their peers. There is no preparation of costumes or set design, but it allows the students to have the practice of reading different parts.

Frequent Independent Reading. The more opportunity students have to practice reading, the more fluent they will become. The key is that the reading is on their independent level and the text is enjoyable for the reader. Students need to have some independent reading time daily.

Paired Reading. Students are sometimes the best teachers. Paired reading is an opportunity for them to provide effective instruction to their peers. For the struggling readers, this is an excellent strategy to increase reading fluency. Sometimes, students can graph the results of their *words correct per minute* (wcpm) with their student helpers to have a visual representation of their progress. There are different things to consider when pairing students, including: reading level, ability to work together and stay on task, and appropriate materials for both partners to read.

Repeated Readings. Repeated reading passages are one of the most effective strategies for increasing oral reading fluency. This can be done individually or in pairs. Tying graphing, paired reading, and repeated oral reading into one time frame within the classroom can provide teachers and students with a specific strategy easily incorporated for a few minutes a day into the classroom routine.

Previously, we described methods used to increase reading fluency. Most teachers would immediately equate fluency with the amount of words per minute read correctly. However, reading fluency is more than reading speed. Students must also demonstrate good prosody. Prosody covers the ideas of reading with expression, appropriate phrasing, and good inflection.

Generally considered a part of fluency, prosody is an important element on all rubrics used to evaluate reading fluency. Prosody is what takes otherwise robotic reading and makes it into something enjoyable to hear. The punctuation we use as part of grammar provides the students the cues for reading with good prosody.

Modeling is one of the most effective strategies a teacher can use with students to enhance their prosody skills. Teachers need to provide examples of good reading, as well as nonexamples where the teacher reads "robotically." In this way, students can hear the differences between good oral reading and poor oral reading.

Prosody can only be built by using oral reading, so any of the already mentioned strategies for improving fluency can also be used to increase the prosody of the same students. It is important for students to clearly understand that reading is not a race. It is not all about the number of words read correctly in a minute, but rather about the number of well-read words.

While the majority of reading will occur silently in the student's head, it is necessary to take the time to practice reading out loud to ensure students develop this more natural flow of language. It will be more likely this phrasing and expression will then transfer into the silent reading if the students are able to perform it orally. If they are unable to do the task orally, the reading in their head may be just as robotic or choppy which can impact comprehension in a negative manner.

Skill 8.2   Demonstrate knowledge of the role of phonics in developing rapid, automatic word recognition; the relationship between decoding and reading comprehension; and strategies for strengthening students' decoding skills

Mature readers identify words with remarkable speed and accuracy. Fluent, automatic word recognition is a prerequisite for comprehending text. If a reader must slowly analyze many of the words in a text, memory and attention needed for comprehension are drained by word analysis.

To decode means to change communication signals into messages. Reading comprehension requires that the reader learn the code within which a message is written and be able to decode it to get the message.

Although effective reading comprehension requires identifying words automatically (Adams, 1990, Perfetti, 1985), children do not have to be able to identify every single word or know the exact meaning of every word in a text to understand it. Indeed, Nagy (1988) says that, children can read a work with a high level of comprehension even if they do not fully know as many as 15 percent of the words within a given text.

Children develop the ability to decode and recognize words automatically. They then can extend their ability to decode to multi-syllabic words.

J. David Cooper (2004) and other advocates of the Balanced Literacy Approach feel that children become literate, effective communicators, able to comprehend by learning phonics and other aspects of word identification through the use of engaging reading texts. Engaging texts, as defined by the balanced literacy group, are those texts which contain highly predictable elements of rhyme, sound patterns, and plot. Researchers, such as Chall (1983) and Flesch (1981), support a phonics-centered foundation before the use of engaging reading texts. This is at the crux of the phonics versus whole language/ balanced literacy/ integrated language arts controversy of teaching reading.

It is important for the new teacher to be informed about both sides of this controversy, as well as the work of theorists who attempt to reconcile these two perspectives, such as Kenneth Goodman (1994). There are powerful arguments on both sides of this controversy, and each approach works wonderfully with some students and does not succeed with others.

As far as the examinations go, all that is asked of the teacher is the ability to demonstrate a familiarity with these varied perspectives. If asked on a constructed response question, teachers need to be able to show an ability to talk about teaching some aspect of reading using strategies from one or the other or a combination of both approaches.

This guide is designed to provide you with numerous strategies representing both approaches.

The working teacher can, depending on the perspective of his /her school administration and the needs of the particular children he/she serves, choose from the strategies and approaches which work best for the children concerned.

Blending Letter Sounds

Prompts for Graphophonic Cues

> You said _(the child's incorrect attempt)_ . Does that match the letters you see?
>
> If it were the word you just said, _(the child's incorrect attempt)_ , what would it have to start with?
>
> If it were the word you just said _(the child's incorrect attempt)_ , what would it have to end with?
>
> Look at the first letter/s . . . look at the middle letter/s . . . look at the last letter. What could it be?
>
> If you were writing _(the child's incorrect attempt)_ what letter would you write first? What letters would go in the middle? What letters would go last?

A good strategy to use in working with individual children is to have them explain how they finally correctly identified a word that was troubling them. If prompted and habituated through one-on-one teacher/tutoring conversations, they can be quite clear about what they did to "get" the word.

If the children are already writing their own stories, the teacher might say to them: "You know when you write your own stories, you would never write any story which did not make sense. You wouldn't, and probably this writer didn't either. If you read something that does make sense, but doesn't match the letters, then it's probably not what the author wrote. This is the author's story, not your story right now, so go back to the word and see if you can find out the author's story. Later on, you might write your own story."

Skill 8.3   **Demonstrating knowledge of the role of vocabulary knowledge in facilitating reading comprehension (e.g., familiarity with grade-level vocabulary, common idioms, figurative phrases, and playful use of language [puns, wordplay, and palindromes]) and strategies for preteaching vocabulary to support comprehension**

Andrew Biemiller's (2003) research documents that those children entering fourth grade with significant vocabulary deficits demonstrate increasing reading comprehension problems. Evidence shows that these children do not catch up, but rather continue to fall behind.

Strategy One: Word Map Strategy. This strategy is useful for children in grades 3–6 and beyond. The target group of children for this strategy includes those who need to improve their independent vocabulary acquisition abilities. The strategy is essentially teacher-directed learning where children are "walked through" the process. The teacher helps the children to identify the type of information that makes a definition. Children are also assisted in using context clues and background understanding to construct meaning.

The *word map graphic organizer* is the tool teachers use to complete this strategy with children. Word map templates are available online from the Houghton Mifflin web site and from *ReadWriteThink*, the web site of the NCTE (see webliography section). The word map helps children to visually represent the elements of a given concept.

The children's literal articulation of the concept can be prompted by three key questions: What is it? What is it like? What are some examples?
For instance, the word "oatmeal" might yield a word map with boxes that have the answers to each of the three key questions. What is it? (A hot cereal) What's it like? (Mushy and Salty) What are some examples? (Plain or Apple-Flavored)

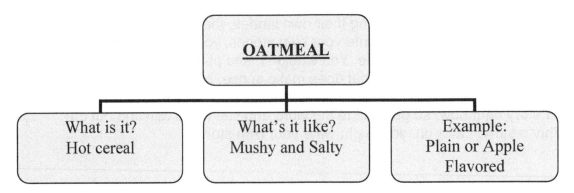

To share this strategy with children, the teacher selects three concepts familiar to the children and shows them the template of a word map with the three questions asked on the map. The teacher then helps the children to fill in at least two word maps with the topic in the top box and the answers in the three question boxes. The children should then independently complete the word map for the third topic. To reinforce the lesson, the teacher has the children select a concept of their own to map either independently or in a small group. As the final task for this first part of the strategy, the children, in teams or individually, write a definition for at least one of the concepts using the key things about it listed on the map. The children share these definitions aloud and talk about how they used the word maps to help them with the definitions.

For the next part of this strategy, the teacher picks an expository text or a textbook the children are already using to study mathematics, science, or social studies. The teacher either locates a short excerpt where a particular concept is defined or uses the content to write original model passages of definition.

After the passages are selected or authored, the teacher duplicates them. Then they are distributed to the children along with blank word map templates. The children will be asked to read each passage and then to complete the word map for the concept in each passage. Finally, the children share the word maps they have developed for each passage, and explain how they used the word in the passage to help them fill out their word map. Lastly, the teacher reminds the children that the three components of the concept—class, description, and example—are just three of the many components for any given concept.

This strategy has assessment potential because the teacher can literally see how the students understand specific concepts by looking at their maps and hearing their explanations. The maps the students develop on their own demonstrate whether they have really understood the concepts in the passages. This strategy serves to ready students for inferring word meanings on their own. By using the word map strategy, children develop concepts of what they need to know to begin to figure out an unknown word on their own. It assists the children in grades 3 and beyond to connect prior knowledge with new knowledge

This word map strategy can be adapted by the teacher to suit the specific needs and goals of instruction. Illustrations of the concept and the comparisons to other concepts can be included in the word mapping for children grades 5 and beyond. This particular strategy is also one that can be used with a research theme in other content areas.

Strategy Two: *Preview in Context*—This is a direct teaching strategy that allows the teacher to guide the students as they examine words in context prior to reading a passage. Before beginning the strategy, the teacher selects only two or three key concept words. Then the teacher reads carefully to identify passages within the text that evidence strong context clues for the word.

Then the teacher presents the word and the context to the children. As the teacher reads aloud, the children follow along. Once the teacher has finished the read-aloud, the children reread the material silently. After the silent rereading, the children are coached by the teacher on a definition of one of the key words selected for study. This is done through a child-centered discussion. As part of the discussion, the teacher asks questions that can help the children activate their prior knowledge and use the contextual clues to figure out the correct meaning of the selected key words. The teacher makes certain that the definition of the key concept word is finally made by the children.

Next, the teacher helps the children to expand the word's meaning by having them consider the following for the given key concept word: synonyms, antonyms, other contexts, or other kinds of stories/texts where the word might appear. This is the time the children check their responses to the challenge of identifying word synonyms and antonyms by having them go to the thesaurus or the dictionary to confirm their responses. In addition, the children are asked place the synonyms or antonyms they find in their word boxes or word journals. The recording of their findings will guarantee them ownership of the words and deepen their capacity to use contextual clues.

The main point to remember in using this strategy is that it should only be used when the context is strong. It will not work with struggling readers who have less prior knowledge. Through listening to the children's responses as the teacher helps them to define the word and its potential synonyms and antonyms, the teacher can assess students' ability to successfully use context clues. The key to this simple strategy is that it allows the teacher to draw the children out and to learn about their thinking process through their responses. The more talk from the child the better.

The Role of Systematic, Noncontextual Vocabulary Strategies

Hierarchical and Linear Arrays. The very complexity of the vocabulary used in this strategy description, may be unnerving for the teacher. Yet this strategy included in the Cooper (2004) literacy instruction is really very simple once it is outlined directly for children.

By using the term "hierarchical and linear" arrays, Cooper really is talking about how some words are grouped based on associative meanings. The words may have a "hierarchical" relationship to one another. For instance, the sixth grader is lower in the school hierarchy than the eighth grader. Within an elementary school, the fifth or sixth grader is at the top of the hierarchy and the pre-K or kindergartener is at the bottom of the hierarchy. By the way, the term for this strategy obviously need not be explained in this detail to K–3 children, but might be shared with some grade and age appropriate modifications with children in grades 3 and beyond. It will enrich their vocabulary development and ownership of arrays they create.

Words can have a linear relationship to one another in that they run a spectrum from bad to good. An example for K–3 children might be *pleased–happy–overjoyed*. These relationships can be displayed in horizontal boxes connected with dashes. Below is another way to display hierarchical relationships.

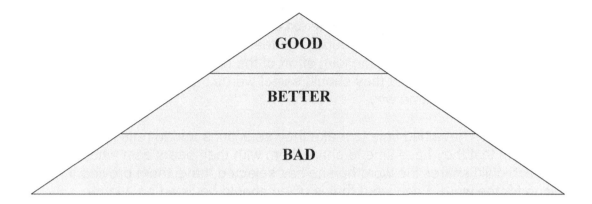

Once you get past the seemingly daunting vocabulary words, the arrays turn out to be another excellent graphic organizer tool which can help children "see" how words relate to one another.

To use this graphic organizer, the teacher should pre-select a group of words from a read-aloud or from the children's writing. Show the children how the array will look using arrows for the linear array and just straight lines for the hierarchy. In fact, invite some children up to draw the straight hierarchy lines as the array is presented. This lets the children have a role in developing even the first hierarchical model.

Create one hierarchy array and one linear array of the pre-selected word with the children. Talk them through filling in (or helping the teacher to fill in) the array. After the children have had their own successful experience with arrays, they can select the words from their independent texts or familiar, previously read favorites to study. They will also need to decide which type of array, hierarchical or linear, is appropriate. For fifth and sixth graders, this choice can and should be voiced using the now "owned" vocabulary words "hierarchical array" and "linear array."

This strategy is best used *after* reading because it will helps children to expand their word banks.

Contextual Vocabulary Strategies

Vocabulary Self-Collection. This strategy is one in which children, even on the emergent level from grade 2 and up, take responsibility for their learning. It is also by definition, a student centered strategy, which demonstrates student ownership of their chosen vocabulary.

This strategy is one that can be introduced by the teacher early in the year, perhaps even the first day or week. The format for self-collection can then be started by the children. It may take the form of a journal with photocopied template pages. It can be continued throughout the year.

To start, ask the children to read a required text or story. Invite them to select one word for the class to study from this text or story. The children can work individually, in teams, or in small groups. The teacher can also do the self-collecting so that this becomes the joint effort of the class community of literate readers. Tell the children that they should select words that particularly interest them or are unique in some way.

After the children have had time to make their selections and to reflect on them, make certain that they have time to share them with their peers as a whole class. When each child shares the word he/she has selected, have them provide a definition for the word. Each word that is given should be listed on a large experiential chart or even in a BIG BOOK format, if that is age and grade appropriate. The teacher should also share the word he/she selected and provide a definition. The teacher's definition and sharing should be somewhere in the middle of the children's recitations.

The dictionary should be used to verify the definitions. When all the definitions have been checked, a final list of child-selected and teacher-selected words should be made.

Once this final list has been compiled, the children can choose to record all or part of the list in their word journals. Some students may record only those words they find interesting. It is up to the teacher at the onset of the vocabulary self-collection activity to decide whether the children have to record all the words on the final list or can eliminate some. The decision made at the beginning by the teacher must be adhered to throughout the year.

To further enhance this strategy, children, particularly those in grades 3 and beyond, can be encouraged to use their collected words as part of their writings or to record and clip these words as they appear in newspaper stories or online. This type of additional recording demonstrates that the child has truly incorporated the word into his/her reading and writing. It also habituates children to be lifelong readers, writers, and researchers.

One of the nice things about this simple but versatile strategy is that it works equally well with either expository or narrative texts. It also provides children with an opportunity to use the dictionary.

Assessment is built into the strategy. As the children select the word for the list, they share how they used contextual clues. Further, as children respond to definitions offered by their peers, their prior knowledge can be assessed.

What is most useful about this strategy is that it documents that children can learn to read and write by reading and writing. The children take ownership of the words in the self-collection journals, which can be used later to develop writer observation journals. Children also use the word lists as a start for writers' commonplace books. These books are filled with newspaper, magazine, and functional document clippings using the journal words.

This activity is a good one for demonstrating the balanced literacy belief that vocabulary study works best when the words studied are chosen by the child.

The Relationship between Oral Vocabulary and the Process of Identifying and Understanding Written Words

One way to explore the relationship between oral vocabulary and the comprehension of written words is through the use of oral records (which are discussed at length in the appendix).

In *On Solid Ground: Strategies for Teaching Reading K–3*, Sharon Taberski (2000) discusses how oral reading records can be used by the K–3 teacher to assess how well children are using cueing systems. She notes that the running record format can also show visual depictions for the teacher of how the child "thinks" as the child reads. The notation of miscues in particular shows how a child "walks through" the reading process. These notations indicate if and what types of "guided" support the child may require to understand the words he/she reads aloud. Taberski notes that children need to think about several things at once when they read. First, they must consider whether what they are reading makes sense (semantic or meaning cues). Next, they must know whether their reading "sounds right" in terms of Standard English (syntactic and structural cues). Third, they have to weigh whether their oral language actually and accurately matches the letters the words represent (visual or graphophonic cues).

In taking the running record and having the opportunity first-hand to listen to the child talk about the text, the teacher can analyze the relationship between the child's oral language and word comprehension. Information from the running record provides the teacher with a road map for differentiated cueing system instruction.

For example, when a running record is taken, a child often makes a mistake but then self-corrects. The child may select from various cueing systems when he/she self-corrects. These include: "M" for meaning, "S" for syntax, and "V" for visual. The use of a visual cue means that the child is drawing on his/her knowledge of spelling patterns. Of course, Taberski cautions that any relationship between oral language and comprehension that the teacher draws from an examination of the oral-reading records, must be drawn from not just one, but a series of three or more of the child's oral reading records, taken over time.

A teacher can review children's running records over time to note their pattern of miscues and which cues they have the greatest tendency to use in their self-corrections. Whichever cueing system the children use to the greatest extent, it is necessary for the teacher to offer support in also using the other cueing systems to construct correct meaning. Taberski suggests that while assessing running records to determine the relationship between oral language and meaning, the children read from "just right" books defined as those books that children can read on their own at between 92% and 97% accuracy level.

Strategies for Promoting Oral Language Development and Language Comprehension

Read Alouds. (This is the cornerstone of the *Balanced Literacy Approach* for teaching reading. Therefore, it is advised that the teacher candidate and new teacher read this material carefully. This may well appear as an essay topic in the Constructed Response section of the test.)—Within the context of the *Balanced Literacy Approach* and the *Literacy Block,* the *Read-Aloud* is part of *Whole Class Activities. The book should be selected from the classroom library and be appropriate for a read-aloud.* Before reading the book to the class, the teacher needs to be familiar with it. The teacher should also *plan* or at least *know* what nuances of content, style, rhythm, and vocabulary will be emphasized in the reading.

In addition, specifically for the younger grades, the teacher should select a text that also enhances the development of phonemic awareness. This might include a text that can be used to teach rhyming, alliteration, or poetry.

Sometimes, read-aloud texts are selected for their tie-ins with the science, social studies, and mathematics curriculum.

Teachers generally aim to teach one strategy during the read-aloud, which the children will practice in small groups or independently. Among these strategies for the first grader could be print strategies and talking about books.

As the teacher reads aloud, the teacher's voice quality should highlight his/her enjoyment of the book and involvement with its text. Often in a balanced literacy classroom, the teacher reads from a specially decorated *Reader's Chair,* as do the guest readers. This chair's decorativeness, complete with comfortable throwback pillows or rocking chair style frame, is meant to set an atmosphere that will promote the children's engagement in and love for lifelong reading.

The Balanced Literacy Approach also advocates that teachers select books which children will enjoy reading aloud. Particularly accessible texts for the elementary school classroom read-alouds are collections of poetry.

Teachers must allow time for discussion during and after each Read-Aloud period. After the children have made comments, the teacher should also talk about the reading.

Knowledge of Common Sayings, Proverbs, and Idioms

Strategy: The Fortune Cookie Strategy (Reissman, 1994). Grades 3 and up—Distribute the fortune cookies to the children. Have them eat the cookies and then draw their attention to the enclosed fortunes.

First, the teacher will model by reading aloud his/her own fortune. After reading the fortune aloud, the teacher will explain what the fortune means using its vocabulary as a guide. Finally, the teacher may share whether or not the teacher agrees with the statement made in the fortune.

Similarly, children can read their fortunes aloud, explain the saying, and tell whether they agree with the proverb or prediction.

Following this activity, children can be asked to go home and interview their parents or community members to get family proverbs and common sayings.

Once the children return with the sayings and proverbs, they can each share them and explain their meaning. The class as a whole can discuss to what extent these sayings are true for everyone. Proverbs and sayings can become part of a word wall or be included in a special literacy center. The teacher can create fill-in, put-together, and writing activities to go with the proverbs. These tie in nicely with cultural study in grade 3–6 including the study of Asian, Latin American, and African nations.

What makes proverbs particularly effective for vocabulary development are the limited number of words in their texts and the fact that these short texts allow for guided and facilitated reading instruction.

This strategy also highlights, in a positive way, both the uniqueness and commonality of the family proverbs contributed by children from ELL backgrounds. If possible their proverbs can also be posted in their native languages as well as in English.

To see more proverbs, go to:

http://www.serve.com/shea/germusa/prov1.htm

Write like a Babylonian: http://www.upennmuseum.com/cuneiform.cgi

Write like an Egyptian: http://www.upennmuseum.com/hieroglyphsreal.cgi

Knowledge of Foreign Words and Abbreviations Commonly Used in English (e.g., RSVP)

Strategy: RSVP your foreign language in English literacy

Of course, the English language is replete with abbreviations that are shortened forms of words from other languages. Not only can this be used for expanding children's vocabulary and writing variety, it can also help to positively highlight the bilingual and sometimes trilingual abilities of ELL students.

The teacher should develop a word-strip mix-and-match game with commonly found foreign words and abbreviations. These words should, if possible, be cut out of newspapers, flyers, and magazines to highlight their authenticity as items from everyday life and demonstrate concretely the influence of other languages on the English language. Among those common words and abbreviations might be: perfume, liqueur (chocolate, of course), latte, cappuccino, brioche, latkes, etc. To get sufficient material to cut out to start the game, just get an extra Sunday newspaper or pick up a few circulars from a large supermarket.

Model for the children how to play the game and use the dictionary to find out the common words' or abbreviations' meanings. Next, have the children work as a whole class or in small groups to identify the derivations of the foreign words and even map them on a world map.

For additional foreign word activities, children can choose from a number of options. These can include maintaining a *Big Book of Foreign Words or Abbreviations,* to which many contribute; using the weekly food circulars and collecting labels with foreign words which can then be collaged with an accompanying product list; and authoring stories and true accounts featuring as many foreign words as possible.

What is productive about this strategy is that it enhances vocabulary development while also highlighting the extent to which the English language as currently used in the United States is embedded with foreign language words and terms. This, of course, makes the native language talents of the ELL child stand out as positive and important ones.

Extending a Reader's Understanding of Familiar Words

Dictionary Use. Dictionaries are useful for spelling, writing, and reading. It is very important to initially expose and habituate students to enjoy using the dictionary.

Cooper (2004) suggests that the following be kept in mind as the teacher of grades K–6 introduces and then habituates children to a lifelong fascination with the dictionary and vocabulary acquisition.

Requesting or suggesting that children look up a word in the dictionary should be an invitation to a wonderful exploration, not a punishment or busy work that has no reference to their current reading assignment.

Model the correct way to use the dictionary for children even as late as the third to sixth grade. Many have never been taught proper dictionary skills. The teacher needs to demonstrate to the children that as an adult reader and writer, he/she routinely and happily uses the dictionary and learns new information that makes him or her better at reading and writing.

Cooper believes in beginning dictionary study and use as early as kindergarten; this is now very possible because of the proliferation of lush picture dictionaries that can be introduced at that grade level. He also suggests that children not only look at these picture dictionaries, but also begin to make dictionaries of their own at this grade level filled with pictures and beginning words. As children join the circle of lexicographers, they will begin to see themselves as compilers and users of dictionaries. Of course, this will support their ongoing vocabulary development.

In early grade levels, use of the dictionary can nicely complement the children's mastery of the alphabet. They should be given whole-class and small-group practice in locating words.

As the children progress with their phonetic skills, the dictionary can be used to show them phonetic re-spelling using the pronunciation key.

Older children in grades 3 and beyond need explicit teacher demonstrations and practice in the use of guide words. They also need to begin to learn about the hierarchies of various word meanings. In the upper grades, children should also explore using special content dictionaries and glossaries located in the backs of their books.

Strategies for Promoting Comprehension across the Curriculum by Expanding Knowledge of Content Area Vocabulary

Key Words. Cooper (2004) feels that it is up to the teacher to preview the content area text to identify the main ideas. Then the teacher should compile a list of terms related to the content thrust. These terms and words become part of the key concepts list.

Next, the teacher sees which of the key concept words and terms are already defined in the text. These will not require direct teaching. Words for which children have sufficient skills to determine their meaning through base, root, prefixes, or suffixes also will not require direct teaching.

Instruction in the remaining key words, which should not be more than two or three in number, can be provided before, during, or after reading. If students have previewed the content area and identified those words with which they need support, the instruction should be provided before reading. Instruction can also easily be provided as part of guided reading support. After reading support is indicated, the text offers the children an opportunity to enrich their own vocabularies.

Having children work as a whole class or in small groups on a content-specific dictionary for a topic regularly covered in their grade level social studies, science, or mathematics curriculum offers an excellent collaborative opportunity for children to design a dictionary/word resource that can celebrate their own vocabulary learning. Such a resource can then be used with the next year's classes as well.

Development of Vocabulary Knowledge and Skills in Individual Students

Hierarchical and linear array vocabulary-development strategies lend themselves well to support struggling learners or second language learners. The use of arrays allows these learners to use a visual format to "see" and diagram word relationships. Furthermore, the diagrams are easy to make and can be illustrated. With sufficient support and modeling, many special needs children can do simple linear and hierarchical arrays on their own. The arrays can also be attractively displayed in resource rooms and in regular education classrooms as a demonstration of these individual students' ownership of their words.

English Language Learners should first capably demonstrate their capacity to fill out hierarchical and linear arrays in their native language and then can work with this same format to hone their English Language vocabulary development. Their native language hierarchical relationships and arrays can be displayed in their general education classrooms. Teachers may also want to encourage children in grades 3 and beyond to make connections between some of the native, other than English, words and words derived from them in English. This could be a "buddy" (ELL child and native English Language speaker) investigation or could be an activity for ELL children alone. At any rate, use of the array with the ELL child's native language makes that child a second language vocabulary owner which immediately includes the child positively in ongoing vocabulary development.

Cooper (2004) suggests that teachers who have children from different language backgrounds use any unscheduled or "extra" time that emerges for read-alouds.

Using the Semantic Feature Analysis Grid

Highly proficient readers can be asked to help same-grade peers or better yet younger peers with their word-analysis skills by having them work with these struggling readers on filling out teacher-developed semantic analysis grids. Some highly proficient readers from fifth and sixth grade may even desire to create their own semantic-analysis grids for their peers or younger tutees. In this way, highly proficient readers can gain insight at an early age into the field of teaching reading. At the same time, struggling readers can have the edge taken off their struggles by working with a peer or an older student. For both groups of students—the proficient and the struggling readers—this experience promotes and celebrates word-analysis skills and nurtures the concept of a literate and caring community of readers.

When the class is making semantic-analysis grids, ELL students can add in items that reflect their cultures. For instance, Latino children can add in plantains and guava to the list of fruit which their non-Latino peers might list. This puts the ELL learners in a positive light, providing them an opportunity to enrich the knowledge base of their peers' subject category inventory. The easy notations on the grid are accessible to even ELL children with limited English language writing and speaking capacities.

Special needs learners can benefit from the grid, too. While the grid may be developed by teachers, paraprofessionals, or tutors, the children can make the notations themselves and illustrate the grid. The grid can be posted or kept in the word center. It provides special needs learners, who are often spatial learners, with a concrete demonstration of their word-analysis achievement.

Biemiller's research indicates that the listening vocabulary of a sixth grader who tests at the 25th percentile in reading is equivalent to that of a 75th percentile third grader. This deficit in vocabulary presents a formidable challenge for the sixth grader to succeed, not only on reading tests, but in various content subjects in elementary school and beyond.

Skill 8.4 **Demonstrate knowledge of the relationship between students' oral language proficiency and their ability to comprehend text at the word level, the sentence level, and the paragraph level**

Generalization of tasks from specific skill instruction to broader areas is a complex skill that some students have difficulty obtaining. Understanding how English grammar, spelling, and the other language conventions cross all of the language arts disciplines is a skill students need in order to be successful.

Reading. When reading, students are exposed to all of the grammar, spelling, and other reading conventions on a regular basis. As the teacher, it is important to take time to point out these areas to the students who may otherwise pass them by without a second thought. One important strategy for helping in this area is called Directed Reading Thinking Activities (DRTA). This strategy developed by Russell Stauffer (1969) allows the teacher to guide the thinking of the student to make predictions and improve comprehension. An adaptation of this strategy would allow the teacher to guide the thinking of the students to recognize and identify the conventions.

Writing. Since writing is a more formal skill than oral language, the conventions are slightly different. Many times students write the same way they speak, which is usually unacceptable for written language. The editing process is probably the most effective method for helping students achieve improved use of grammar, spelling, syntax, and semantics. Peer editing and teacher editing provide excellent tools for students.

Listening. Listening is an art. Many times it is obvious that students are hearing what the speaker is saying, but are not actively listening. Setting the purpose for an oral presentation and providing graphic organizers are two strategies that help structure listening activities. Having to develop graphic organizer gives students a purpose for listening and makes them focus on distinguishing between relevant and irrelevant information. Demonstration of correct and incorrect language conventions provides students with the opportunity to complete a compare-and-contrast situation.

Speaking. When orally presenting information, it is important that the student realize the necessity of using correct language. Having the students practice the presentation aloud into a tape recorder is a technique that will allow the students the opportunity to critique themselves or others and provide valuable feedback.

Skill 8.5   **Recognize the role of prior knowledge in supporting fluent reading and reading comprehension and demonstrating knowledge of ways to activate students' prior knowledge and scaffold reading tasks to support comprehension**

The Balanced Reading Approach is taking on new meaning after publication of the well-known report, *Teaching Children to Read* from the National Reading Panel (2000). A comprehensive and well-balanced reading program is becoming more complex and difficult to define.

In general, such a program should include instruction in phonemic awareness, phonics, fluency, comprehension, and vocabulary. There also needs to be time when the teacher reads *to* the children, when the teacher reads *with* the children, and where the children read for themselves. The catch phrase, "To, With, and By," has often been used to remind teachers of the types of reading that must occur within the classroom.

In reading *to* students, teachers generally use a read-aloud approach. The read-aloud helps build vocabulary and listening comprehension. It allows modeling of fluent reading and builds a love of reading.

When reading *with* students, teachers use two different approaches: shared reading and guided reading. Shared reading allows the teacher to share more difficult texts with the students than they might be able to read on their own. The teacher generally focuses on comprehension skills and will often complete think alouds or use other comprehension strategies to increase the development of these skills. Vocabulary development and modeling appropriate fluency are also key factors in shared reading. In guided reading, the students are reading texts on their instructional levels. In these small groups, skill development occurs regularly. This is where the phonics skills and phonemic awareness skills can be focused on specifically for a small group of students.

Finally, independent reading (*by* students) provides each child the opportunity to practice all of the parts of reading. Children are able to get multiple repetitions of the same skills taught otherwise to build the automatic nature with which they read.

No one part of the reading program as described above would be sufficient to help the students develop and become proficient readers. It is the inter-relationship of all these parts that makes the program work. If one part is removed, not only are skills missed, but also the practice opportunities and modeling opportunities are lost.

While all of the components of good reading instruction can be taught or practiced in each section individually, it is when they are combined that the most economical use of the time occurs.

Teachers should have a toolkit of instructional strategies, materials, and technologies to encourage and teach students how to solve problems and think critically about subject content. With each curriculum chosen by a district for school implementation, comes an expectation that students must master benchmarks and standards of learning skills. There is an established level of academic performance and proficiency in public schools that students are required to master in today's classrooms. Research of national and state standards indicate that there are additional benchmarks and learning objectives in the subject areas of science, foreign language, English language arts, history, art, health, civics, economics, geography, physical education, mathematics, and social studies that students are required to master in state assessments (Marzano and Kendall, 1996).

Students use basic skills to understand things that are read such as a reading passage or a math word problem or directions for a project. However, students apply additional thinking skills to fully comprehend how what was read could be applied to their own life or how to make comparisons or choices based on the factual information given. These higher-order thinking skills are called *critical thinking skills* as students think about thinking and teachers are instrumental in helping students use these skills in everyday activities.

- Comparing shopping ads or catalogue deals
- Finding the main idea from readings
- Applying what's been learned to new situations
- Gathering information/data from a diversity of sources to plan a project
- Following a sequence of directions
- Looking for cause and effect relationships
- Comparing and contrasting information and synthesizing information

Teachers who couple diversity in instructional practices with engaging and challenging curriculum and the latest advances in technology can create the ultimate learning environment for creative thinking and continuous learning for students. Teachers who are innovative and creative in instructional practices are able to model and foster creative thinking in their students. Encouraging students to maintain journals and portfolios of their valued work from projects and assignments will allow students to make conscious choices on including a diversity of their creative endeavors in a filing format that can be treasured throughout the educational journey.

Helping students become effective note-takers and stimulating a diversity of perspectives for spatial techniques that can be applied to learning is a proactive teacher strategy in creating a visual learning environment where art and visualization become natural art forms for learning. In today's computer environment, students must understand that computers cannot replace the creative thinking and skill application that comes from the greatest computer on record, the human mind.

Strategic reading occurs when students are reading to gain information. The purpose for reading is simply to learn. Typically, strategic reading occurs with nonfiction or expository texts. The students are generally given some guidance on what information they are to find.

In strategic reading however, it is not a simple recall of facts. This is not literal comprehension. The students are required to read a great deal of information about a topic. Then they need to take all of that information and build their own foundation of knowledge. Constructing knowledge is what makes strategic reading different from simple literal recall. It is through this process that information is connected to prior knowledge.

These connections are key factors in the success of comprehension. Strategic reading requires the reader to be able to tie new and old learning together to compound it into useful information. This process of thinking about reading and manipulating all *that is* learned is known as metacognition.

Metacognition is a complex set of variables for the reader. The reader needs to be aware of the reading process and be able to recognize when information does not make sense to. At this point, the reader needs to adjust the things they are doing in order to clarify and make the necessary connections. Throughout this process, the reader must continue to integrate the new and old.

Strategic readers call into play their meta-cognitive capacities as they analyze texts so they are aware of the skills needed to construct meaning from the text structure.

When reading strategically, students need to keep in mind several factors:

Self-Monitoring. When students self-monitor, they are able themselves to keep track of all the factors involved in the process. In this way, they are able to process the information in the manner that is best for them.

Setting the Purpose for Reading. In strategic reading, the child has a specific reason for reading the text—to gain information. This reason should be clear to the student. If it is unclear, the student will not be successful.

Rereading. Rereading is probably one of the most used methods for taking in an overwhelming amount of information. By revisiting the text more than once, the student is able to note and take in smaller pieces of information that he/she might have missed during the first read.

Adjusting Reading Rates and Strategies. Similar to self-monitoring, students must be able to understand that sometimes it will be necessary to read slower than at other times. Sometimes they will need to make adjustments to the way they are reading in order to be successful at gaining the information they want to gain.

Text Factors and Structure. Understanding the arrangement of nonfiction text with section and chapter titles, heads and subheads, (set in bold type) and other unique organizational devices can provide students with other tools to be successful. Students who use these as the main points can than fill in additional learning by reading the information below that heading. Also, if looking for a specific piece of information students can utilize Table of Contents and Indexes, which are generally a part of expository writing. By understanding the structure of the text, students save valuable time and decrease the amount of rereading required.

Generally, there is so much known and valuable information about topics that authors try to share all of that information with the reader. Since there is a large amount of information to be conveyed, authors use specific organizational tools to break the text into smaller, more manageable, chunks. These different structures require the reader to make adjustments to their own personal reading style in order to successfully manage the intake of the new learning.

Note Taking. Learning how to take notes when reading is a tough skill to master and to teach. It requires the reader to understand the main ideas in a passage and immediately be able to summarize those ideas into something meaningful. This process requires a great deal of higher-order thinking and may need to be scaffolded for younger students. A method of providing support is to provide a rough outline with some information missing that the students can find when they are reading.

Mapping. Mapping is a strategy that can be used to reach all learning styles and therefore is an important one to teach. It is exactly what its name implies—a map of the reading. Just as a road map helps the driver get from point A to point B, so it is for a reading map. It helps the reader maneuver through the information in a meaningful manner. Maps can use words with key ideas connected to smaller chunks of information. They can also use pictures instead of words to help the more visual learner. Adding color to a map can help certain ideas stand out. This can be particularly helpful for students to begin to understand the process of prioritization in skills. Combining words and pictures is probably the most commonly used type of map. Lines are drawn between connecting concepts to show relationships and because the reader is creating it himself or herself, it is meaningful only to them. Maps are individual creations and revolve around the reader's learning and prior knowledge.

Skill 8.6 Recognize how differences in students' backgrounds (e.g., cultural and linguistic) can affect their reading comprehension

Adolescent literature, because of the age range of readers, is extremely diverse. Fiction for the middle group, usually ages 10 and 11 to 14 and 15, deals with issues of coping with internal and external changes in their lives. Because children's writers in the twentieth century have produced increasingly realistic fiction, adolescents can now find problems dealt with honestly in novels.

Teachers of middle/junior high school students see the greatest change in interests and reading abilities. Fifth and sixth graders, included in elementary grades in many schools, are viewed as *older children* while seventh and eighth graders are considered *preadolescent.* Ninth graders, included sometimes as top dogs in middle school and sometimes as underlings in high school, definitely view themselves as *teenagers.* Their literature choices are often governed more by interest than by ability. As a result, a wealth of high-interest, low-readability books have flooded the market in recent years. Tenth through twelfth graders will still select high-interest books for pleasure reading but are also easily encouraged to stretch their literature muscles by reading more classics.

Because of rapid social changes in recent years, topics that once did not interest young people until they reached their teens — suicide, gangs, and homosexuality — are now subjects of books for even younger readers. The plethora of commercial high-interest books reveals how desperately schools have failed to produce on-level readers and how the market has adapted to that need. However, these high-interest books are now readable for younger children whose reading levels are at or above normal. No matter how tastefully written, some contents are inappropriate for younger readers. The problem becomes not so much steering them toward books that they have the reading ability to handle, but encouraging them toward books whose content is appropriate to their levels of cognitive and social development. A fifth-grader may be able to read V. C. Andrews' book *Flowers in the Attic* but not possess the social and/or moral development to handle the deviant behavior of the characters. At the same time, because of the complex changes affecting adolescents, the teacher must be well versed in child development and learning theory as well as be competent to teach the subject matter of language and literature.

COMPETENCY 9.0   UNDERSTAND STRATEGIES FOR DEVELOPING AND
                  REINFORCING STUDENTS' READING
                  COMPREHENSION SKILLS AS THEY RELATE TO
                  LITERARY TEXTS

Skill 9.1   Identify levels of comprehension (e.g., literal, inferential, and
             evaluative) of literary texts and demonstrate knowledge of
             strategies for promoting comprehension of literary texts at all
             three levels

If there were two words synonymous with reading comprehension as far as the
Balanced Literacy Approach is concerned, they would be *constructing meaning.*
Cooper, Taberski, Strickland, and other key theorists and classroom teachers
conceptualize the reader as interacting with the text and bringing his/her prior
knowledge and experience to it. Writing is interlaced with reading and is a
mutually integrative and supportive parallel process. Hence the division of
literacy learning by the balanced literacy folks into reading workshop and writing
workshop, with the same anchor "readings" or books being used for both.

Consider the sentence, "The test booklet was white with black print, but very
scary looking." According to the idea of constructing meaning as the reader read
this sentence, the schemata (generic information stored in the mind) of tests the
reader had experienced was activated by the author's notion that tests are scary.
Therefore the ultimate meaning that the reader derives from the page is from the
reader's own responses and experiences coupled with the ideas the author
presents. The reader constructs a meaning that reflects the author's intent and
also the reader's response to that intent.

It is also to be remembered that, generally, readings are fairly lengthy passages,
composed of paragraphs which in turn are composed of more than one
sentence. With each successive sentence, and every new paragraph, the reader
refocuses. The schemata are reconsidered, and a new meaning is constructed.

**Knowledge of levels of reading comprehension and strategies for
promoting comprehension of imaginative literary texts at all levels**

Taberski (2000) recommends that, initially, strategies for promoting
comprehension of imaginative literary texts be done with the whole class.
Here are Taberski's four main strategies for promoting comprehension of
imaginative literary texts. She feels that if repeated sufficiently during the K–3
years and even if introduced as late as grade 4, these strategies will even serve
the adult lifelong reader in good stead.

Strategy One: *Stopping to Think* —**Reflects on the text as a whole.** As part of this strategy, the reader is challenged to come up with the answer to these three questions:

- What do I think is going to happen? (Inferential)
- Why do I think this is going to happen? (Evaluative and inferential)
- How can I prove that I am right by going back to the story? (Inferential)

Taberski recommends that teachers introduce these key instructive strategies with books that can be read in one sitting and with the use of picture books.

Taberski also suggests that books which are read aloud and used for this strategy also contain a strong storyline, some degree of predictability, a text that invites discussion, and a narrative with obvious stopping points.

Strategy Two: *Story Mapping*—**Promotes comprehension of imaginative/literary texts.** For stories to suit this strategy, they should have distinct episodes, few characters, and clear-cut problems to solve. In particular, Taberski tries to use a story where a single, central problem or issue is introduced at the beginning of the story and is then resolved, or at least followed through, by the close of the story.

To make a story map of a particular story, Taberski divides the class into four groups. She asks the first group of children to illustrate the *characters* in the book, the second to draw the *setting,* the third group to tackle the *problem,* and the fourth group to address the *resolution.* The story map may also help children hold together their ideas for writing in the writing workshop as they take their reading of an author's story to a new level.

Strategy Three: *Character Mapping*—**Focuses readers on the ways in which the main character's personal traits can determine what will happen in the story.** In this strategy, character mapping works best when the character is a non-stereotypical individual, has been featured perhaps in other books by the same author, has a personality that is somewhat predictable, and is capable of changing behavior as a consequence of what happens. Using writing to share, deepen, and expand understanding of literary texts is a cornerstone of the Balanced Literacy Approach.

Strategy Four: *Read and Record*—Taberski advocates reading sections of stories aloud and then having the teacher pause to reflect on what's happened in the story and model writing down a response to it. The teacher can use a chart to record his/her response to the events or characters of a particular story being read and the children can contribute their comments as well. Later on, the children can start reflective reader's notebooks or journals and independently record their reactions to their readings.

The best types of texts for this type of response are those that relate to age-appropriate issues for young children (e.g., homework, testing, bullies, and friendship), a plot that can be interpreted in different ways, a text that is filled with questions, and a text full of suspense or wonder.

Development of Literary Response Skills

Literary response skills are dependent on prior knowledge, schemata, and background. Schemata (the plural of schema) are those structures which represent concepts stored in our memory.

Without schemata and experiences to call upon as they read, children have little ability to comprehend. Of course, the reader's schemata and prior knowledge have more influence on the comprehension of plot or character information that is implied rather than directly stated.

Prior Knowledge. Prior knowledge can be defined as all of an individual's prior experiences, learning, and development preceding the child's entry into a specific learning situation or attempt to comprehend a specific text. Sometimes prior knowledge can be erroneous or incomplete. Obviously, if there are misconceptions in a child's prior knowledge, these must be corrected so that the child's overall comprehension skills can continue to progress. Prior knowledge of children includes their accumulated positive and negative experiences both in and out of school.

These experiences might range from wonderful family travels, watching television, or visiting museums and libraries to visiting hospitals, prisons, and surviving poverty. Whatever prior knowledge the child brings to the school setting, the independent reading and writing the child does *in school* immeasurably expands his/her total knowledge and hence broadens his/her reading comprehension capabilities.

Before beginning any imaginative/literary text, the teacher must consider the following about the students' level of prior knowledge:

1. What prior knowledge needs to be activated for the text and theme or for the writing to be done successfully?

2. How independent are the children in using strategies to activate their prior knowledge?

Holes and Roser (1987) have suggested five techniques for activating prior knowledge before starting an imaginative/literary text:

- *Free Recall:* Tell us what you know about.

- *Unstructured Discussion:* Let's talk about.

- *Structured Question:* Who exactly was Jane Aviles in the life of the hero of the story?

- *Word Association:* When you hear these words—hatch, elephant, who, think— What author do you think of?

- *Recognition:* Mulberry Street—What author comes to mind?

Previewing, predicting, and story mapping are also excellent strategies for activating prior knowledge.

Development of Literary Analysis Skills

There are many exciting ways to sensitize and to teach children about the features and formats of different literary genres.

Strategy One: *Genre Switch-Reader and Writer Transformation.* This strategy should be introduced as a read-aloud with young children or with children who are struggling readers. In a similar fashion, it would be introduced as a read-aloud for ELL learners. Older children in grades 3–6 might just be "started off" by a teacher prompt and do the required reading on their own.

To begin, the teacher selects a particular genre book. If it is close to Halloween, a goblin or suspense story will do well. The teacher begins to read the story with an open invitation to the students to determine, as the story is being read, what type of story it is and what makes it that type of story.

Older children take notes in their reading journals, while younger children and those more in need of explicit teacher support contribute their ideas and responses as part of the discussion in class. Their responses are recorded on a chart.

As the reading continues, the story type components are listed on the chart (most of the responses are those which have been elicited from the children). At some point, in what is either an oral read-aloud, guided reading, or independent reading, the teacher directs the children's attention to the components which have emerged on the chart. They then use these components—generally components of character, setting, plot, style, conflict, and language—to identify the story genre.

The teacher provides the children with an opportunity to expound at length on why this story is an example of the genre they have identified. Once they have done so, the teacher challenges them to consider how this story—with its given characters, plot, and setting—would change if the genre were different. The teacher can challenge the class as a whole with the idea of changing the story to a radically different genre, for example, from suspense to a fairy tale or a comedy, or allow the children to come up with another genre. Then, depending on the children's developed writing abilities, they might be given time to rewrite the story on their own or retell it in class prior to writing and illustrating it.

In the Balanced Literacy Approach, this transformation of the story into another genre is done as part of the Writing Workshop component. (The same reading material is used as the source for writing.) With the implementation of this strategy, children get experience in doing an in-depth analysis of a particular genre or engaging in hands-on writing that transforms the basic plot and characters into another genre. (In trying hands-on writing, they can even assess if they cannot yet write or cannot yet write in English.) This authenticates the children's participation as readers and writers.

Strategy Two: *Analyzing Story Elements.* Story elements include plot (conflict and resolution), setting (time and place), characters (flat and round/static and dynamic), and theme (the main idea of the story). Students can use graphic organizers such as story maps, compare/contrast displays, and sequence boxes to display their understanding of these critical features of fiction.

Strategy Three: *Analyzing Character Development.* Characters in children's literature may be flat or round. A flat character is one-dimensional and is often defined by one characteristic. Rosie in *Rosie's Walk* is an example. A round character seems like someone you know, such as Jess in *Bridge to Terabithia*. Static characters do not change from the beginning to the end of the story, while dynamic ones do. Characters reveal themselves through their actions, interactions, and what they say.

Strategy Four: *Interpreting Figurative Language.* Similes are direct comparisons between two things using *like* or *as.* "Her eyes were like stars" is a simile. Metaphors are indirect comparisons, such as "The earth is a big blue marble." Personification is giving human characteristics to non-animal beings. Frances, Shrek, or the animals in *Mr. Gumpy's Outing* are all examples of personification.

Strategy Five: *Identifying Literary Allusions.* Children can understand allusions best when they read a lot. A literary allusion that appears in a story is also called *intertextuality.* That is when a reference, character, or symbol from one story appears or is alluded to in another. Recently, many popular children's books use literary allusions from Albert and Janet Ahlbergs' *Each Peach Pear Plum* to Jon Scieszka's *The True Story of the Three Little Pigs.* Note that any character or plot element can become allusions, not just references from fairy tales.

Strategy Six: *Analyzing the Author's Point of View.* In fiction, point of view is the vantage point from which the narrator tells the story. We determine point of view by asking: Where is the narrator standing in relation to the characters? Is the narrator inside or outside of the story? If inside, is the narrator one of the characters? This is *first person point of view.* If outside, can the narrator "see" into anyone else's mind besides his/her own? If the narrator cannot see into the mind and heart of other characters, then the point of view is *third person limited.* Narrators who can see what other characters are thinking and feeling are using *third person omniscient point of view.*

Use of Comprehension Strategies Before, During, and After Reading

Cooper (2004), Taberski (2000), Cox (2005) and other researchers recommend a broad array of comprehension strategies before, during, and after reading. Cooper suggests a broad range of classroom posters on the walls plus explicit instruction that provides children with prompts to monitor their own reading Such as *My Strategic Reading Guide:*

1. Do I infer/predict important information, use what I know, and think about what may happen or what I want to learn?

2. Can I identify important information about the story elements?

3. Do I generate questions and search for the answers?

4. Does this make sense to me? Does this help me meet my purpose in reading?

5. If lost, do I remember the remedies to use: reread, read further ahead, look at the illustrations, ask for help, think about the words, and evaluate what I have read?

6. Do I remember to think about how the parts of the stories that I was rereading came together?

Storyboard panels—used by comic strip artists, artists who do advertising campaigns, television and film directors—are perfect for engaging children K–6 in a variety of comprehension strategies before, during, and after reading. They can storyboard the beginning of a story, read aloud, and then storyboard its predicted middle or end. Of course, after they experience or read the actual middle or ending of the story, they can compare and contrast what they produced with its actual structure. They can play literature identification games with a buddy or as part of a group by storyboarding one key scene or characters from a book and challenging a partner or peers to identify the book and characters correctly.

Use of Oral Language Activities to Promote Comprehension

Retelling. Retelling needs to be very clearly defined so that the child reader does not think that the teacher wants him or her to repeat verbatim the WHOLE story back in the retelling. A child should be able to talk comfortably and fluently about the story he/she has just read. He/she should be able to tell the main things that have happened in the story.

When a child retells a story to a teacher, the teacher needs ways to help in assessing the child's understanding. Ironically, the teacher can use some of the same strategies he/she suggests to the child to assess the child's understanding of a book with which the teacher is not familiar. These strategies include: back cover reading, scanning the table of contents, looking at the pictures, and reading the book jacket.

If the child can explain how the story turned out and provide examples to support these explanations, the teacher should try not to interrupt the child with too many questions. Children can use the text of the book to reinforce what they are saying and they can even read from it if they wish. It is also important to note that some children need to reread the text twice with the second reading being for enjoyment.

When the teacher plans to use the retelling as a way of assessing the child, then the following ground rules have to be set and made clear to the child. The teacher explains the purpose of the retelling to determine how well the child is reading at the outset of the conference.

The teacher maintains in the child's assessment notebook or in his/her assessment record what the child is saying in phrases, not sentences. Just enough is recorded to indicate whether the child actually understood the story. The teacher also tries to analyze from the retelling why the child cannot comprehend a given text. If the child's accuracy rate with the text is below 95 per cent, then the problem is at the word level, but if the accuracy rate for the text is above 95 per cent, the difficulty lies at the text level.

Development of the Reading Comprehension Skills and Strategies of Individual Students

ELL Learners bring to their classrooms different prior-knowledge concerns than do their native English language speaking peers. Some ELL students have extensive prior knowledge in their native language and can read well on or above their chronological age level in their native language. Other ELL learners come to the United States from cultures where reading was not emphasized or from circumstances where their families did not have native language literacy opportunities. Rigg and Allen (1999) offer the following four principles regarding the literacy development and prior knowledge of ELL/second-language learners:

1. In learning a language, you learn to do the things you want to do with people who are speaking that language.

2. A second language, like the first, does not develop linearly, but rather globally.

3. Language can develop in rich context.

4. Literacy develops parallel to language. So, as speaking and listening for the second language develop, so do writing and reading.

As far as retelling, it needs to be noted that English language learners have the problem of not bringing rich oral English vocabulary to the stories they are decoding. Therefore, often they "sound the stories out" well, but cannot explain what they are about, because they do not know what the words mean.

Use of Oral Reading Fluency in Facilitating Comprehension

At some point it is crucial that just as the nervous, novice bike rider finally relaxes and speeds happily off, so too must the early reader integrate graphophonic cues with semantic and structural ones. Before this is done, the oral quality of early reader's has a stilted beat to it, which of course does not promote reading engagement and enjoyment.

The teacher needs to use all of his/her drama skills to effectively model the beauty of the voice and other nuances of the text that the class is following. Children love nothing more than to mimic their teacher. If the teacher takes time each day to recite a poem with the students, the students will begin to mimic the teacher legitimately and unhesitatingly. The poem might be posted on chart paper and be up on the wall for a week.

First the teacher can model the fluent and expressive reading of this poem. Then with a pointer, the class can recite it with the teacher. As the week progresses, the class can recite it on their own.

Use of Writing Activities to Promote Literary Response and Analysis

In addition to the activities already mentioned, the activities below will promote literary response and analysis:

- Have children take a particular passage from a story and retell it from another character's perspective.

- Challenge children to suggest a prequel or a sequel to any given story they have read.

- Ask the children to recast the key male characters as female (or vice versa). Have them explain how these changes alter the narrative, plot, or outcome of the story.

- Encourage children to transform a story or book into a Reader's Theater format and record it complete with sound effects for the audio-cassette center of the classroom.

- Have the children produce a newspaper where the characters of a given story report the news as it would be reported in their community.

- Transform the story into a ballad poem or a picture book version for younger peers.

- Give ELL children an opportunity to translate stories into their native language or to author in English (with a buddy) a favorite story that was originally published in their native language.

Skill 9.2   Demonstrate knowledge of strategies for promoting students' ability to evaluate the structural elements of plot (e.g., subplots, parallel episodes, and climax), development of plot, and the ways in which conflicts are or are not addressed or resolved

See Skill 2.2.

Skill 9.3   Demonstrate knowledge of strategies for promoting students' ability to analyze an author's purpose, point of view, and voice

The ability to analyze, synthesize, and evaluate information is critical for success in these skills. The students should practice the following activities:

Define Author's Purpose. Is the purpose to inform, to entertain, or to persuade? *Student activity:* A title can often set the tone of the passage. Reading newspaper headings is one way to practice determining the author's purpose.

Cause and Effect. Cause and effect may occur in fiction, nonfiction, poetry, and plays. Sometimes one cause will have single or multiple effects. Other times, multiple causes lead to a single effect. *Student activity:* Creating cause and effect diagrams helps students identify these components.

Chronological Order. Recognize the order of events in a selection. A text that is chronologically organized features a sequence of events that unfold over a period of time. *Student activity:* Read a passage to the students then complete a timeline by matching the major events to their corresponding dates.

Probable Passage. Probable passage is a strategy to improve comprehension, develop an awareness of story structure, and increase vocabulary development. *Student activity:* Have a story prepared to read to the students. Then put together a chart similar to the graphic organizer below. Ask the students, "Can you predict what comes next in the story you will be reading? Use the vocabulary words from your story frame to complete the probable passage by placing words into the blanks."

Selective Underlining. Selective underlining is an effective tool for enhancing the recall of facts. It can be used both for initial reading and response, and as a reference when studying for tests. Have students identify the main idea of various short stories and articles.

Story Mapping. Story mapping is a technique used after a story has been read. It includes identifying the main elements and categorizing them in sequential order. A graphic representation is often used to illustrate the story structure and sequence of events.

Graphic organizers: Graphic organizers help readers think critically about an idea, concept, or story by pulling out the main idea and supporting details. These pieces of information can then be depicted graphically through the use of connected geometric shapes. Readers who develop this skill can use it to increase their reading comprehension. An example of a graphic organizer is below.

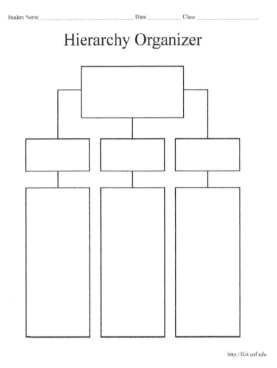

Student Name_____ Date_____ Class_____

Hierarchy Organizer

http://fcit.usf.edu

Vocabulary:
    Zeus
    recognized
    pardoned
    arena
    forest
    bound
    freed
    capture
    lion

Setting: _____

Characters: _____

Problem: _____

Solution: _____

Ending: _____

Skill 9.4 Demonstrate knowledge of strategies for promoting students' ability to interpret a character's traits, emotions, and motivations

The use of graphic organizers is one instructional strategy teachers can use to help students interpret a character's traits, emotions, and motivations. The following chart is useful in helping students organize their ideas:

(what the dialogue reveals about the character)

(physical characteristics)　　　(character's name)　　　(character's thoughts)

(what the character's actions reveal)　　　(what others think of the character)

Students can also use a list of adjectives to describe a character or write an acrostic poem using the letters of the character's name. Having the students create a T-shirt displaying a slogan that captures the essence of the character is an activity students of all ages like to do.

Skill 9.5 **Demonstrate knowledge of strategies for promoting students' ability to identify the speaker and determine if a text is narrated in the first or third person**

When reading a story to students, ask them "Who is telling the story?" Point out the clues that tell who is narrating the story and provide evidence to prove who the speaker is. Through modeling by the teacher, students should be able to identify first or third person. The students learn that when "I" is used, the story is being narrated in the first person; when "he," "she," and "they" are the pronouns used as the main method of telling the story, then the story is being narrated in the third person.

Students will realize that when a story is told in the first person, the speaker is actually a part of the story. Usually, the speaker relates incidents as they take place. The third person denotes that the person is telling the reader something about someone else and is not actually there when the action takes place. As a rule, most stories are told in the third person with the use of "they," "them," etc. Students are used to hearing these words in stories and automatically assume that the story is being told by someone else.

Teachers can also have students use a chart for students to determine the speaker of the story and the person the author uses.

Skill 9.6 **Recognize that theme refers to the meaning of a selection, whether implied or stated, and demonstrate knowledge of strategies for promoting students' ability to analyze theme as it relates to a literary text (e.g., identify and analyze symbols used to develop a text's theme)**

See Skill 2.2.

COMPETENCY 10.0 UNDERSTAND STRATEGIES FOR DEVELOPING AND REINFORCING STUDENTS' READING COMPREHENSION SKILLS AS THEY RELATE TO INFORMATIONAL TEXTS

Skill 10.1 Identify levels of comprehension (e.g., literal, inferential, and evaluative) of informational texts and demonstrate knowledge of strategies for promoting comprehension of informational texts at all three levels

There are five key strategies a child uses to read informational/expository texts: Inferencing, identifying main ideas, monitoring, summarizing, and generating questions.

Inferencing is a process that involves the reader in making a reasonable judgment based on the information given. It engages children to literally construct meaning. In order to develop and enhance this key skill in children, they might have a mini-lesson where the teacher demonstrates this by reading an expository book aloud (e.g., one on skyscrapers for young children) and then demonstrates for them the following reading habits: looking for clues, reflecting on what the reader already knows about the topic, and using the clues to figure out what the author means/intends.

Identifying main ideas in an expository text can be improved when the children have an explicit strategy for identifying important information. They can make this strategy part of their everyday reading style, "walking" through the following exercises during guided reading sessions:

1. The child should read the passage so that the topic is readily identifiable to him or her. It will be what most of the information is about.

2. The child should then be asked to be on the lookout for a sentence within the expository passage that summarizes the key information in the paragraph.

3. Then the child should read the rest of the passage or excerpt in light of this information and also note which information in the paragraph is less important. The important information the child has identified in the paragraph can be used to pinpoint the author's main idea. The child reader may even want to use some of the author's own language in stating that idea.

Monitoring means self-clarifying. As one reads, he/she may often realize that what is being read does not make sense. The reader then has to have a plan for making sensible meaning out of the excerpt. Cooper and other balanced literacy advocates have a "stop and think" strategy they use with children. The child reflects, "Does this make sense to me?" When the child concludes that it does not, the child then either rereads, reads ahead in the text, looks up unknown words, or asks for help from the teacher. What is important about monitoring is that some readers ask these questions and try these approaches without ever being explicitly taught them in school by a teacher. However, these strategies need to be explicitly modeled by most, if not all, child readers and practiced under the guidance of the teacher.

Summarizing engages the reader in pulling together, into a cohesive whole, the essential bits of information within a longer passage or excerpt of text. Children can be taught to summarize informational or expository text by following these guidelines:

1. Look at the topic sentence of the paragraph or the text and ignore the trivial information.

2. Search for information which has been mentioned more than once and make sure it is included only once in their summary.

3. Find related ideas or items and group them under a unifying heading.

4. Search for and identify a main idea sentence.

5. Put the summary together using all these guidelines.

Generating questions can motivate and enhance children's comprehension of reading in that they are actively involved. The following guidelines will help children generate meaningful questions that will trigger constructive reading of expository texts:

1. Have the children preview the text by reading the titles and subheadings.

2. Have the children look at the illustrations and the pictures. Then ask them to read the first paragraph. These first previews should yield an impressive batch of specific questions.

3. Have the children get into a Dr. Seuss mode and ask themselves a "THINK" question. Make certain that the children write down the question.

4. The children should read to find important information to answer their "think" question. and write down the answer they found and copy the sentence or sentences where they found the answer.

5. Also have the children consider whether, in light of their further reading through the text, their original question was a good one or not. Ask them to be prepared to explain why their original question was a good one or not.

6. Once the children have answered their original "think" question, have them generate additional ones and then find their answers and judge whether these questions were "good" ones in light of the text.

Strategies for Identifying Point of View, Distinguishing Facts from Opinions and Detecting Faulty Reasoning in Informational/Expository Texts

Expository texts are full of information which may or may not be factual and which may reflect the bias of the editor or author. Children need to learn that expository texts are organized around main ideas. Expository content is commonly found in newspapers, magazines, content textbooks, and informational reference books (i.e. atlas, almanac, yearbook, or encyclopedia).

The five types of expository texts (also called "text structures") to which the children should be introduced through modeled reading and a teacher facilitated walk through are: *description text, cause and effect (or causation) text, comparison text, collection text, and response structure expository texts.*

Description Text. This type of text gives the characteristics or qualities of a particular topic. It can be depended upon to be factual. Within description text, the child reader has to use all of his/her basic reading strategies, because these types of expository texts do not have explicit clue words.

Cause and Effect (or Causation) Text. This type of text is one where faulty reasoning may come into play and the child reader has to use inferential and self-questioning skills to assess whether the stated cause-and-effect relationship is a valid one. Clue words to look for are: *therefore, the reasons for, as a result of, because, in consequence of,* and *since.* The reader must then decide whether the relationship is valid. For example, "The children ran very fast. Therefore, they were out of breath."

Comparison Text. This expository text gives contrasts and similarities between two or more objects and ideas. Many social studies, art, and science text books used in class, as well as other nonfiction books, include these aspects contrast and comparison. Key words and phrases to look out for are: *like, unlike, resemble, different, different from, similar to, in contrast with, in comparison to,* and *in a different vein.* It is important that as children examine texts which are talking about illustrated or photographed entities can review the graphic representations for clues to support or contradict the text.

Collection Text. This text presents ideas in a group. The writer presents a set of related points or ideas. This text structure is also called a listing or a sequence. The author frequently uses clue words such as: *first, second, third, finally,* and *next* to alert the reader to the sequence. Based on how well the writer structures the sequence of points or ideas, the reader should be able to make connections.

It is important the writer make clear in the expository text how the items are related and why they follow in that given sequence. Simple collection texts that can be literally modeled for young children include following a simple recipe for making a favorite dessert. The children can construct meaning from a live five-minute class demonstration and would, in the future, pay closer attention to collection texts on other food and product boxes because this text had become an authentic part of their lives.

Response Structure Expository Texts. These present a question or response followed by an answer or a solution. Of course, entire mathematics text books and some science and social studies text books are filled with these types of structures. Again, it is important to walk the child reader through the excerpt and to sensitize the child to the clue words which signal this type of structure. These words include, but are not limited to: *the problem is, the question is, you need to solve for, one probable solution would be, an intervention could be, the concern is,* and *another way to solve this would be.*

Newspapers provide wonderful features which can be used by the teacher as read-alouds to introduce children grades 3–6 to point-of-view distinctions, specifically, editorials, editorial cartoons, and key sports editorial cartoons. Children can also come to understand the distinction between fact and fiction. For example, when they examine a newspaper advertisement or a supermarket circular for a product they commonly use, eat, drink, or wear, they might realize that the ad includes exaggerated claims about what the product can actually do for the individual.

Finally, the fact-versus-opinion distinction can be nicely explored if the teacher takes the children online to look at some celebrity web sites and walks them through some exaggerated claims made about their particular favorite movie star. If children have access to the internet, it is very important at some point, for the teacher to show them how to critically examine web sites, look at who developed a particular web site, and consider the credibility of the web site developers.

Use of Reading Strategies for Different Texts and Information-Gathering Goals

As children progress to the higher grades (3–6) and learn to use expository informational texts to conduct research for social studies or science projects, for example, it is important for the teacher to point out that it may not be necessary to read every single word in the text. For instance, if the child is trying to find out about hieroglyphics, he/she might only read through those sections of a book on Egyptian or Sumerian civilization which deal with picture writing. The teacher should model with a child how to go through the table of contents and the index of the book to identify those pages which specifically deal with picture writing. In addition, other children should come to the front of the room or to the center of the area where the reading group is meeting. They should then, with the support of the teacher, skim through the book for illustrations or diagrams of picture writing—the focus of their study.

Children can practice the skills of skimming texts and scanning for particular topics that connect with their grade's social studies, science, and mathematics content areas.

Use of Text Features (e.g., Index and Glossary), Graphic Features (e.g., Charts and Maps), and Reference Materials

Traditionally, the use of expository texts has been taught in a dry format that involves reference books from the school or public library, particularly, the Atlas, Almanac, and large geography volumes.

Although these worthy books from public and classroom libraries can still be used, it is much easier to take a simple newspaper to introduce and provide children with daily, ongoing, and authentic experiences in learning these necessary skills. As an added benefit, children can keep up with real world events that affect their daily lives.

Children can go on a chronological hunt through the daily newspaper and discover the many formats of schedules printed in the paper. For instance, some newspapers include a calendar of the week with literary, sports, social, movie and other public events. Children can also go on scavenger hunts through various sections of the newspaper and, on certain days, find full-blown timelines detailing famous individuals' careers, business histories, milestones in the political history of a nation, or even key movies made by a famous movie director up for an Oscar.

Newspaper stories address the public's need to know the "why" and "wherefore" behind natural disasters, company takeovers, political downfalls, national uprisings, and the like with the support of such elements as graphic representations, cause /effect diagramming, and comparison/contrast wording. If the teacher wants to make certain that the students come away recognizing and understanding these elements, he/she can pre-clip news stories to introduce in a special NEWS center and use as "teaching" tools.

After children have been walked through these comparison/contrast news writings and cause/effect diagrams as they have appeared in the newspaper, they can be challenged to find additional examples of these text structures in the news or to rewrite familiar stories using these text structures. They can even use desktop publishing to re-author the stories using the same text structures.

If a class participates in a local Newspaper in Education program, where the classroom receives a free newspaper two to three times a week, the teacher can teach index skills. Using the index of the newspaper, children compete or cooperate in small groups to find various features.

Map and chart skills take on much more relevance and excitement when the children work on these skills using what is familiar or interesting to them—such as sports charts detailing the batting averages and pass completions of their favorite players or perhaps the box scores of their older siblings' football and baseball games. Maps dealing with holiday weather become meaningful to children as they anticipate a holiday or vacation.

Skill 10.2 Demonstrate knowledge of strategies for promoting students' ability to distinguish fact from opinion and nonfiction from fiction

In order for students to be able to distinguish between fact and opinion, they need instruction in how to read context clues and vocabulary in various types of texts. The teacher has to instruct them in the difference between the two terms and provide examples. The definitions of "fact" and "opinion" should be posted in the classroom along with examples. Students can add to the list by providing examples of their own.

Ask students why it is important to tell the difference between the two. When reading a nonfiction text, ask the students to find proof for a fact you state. Then state an opinion you might have about the topic and see if the students identify the statement as an opinion. Teach the students how to recognize clue words that tell them a statement is an opinion. These include such words or phrases as: *I think, my favorite, all, everyone, no one, never, always,* etc.

When teaching the difference between nonfiction and fiction, one strategy to use is to ask students if a specific situation in a work of fiction could be true. Students should also know the types of text included in the nonfiction genre and be able to explain why a text is either fiction or nonfiction.

Students can complete a chart or Venn diagram comparing fiction and nonfiction. They will identify elements that are common to both and the elements that are unique to each one. One example of how teachers can do this is to read a fiction book and a nonfiction book about the same topic. Then have the students complete the chart to show they understand the differences. This same technique can be used to help students understand the difference between fact and opinion.

Skill 10.3   Demonstrate knowledge of strategies for promoting students' ability to recognize and trace the development of author's argument, point of view, or perspective in an informative text

See Skill 4.4.

Skill 10.4   Demonstrate knowledge of strategies for promoting students' ability to identify evidence to support an argument and to locate information to answer questions and draw conclusions

See Skill 4.4.

Skill 10.5   Demonstrate knowledge of strategies for promoting students' ability to use various methods for summarizing main ideas, supporting ideas, and supporting details

As proficient readers, students must master strategies to monitor their comprehension. Teachers need to model these skills effectively, helping students eventually apply them independently to their own reading.

Self-Questioning. In this technique, the students will ask themselves a series of questions about the text to ensure they understand the progression of events. These questions generally revolve around the major story elements: characters, plot, setting, events, climax, and resolution. The teacher models for students how to develop questions.

Think Alouds. As previously discussed, thinking aloud is one of the most effective strategies both for teaching comprehension and for working through complex concepts presented in some texts. When using the think-aloud approach, the teacher is simply speaking out loud every thought that would normally be going on silently in her head. As the teacher demonstrates and explains the connections he/she is making while reading, the students begin to understand how the teacher arrived at these connections. Integrating new information with the old information is a valuable skill for students to master.

Visualization. Visualization is the process of creating a mental picture corresponding to the words on the page. Generally, good readers have a mental image of what they are reading. The phrasing and author's voice provide clear details that allow multiple readers to have the same basic vision. When working with visualization it can sometimes be helpful for students to take the additional step of drawing out the picture as they see it in their mind. Working with the teacher, the students can advance their comprehension even if key concepts are missing.

Graphic Organizers. Teacher-prepared graphic organizers are very helpful in providing students with a visual means of organizing and tracking all of the information contained in a text. The next level of appropriate use involves teaching the students how to develop their *own* method of organizing the events and information contained in a text. By becoming less reliant on teacher-prepared organizers, the students will have a better tool that can be used when teachers do not provide organizers or when the students are reading on their own.

Reading Strategies. It is imperative that students understand and are able to utilize the many different types of reading strategies before they can monitor them on their own. Taking the time to teach the skills can provide the foundation that allows students the ability to begin monitoring their own comprehension. These skills include: inferring, questioning, drawing conclusions and making connections, weeding out irrelevant information, and finally, synthesizing information.

Skill 10.6   Demonstrate knowledge of strategies for promoting students' ability to identify and use common text features (e.g., transitions) and organizational structures (e.g., chronological order, logical order, cause and effect, and compare and contrast) of informational texts to enhance comprehension

See Skill 4.4.

Skill 10.7 **Demonstrate knowledge of strategies for promoting students' ability to critically evaluate the merit of texts in all subject areas**

The social changes since World War II significantly affected adolescent literature. The Civil Rights movement, feminism, the protest of the Vietnam Conflict, and issues surrounding homelessness, neglect, teen pregnancy, drugs, and violence bred a new vein of contemporary fiction that helps adolescents understand and cope with the world in which they live.

Popular books for preadolescents deal more with establishing relationships with members of the opposite sex (*Sweet Valley High* series) and learning to cope with their changing bodies, personalities, or life situations, as in Judy Blume's *Are You There, God? It's Me, Margaret*. Adolescents are still interested in the fantasy and science fiction genres as well as popular juvenile fiction. Middle school students still read the *Little House on the Prairie* series and the mysteries of the Hardy boys and Nancy Drew. Teens value the works of Emily and Charlotte Bronte, Willa Cather, Jack London, William Shakespeare, and Mark Twain as much as those of J. K. Rowling, Piers Anthony, S. E. Hinton, Madeleine L'Engle, Stephen King, and J. R. R. Tolkien, because they're fun to read whatever their underlying worth may be.

Older adolescents enjoy writers in these genres:

- Fantasy: Piers Anthony, Ursula Le Guin, Ann McCaffrey

- Horror: V. C. Andrews, Stephen King

- Juvenile fiction: Judy Blume, Robert Cormier, Rosa Guy, Virginia Hamilton, S. E. Hinton, M. E. Kerr, Harry Mazer, Norma Fox Mazer, Richard Newton Peck, Cynthia Voigt, and Paul Zindel

- Science fiction: Isaac Asimov, Ray Bradbury, Robert A. Heinlein, Arthur C. Clarke, Frank Herbert, Larry Niven, H. G. Wells

These classic and contemporary works combine the characteristics of multiple theories. Children ages 11 and 12 who are functioning at the concrete operations stage (Piaget), are of the "good person" orientation (Kohlberg), are still highly dependent on external rewards (Bandura), and exhibit all five needs from Maslow's hierarchy, should appreciate the following titles, grouped by reading level. These titles are also cited for interest at that grade level and do not reflect high-interest titles for older readers who do not read at grade level. Some high interest titles will be cited later.

Reading level 6.0 to 6.9

Barrett, William. *Lilies of the Field*
Cormier, Robert. *Other Bells for Us to Ring*
Dahl, Roald. *Danny, Champion of the World; Charlie and the Chocolate Factory*
Lindgren, Astrid. *Pippi Longstocking*
Lindbergh, Anne. *Three Lives to Live*
Lowry, Lois. *Rabble Starkey*
Naylor, Phyllis Reynolds. *The Year of the Gopher, Reluctantly Alice*
Peck, Robert Newton. *Arly*
Speare, Elizabeth George. *The Witch of Blackbird Pond*
Sleator, William. *The Boy Who Reversed Himself*

For seventh and eighth grades

Most seventh and eighth grade students, according to learning theory, are still functioning cognitively, psychologically, and morally as sixth graders. As these are not inflexible standards, there are some twelve- and thirteen-year-olds who are much more mature socially, intellectually, and physically than the younger children who share the same school. They are becoming concerned with establishing individual and peer group identities that present conflicts with breaking from authority and the rigidity of rules. Some at this age are still tied firmly to the family and its expectations while others identify more with those their own age or older. Enrichment reading for this group must help them cope with life's rapid changes or provide escape and thus must be either realistic or fantastic depending on the child's needs. Adventures and mysteries (the Hardy Boys and Nancy Drew series) are still popular today. Children at this age also become more interested in biographies of contemporary figures rather than legendary figures of the past.

Reading level 7.0 to 7.9

Armstrong, William. *Sounder*
Bagnold, Enid. *National Velvet*
Barrie, James. *Peter Pan*
London, Jack. *White Fang, Call of the Wild*
Lowry, Lois. *Taking Care of Terrific*
McCaffrey, Anne. The Harper Hall Trilogy
Montgomery, Lucy Maud. *Anne of Green Gables* and sequels
Steinbeck, John. *The Pearl*
Tolkien, J. R. R. *The Hobbit*
Zindel, Paul. *The Pigman*

Reading level 8.0 to 8.9

Cormier, Robert. *I Am the Cheese*
McCullers, Carson. *The Member of the Wedding*
North, Sterling. *Rascal*
Twain, Mark. *The Adventures of Tom Sawyer*
Zindel, Paul. *My Darling, My Hamburger*

For ninth grade

Depending upon the school environment, a ninth grader may be top-dog in a middle school or underdog in a high school. Much of his social development and thus his reading interests become motivated by his peer associations. He is technically an adolescent operating at the early stages of formal operations in cognitive development. His perception of his own identity is becoming well-defined and he is fully aware of the ethics required by society. He is more receptive to the challenges of classic literature but still enjoys popular teen novels.

Reading level 9.0 to 9.9

Brown, Dee. *Bury My Heart at Wounded Knee*
Defoe, Daniel. *Robinson Crusoe*
Dickens, Charles. *David Copperfield*
Greenberg, Joanne. *I Never Promised You a Rose Garden*
Kipling, Rudyard. *Captains Courageous*
Mathabane, Mark. *Kaffir Boy*
Nordhoff, Charles. *Mutiny on the Bounty*
Shelley, Mary. *Frankenstein*
Washington, Booker T. *Up from Slavery*

For tenth–twelfth grades

All high school sophomores, juniors, and seniors can handle most other literature except for a few of the most difficult titles like *Moby Dick* or *Vanity Fair*. However, since many high school students do not progress to the eleventh or twelfth grade reading level, they will still have their favorites among authors whose writings they can understand. Many will struggle with assigned novels but still read high interest books for pleasure. A few high interest titles are listed below without reading level designations, though most are 6.0 to 7.9.

> Bauer, Joan. *Squashed*
> Borland, Hal. *When the Legends Die*
> Danzinger, Paula. *Remember Me to Herald Square*
> Duncan, Lois. *Stranger with my Face*
> Hamilton, Virginia. *The Planet of Junior Brown*
> Hinton, S. E. *The Outsiders*
> Paterson, Katherine. *The Great Gilly Hopkins*

Teachers of students at all levels must be familiar with the materials offered by libraries in their own schools. Only then can she guide her students into selections appropriate for their social age and reading level development.

COMPETENCY 11.0   UNDERSTAND METHODS, ACTIVITIES AND TECHNIQUES FOR APPLYING COMPREHENSION STRATEGIES THROUGHOUT THE READING PROCESS

Skill 11.1   Demonstrate knowledge of strategies for orienting students to new texts (e.g., previewing, making predictions, discussing prior knowledge related to the topic, setting a purpose for reading, and generating questions prior to reading)

See Skills 4.4, 7.1, 8.5, and 9.1.

Skill 11.2   Demonstrate knowledge of ways to help students monitor their own comprehension as they read (e.g., visualizing, self-monitoring, self-questioning, rereading, adjusting rate of reading based on passage difficulty, paraphrasing, and note taking)

See Skill 10.5.

Skill 11.3   Demonstrate knowledge of strategies for supporting students' comprehension through oral response (e.g., summarizing, retelling; sharing reactions; making text-to-self, text-to-text, and text-to-world connections) and written response (e.g., journals, semantic maps, Venn diagrams, and other graphic organizers)

See Skill 10.5.

COMPETENCY 12.0   UNDERSTAND THE SELECTION AND USE OF READING MATERIALS FOR DIFFERENT PURPOSES, INCLUDING MATERIALS FOR INTRODUCING OR REVIEWING VARIOUS COMPREHENSION SKILLS AND STRATEGIES

Skill 12.1   Demonstrate knowledge of how to select and use a diverse body of works, authors, U.S. and world literature and other resources to promote students' literary response and analysis skills

See Skill 10.7.

Skill 12.2   Demonstrate awareness of the role of independent reading in the development of comprehension and vocabulary knowledge

Reading emphasis in middle school

Reading for comprehension of factual material—content area textbooks, reference books, and newspapers—is closely related to study strategies in the middle/junior high. Organized study models, such as the SQ3R method (Survey, Question, Read, Recite, and Review Studying), is a technique that makes it possible and feasible to learn the content of even large amounts of text. It teaches students to locate main ideas and supporting details, to recognize sequential order, to distinguish fact from opinion, and to determine cause/effect relationships.

Strategies

1. Teacher-guided activities that require students to organize and to summarize information based on the author's explicit intent are pertinent strategies in middle grades. Evaluation techniques include oral and written responses to standardized or teacher-made worksheets.

2. Reading of fiction introduces and reinforces skills in inferring meaning from narration and description. Teacher-guided activities in the process of reading for meaning should be followed by cooperative planning of the skills to be studied and of the selection of reading resources. Many printed reading- for-comprehension instruments as well as individualized computer software programs exist to monitor the progress of acquiring comprehension skills.

3. Older middle school students should be given opportunities for more student-centered activities: individual and collaborative selection of reading choices based on student interest, small group discussions of selected works, and greater written expression. Evaluation techniques include teacher monitoring and observation of discussions and written work samples.

4. Certain students may begin some fundamental critical interpretation by recognizing fallacious reasoning in news media, examining the accuracy of news reports and advertising, or explaining their reasons for preferring one author's writing to another's. Development of these skills may require a more learning-centered approach in which the teacher identifies a number of objectives and suggested resources from which the student may choose his/her course of study. Self-evaluation through a reading diary should be stressed. Teacher and peer evaluation of creative projects resulting from such study is encouraged.

5. Reading aloud before the entire class as a formal means of teacher evaluation should be phased out in favor of one-to-one tutoring or peer-assisted reading. Occasional sharing of favored selections by both teacher and willing students is a good oral interpretation basic.

Reading emphasis in high school

Students in high school literature classes should focus on interpretive and critical reading. Teachers should guide the study of the elements of inferential (interpretive) reading—drawing conclusions, predicting outcomes, and recognizing examples of specific genre characteristics, for example—and critical reading to judge the quality of the writer's work against recognized standards. At this level students should understand the skills of language and reading that they are expected to master and be able to evaluate their own progress.

Strategies

1. The teacher becomes more facilitator than instructor—helping the student to make a diagnosis of his own strengths and weaknesses, keeping a record of progress, and interacting with other students and the teacher in practicing skills.

2. Despite the requisites and prerequisites of most literature courses, students should be encouraged to pursue independent study and enrichment reading.

3. Ample opportunities should be provided for oral interpretation of literature, special projects in creative dramatics, writing for publication in school literary magazines or newspapers, and speech/debate activities. A student portfolio provides for teacher and peer evaluation.

When preparing to read a book, the reader should become acquainted with the elements of the story such as setting, characterization, style (language, both technically with regard to dialect but also structurally with regard to use of description, length of sentences, phrases, etc.), plot (particularly conflicts and pattern), tone (what is the *attitude* of the writer toward characters, theme, etc.) and particularly theme (the message or point the story conveys). It's not essential to know the writer's biography, but it is often helpful, especially in responding from the reader's point of view.

Literature is written to evoke a personal response in readers. This is why so many books are sold. Once the reader has a grip on the story—a thorough understanding of the story—then an analysis of one's own response to it is in order.

The following questions are useful:

1. Do you respond emotionally to one of the characters? Why? Is a character similar to someone you know or have known?
2. Is the setting evocative for you because of a place, situation, or milieu that you have experienced and that had meaning for you? Why?
3. Did the vocabulary, descriptions, or short or long sentences have impact on you? Why? For example, short, simple sentence after short, simple sentence may be used deliberately, but do you find it annoying?
4. Do you agree with the author's attitude toward the characters, setting, story, etc.? For example, has a character been written unsympathetically that you felt deserved more consideration? Does the author demonstrate distaste for the setting he has chosen, and do you feel he is being unjust? Or do you experience the same distaste? Etc.

Reading is personal. Responding to it personally adds important dimensions to an analysis for others.

See also Skill 1.4.

Skill 12.3 Recognize strategies for facilitating students' selection of appropriate independent reading materials

Many students choose books for reading that are too hard or too easy for them. It is the teacher's job to make sure students choose reading materials with which they will experience success. One method of doing this is to take a reading interest inventory and work with the students to choose books that they are able to read without too much difficulty.

When students choose a book, teach them to use the five finger rule. When using this rule, students should open the book to any page. As they are reading that page, ask them to put up one finger each time they come to a word that they do not understand or cannot figure out from the context. If they raise five fingers by the end of reading the page, then the book may be too far above their reading level. Of course, we want the students to challenge themselves, but we also don't want them to get frustrated and stop reading.

Not everyone continues to read every book they choose. Students may not be aware of this. Tell them that you and other adults often put down a book that is not interesting or too hard. Let the students know that it is acceptable to put back a book and choose another.

Guided reading is an important component of a balanced literacy framework. In this component, teachers assess the students' reading levels to find the text that matches their instructional levels. By using the Fountas and Pinnell method, all texts are leveled using the letters of the alphabet. There should also be books labeled according to this method in the classroom that the students use for their take home reading. Tell the students what letter bin they should use when choosing books.

The levels at which students are reading will change throughout the year. Students will move upwards in the letters and thus get an opportunity to read at several levels throughout the year.

Students often judge a book by the picture on the cover or the size of the book. Read alouds in the classroom will help middle grade students make better choices in the reading material they choose. Simply reading a chapter of a book will hook the students into wanting to continue reading on their own. Show the students how to read the blurb on the back cover or inside the dust jacket to get a brief glimpse of what the book is about. Encourage students to try books with more pages and chapters and inform them that they are not expected to read the book in one night or even one week. This helps to put the students at ease and lets them read at their own pace.

Skill 12.4   Identify ways to facilitate student text selection for specific purposes (e.g., to locate and gather facts to support a persuasive argument, to conduct research, to address student issues, and to allow students to gain insight into themselves and others)

As adults, we read books for a variety of reasons. The same is true for students, and it is just as important for teachers to take time to teach the students how to select appropriate texts based on the reason they have at the moment. Understanding the different types of texts can help students find the information they need in a more efficient manner.

The school librarian or media specialist can be of significant help in this area. In fact, working together with the librarian, teachers can provide students with various examples of not only the different types of texts they may need, but also where they can locate them within the school's media center.

Beginning with understanding the difference between fiction and nonfiction books, it is important to then move the students through the understanding of how different books can be used to provide them with support they may need to accomplish both school-related and personal tasks.

The first step is for the students to clearly understand their purpose and be able to state this purpose. It is important for them to identify whether they are simply conducting research, finding information to support an argument, looking up information to learn about themselves, or seeking supportive data to make a change in school policy regarding some specific student issue.

Modeling is an important strategy to help students see these relationships between books and purpose. When demonstrating how to write a persuasive argument, the teacher should show different passages from books and explain which of these would be good to use in support of the persuasive argument and which would not.

Taking the time to demonstrate how to sift through information using specific criteria is important, and the demonstration must be done through direct instruction. Teaching the students to make these types of judgments will benefit them throughout their lives and help to take their thinking to a higher level.

Skill 12.5   Demonstrate knowledge of strategies for selecting and using materials that provide opportunities for students and construct meaning from various visual/graphic features of text (e.g., tables, charts, graphs, maps, and illustrations)

See Skill 9.1.

COMPETENCY 13.0   UNDERSTAND FORMAL AND INFORMAL
                   TECHNIQUES FOR ASSESSING READING
                   SKILLS

Skill 13.1   Recognize the importance of monitoring student progress on
              an ongoing basis and use a variety of developmentally
              appropriate classroom-reading assessments to provide
              multiple indicators of student progress

Assessment is the practice of collecting information about children's progress, and evaluation is the process of judging the children's responses to determine how well they are achieving particular goals or demonstrating reading skills.

Assessment and evaluation are intricately connected in the literacy classroom. Assessment is necessary because teachers need ways to determine what students are learning and how they are progressing. In addition, assessment can be a tool that helps students take ownership of their own learning and become partners with their teachers and parents in their ongoing development as readers and writers. In this day of public accountability, clear, definite, and reliable assessment creates confidence in public education.

There are two broad categories of assessment. *Informal assessment* utilizes observations and other non-standardized procedures to compile anecdotal and observation data/evidence of children's progress. It includes but is not limited to checklists, observations, and performance tasks. *Formal assessment* is composed of standardized tests and procedures carried out under circumscribed conditions. Formal assessments include: state tests, standardized achievement tests, NAEP tests, and the like.

Effective Assessment Characteristics

1. It should be an *ongoing process* with the teacher making informal or formal assessments on an ongoing basis. The assessment should be a natural part of the instruction and not intrusive.

2. The most effective assessment is *integrated into ongoing instruction*. Throughout the teaching and learning day, the child's written, spoken, and reading contributions to the class or lack thereof, need to and can be continually noted.

3. Assessment should *reflect the child's actual reading and writing experiences*. The child should be able to show that he/she can read and explain or react to a similar literary or expository work.

4. Assessment needs to be a *collaborative and reflective process.* Teachers can learn from what the children reveal about their own individual assessments. Children, even as early as grade two, should be supported by their teacher to continually and routinely ask themselves questions assessing their reading. They might ask:

   a. "Am I understanding what the author wanted to say?"

   b. "What can I do to improve my reading?"

   c. "How can I use what I have read to learn more about this topic?"

   Teachers need to be informed by their own professional observation *and* by children's comments as they assess and customize instruction for children.

5. Quality assessment is *multidimensional* and may include but not be limited to samples of writings, student retellings, running records, anecdotal teacher observations, self-evaluations, and records of independent reading. From this multidimensional data, the teacher can derive a consistent level of performance and design additional instruction that will enhance the child's reading performance.

6. Assessment must *take into account children's age and ethnic/cultural patterns of learning.*

7. Effective assessment *teaches children from their strengths, not their weaknesses.* Find out what reading behaviors children demonstrate well and then design instruction to support those behaviors.

8. Assessment should be *part of children's learning process* and not done *to* them, but rather done *with* them.

Skill 13.2   Demonstrate awareness of the characteristics and uses of standardized tests and other formal reading assessments (e.g., norm-referenced tests, reading rate assessments, curriculum-based measurements, use of rubrics, and reading software assessments)

Criterion-Referenced Tests
Criterion-referenced tests measure children's reading achievement against criteria or guidelines which are uniform for all the test takers. Therefore, by definition, no special questions, formats, or considerations are made for the test taker who is either from a different linguistic/cultural background or is already identified as a struggling reader/writer. On a criterion-referenced test, it is possible that a child test taker can score 100% because the child may have actually been exposed to all of the concepts taught and has mastered them. A child's score on such a test would indicate which of the concepts have already been taught and what additional review or support is needed to master the concept.

Two criterion-referenced tests that are commonly used to assess children's reading achievement are the Diagnostic Indicators of Basic Early Literacy Skills (DIBELS) and the Stanford Achievement Test. DIBELS measures progress in literacy from kindergarten to grade three. It can be downloaded from the Internet free at dibels.uoregon.edu. The Stanford is designed to measure individual children's achievement in key school subjects. Subtests covering various reading skills are part of this test. Both DIBELS and the Stanford Achievement Test are group-administered.

Degrees of Reading Power (DRP)
This test is targeted to assess how well children understand the meaning of written text in real life situations. This test is supposed to measure the process of children's reading, not the products of reading such as identifying the main idea and author's purpose.

CTPIII
This criterion-referenced test measures verbal and quantitative ability in grades 3–12. It is targeted to help differentiate among the most capable students, i.e. those who rank above the 80th percentile on other standardized tests. This is a test that emphasizes higher order thinking skills and process-related reading comprehension questions.

Norm-referenced Test

This test measures children against one another. Scores on this test are reported in percentiles. Each percentile indicates the percent of the testing population whose scores were lower than or the same as a particular child's score. Percentile is defined as a score on a scale of 100 showing the percentage of a distribution that is equal to or below it. This type of state-standardized norm-referenced test is being used in most districts today in response to the *No Child Left Behind Act.* While this type of test does not help tract the individual reader's progress in his or her ongoing reading development, it does permit comparisons across groups.

There are many more standardized norm-referenced tests to assess children's reading than there are criterion-referenced. In norm-referenced tests, scores are based on how well a child does compared to others, usually on the local, state, and national level. If the norming groups on the tests are reflective of the children being tested (e.g., same spread of minority, low income, and gifted students), the results are more trustworthy.

One of the best known norm-referenced tests is the Iowa Test of Basic Skills. It assesses student achievement in various school subjects and has several subtests in reading. Other examples of norm-referenced tests used around the country are the Metropolitan Achievement Tests, the Terra Nova-2, and the Stanford Diagnostic Reading Test-4. These are all group tests. The Woodcock Reading Mastery test is an individual test that reading specialists use with students.

Concepts of Validity, Reliability, and Bias in Testing

Validity is how well a test measures what it is supposed to measure. Teacher-made tests are therefore not generally extremely valid, although they may be appropriate and valid in measuring of the specific concept the teacher wants to assess for his/her own children's achievement.

Reliability is the consistency of the test. This is measured by whether the test will indicate the same score for the child who takes it more than once.

Bias in testing occurs when the information within the test or the information required to be able to respond to a multiple-choice question or constructed response (essay question on the test) is information that is not available to some test takers who come from a different cultural, ethnic, linguistic, or socio-economic background than do the majority of the test takers. Since they have not had the same prior linguistic, social, or cultural experiences that the majority of test takers have had, these test takers are at a disadvantage in taking the test. No matter what their actual mastery of the material taught by the teacher, they may have difficulty addressing the "biased" questions. Generally other "non-biased" questions are given to them and eventually the biased questions are removed from the examination.

To solidify what might be abstract to the reader, on a recent reading test in one school system, the grade four reading comprehension multiple choice had some questions about the well-known fairy tale of *The Gingerbread Boy*. These questions were simple and accessible for most of the children in the class. But two children were recent arrivals from the Dominican Republic where they had learned English. Although they were reading on fourth-grade level, the story of *The Gingerbread Boy* was not read in their Dominican grade school. Therefore, a question about this story on the standardized reading test *did* demonstrate examiner bias and was not fair to these test takers.

See also in skill 13.3 and 14.5

Skill 13.3   Demonstrate awareness of the characteristics and uses of a variety of informal classroom-reading assessments (e.g., informal reading inventories, miscue analyses, anecdotal notes, and student retellings)

Informal Assessments

Running Records. A running record of children's oral reading progress in the early grades K–3 is a pivotal informal assessment. It supports the teacher in deciding whether a book a child is reading is matched to his/her stage of reading development. In addition this assessment allows the teacher to analyze a child's miscues to see which cueing systems and strategies the child uses and to determine which other systems the child might use more effectively. Finally the running record offers a graphic account of a child's oral reading.

Generally, a teacher should maintain an annotated class notebook with pages set aside for all the children or individual notebooks for each child. One of the benefits of using running records as an informal assessment is that they can be used with any text and can serve as a tool for teaching, rather than an instrument to report on children's status in class.

Running records are meant to be updated frequently by the teacher so that the educator can truly observe a pattern of errors and provides the educator with sufficient information to analyze the child's reading progress over time. As any mathematician or scientist knows, the more samples of a process you gather over time, the more likely the teacher is to get an accurate picture of the child's reading needs.

Using the notations Marie Clay developed and shared in *An Observation Study of Early Literacy Achievement,* Sharon Taberski offers in her book, *On Solid Ground,* a lengthy walk through keeping a running record of children's reading. Taberski writes in the child's miscue on the top line of her running record above the text word. Indeed she records all of the child's miscue attempts on the line above the text word. Taberski advises the teacher to make all the miscue notations as the child reads, since this allows the teacher to get additional information about how and why the child makes miscue choices. Additionally, the teacher should note all self-corrections (coded SC) made when the child is monitoring his/her own reading, crosschecks information, and uses additional information.

As part of the informal assessment of primary grade reading, it is important to record the child's word insertions, omissions, requests for help, and attempts to get the word. In informal assessment the rate of accuracy can be estimated by dividing the child's errors by the total words read.

Results of a running record assessment can be used to select the best setting for the child's reading. If a child reads from 95%–100% correct, the child is ready for independent reading. If the child reads from 92%–97% right, the child is ready for guided reading. Below 92% the child needs a read-aloud or shared reading activity. Note that these percentages are slightly different from those one would use to match books to readers.

Literacy Portfolios. Compiling literacy portfolios is an increasingly popular and meaningful form of informal assessment. It is particularly compelling because artists, television directors, authors, architects, and photographers use portfolios in their careers and jobs. It is also a most authentic format for documenting children's literacy growth over time. The portfolio is not only a significant professional informal assessment tool for the teacher, but a vehicle and format for the child reader to take ownership of his/her progress over time. It models a way of compiling one's reading and writing products as a lifelong learner, which is the ultimate goal of reading instruction.

Portfolios can include the following four categories of materials:

- *Work Samples:* These can include children's story maps, webs, KWL charts, pictures, illustrations, storyboards, and writings about the stories they have read.

- *Records of Independent Reading and Writing:* These can include the children's journals, notebooks, or logs of books read with the names of the authors, titles of the books, date completed, and pieces related to books completed or in progress.

- *Checklists and Surveys:* These include checklists designed by the teacher for reading development, writing development, ownership checklists, and general interest surveys.

- *Self-Evaluation Forms:* These are the children's own evaluations of their reading and writing process framed in their own words. They can be simple templates with starting sentences such as:

  - I am really proud of the way I _____.
  - I feel one of my strengths as a reader is _____.
  - To improve the way I read aloud I need to _____.
  - To improve my reading I should _____.

Generally, child's portfolio in Grade 3 or above begins with a letter to the reader explaining the work that will be found in the portfolio. In Grade 4 and up, children write a brief reflection detailing their feelings and judgments about their growth as readers and writers.

When teachers maintain student portfolios for mandated school administrative review, district review, or even for their own research, they often prepare portfolio summary sheets. These provide identifying data on the children and then a timeline of their review of the portfolio contents. The summary sheets also contain professional comments on the extent to which the portfolio documents satisfactory and ongoing growth in reading.

Portfolios can be used beneficially for child-teacher and parent/teacher conversations to review the child's progress, discuss areas of strength, set future goals, make plans for future learning activities, and evaluate what should remain in the portfolio and what needs to be cleared out for new materials.

Rubrics. Holistic scoring involves assessing a child's ability to construct meaning through writing. It uses a scale called a *Rubric* usually ranges can range from 0 to 4:

> 0—Indicates the piece cannot be scored. It does not respond to the topic or is illegible.
>
> 1—The writing responds to the topic but does not cover it accurately.
>
> 2—The writing responds to the topic but lacks sufficient details or elaboration.
>
> 3—This piece fulfills the purpose of the writing assignment and has sufficient development (which refers to details, examples, and elaboration of ideas).
>
> 4—This response has the most details, best organization, and presents a well expressed reaction to the original writer's piece.

Miscue Analysis. This is a procedure that allows the teacher a look at the reading process. By definition, the miscue is an oral response different from the text being read. Sometimes miscues are also called unexpected responses or errors. By studying a student's miscues from an oral reading sample, the teacher can determine which cues and strategies the student is correctly using or not using in constructing meaning. Of course, the teacher can customize instruction to meet the needs of this particular student.

Informal Reading Inventories (IRI). These are a series of samples of texts prearranged in stages of increasing difficulty. Listening to children read through these inventories, the teacher can pinpoint their skill level and the additional concepts they need to work on.

See also Skill 13.2

Skill 13.4 Demonstrate knowledge of how to administer various formal and informal assessments

Characteristics and uses of Group versus Individual Reading Assessments

In assessment, tests are used for different purposes. They have different dimensions or characteristics whether they are given individually or in a group and whether they are standardized or teacher-made. The chart below shows the relationships of these elements.

	Standardized	**Teacher-made**
Individual	*Characteristics* • is uniformly administered *Uses* • is best for younger children • helps with placement for special services	*Characteristics* • has more flexibility *Uses* • assists teaching decisions • used for diagnostic purposes
Group	*Characteristics* • is uniformly administered • is time efficient *Uses* • permits comparisons across groups • used for policy decisions by administrators	*Characteristics* • has high face validity • is time efficient *Uses* • informs teach-reteach and enrichment decisions • documents students' learning

Techniques for Assessing Particular Reading Skills

Sharon Taberski recommends that the teacher build in one-on-one time for supporting individual children as needed in considering what makes sense, sounds right, and matches the letters. She notes that emergent and early readers tend to focus on meaning without adequate attention to graphophonic cues. She suggests using the following prompts for children who are having problems with graphophonic cues:

- Does what you said match the letters?

- If the word you said were _____, what letter would it have to start with?

- Look carefully at the first letters. Then, look at the middle letters. Then, look at the last letters. What could it be?

- If it word were _____, what letter or letters would it end with?

Oral retellings can be used to test children's comprehension. Children who are retelling a story to be tested for comprehension should be told that that is the purpose when they sit down with the teacher.

It is a good idea to let the child start the retelling on his/her own, because then the teacher can see whether he/she needs prompts to retell the story. Many times, more experienced readers summarize what they have read. This summary usually flows out along with the characters, the problem of the story, and other details.

Other signs that children understand what they are reading when they give an oral retelling include:

- Their use of illustrations to support the retelling

- References to the exact text in the retelling

- Emotional reaction to the text

- Making connections between the text and other stories or the readers' own experiences

- Giving information about the text without the teacher's asking for it

Awareness of Text Leveling

The classroom library, in the context of the Balanced Literacy Approach to reading instruction, is focused on leveled books. These books have been leveled with the support of Fountas and Pinnell's *Guided Reading: Good First Teaching for All Children* and *Matching Books to Readers: Using Leveled Reading in Guided Reading, K–3.*

The books are leveled according to the designations in these reference books and need to be stored in bins or crates with front covers facing out. This makes them much easier for the children to identify. In that way the children can go through the appropriate levels and find those books of particular interest to them while staying in the level that is right for them to read. These are books that the children can read with the right degree of reading accuracy. When young children can see the cover of a book, they are more likely to flip through the book until they can independently identify an appealing book. Then they will read a little bit of the book to see if it's "just right."

"Just right" leveled books—books that children can read on their own—need to be available for them to read during independent reading. The goal is for the more fluent readers to select books on their own. Ultimately, the use of leveled books helps the children, in addition to the teacher, to decide which books are "good" or "just right" for them.

Levels are indicated by means color-coded stickers. A blue, yellow, red, or green dot sticker is placed in the upper right corner of each book to indicate emergent, early, transitional, and fluent reading stages, respectively. The books are then kept in containers with other "blue," "yellow," "red," and "green" books.

Other lists and resources other than Fountas and Pinnell which can be used to match children with "just right" books include the Reading Recovery level list. Ultimately, the teacher has to individualize whatever leveling is used in the library to address the individual learner's needs.

Awareness of the Challenges and Supports in a Text

Illustrations can be key supports for emergent and early readers. Teachers should not only use wordless stories (books which tell their narratives through pictures alone), but can also make targeted use of Big Books for read-alouds, so that young children become habituated to the use of illustrations as an important component for constructing meaning. The teacher should model for the child how to reference an illustration for help in identifying a word in the text the child does not recognize. Of course, children can also go on a picture walk with the teacher as part of a mini-lesson or guided reading and anticipate the story (narrative) using the pictures alone to construct meaning.

Decodability. Use literature that contains examples of letter sound correspondences you wish to teach. First, read the literature with the children or read it aloud to them. Then take a specific example from the text and have the children reread it as the teacher points out the letter-sound correspondence to the children. Then ask the children to go through the now-familiar literature to find other letter-sound correspondences. Once the children have correctly made the letter-sound correspondences, have them share similar correspondences they find in other works of literature.

Cooper (2004) suggests that children can become word detectives so that they can independently and fluently decode on their own. The child should learn the following *word detective routines* so that he/she can function as an independent fluent reader who can decode words on his/her own:

- First the child should read to the end of a sentence.

- Then the child should search for word parts which he/she knows.

- The child should also try to decode the word from the letter sounds.

- As a last resort, the child should ask someone for help or look up the word in the dictionary.

Assessment of the Reading Development of Individual Students

For young readers who are from ELL backgrounds, even if they have been born in the United States, the use of pictures validates their story-authoring and storytelling skills and provides them with access and equity to the literary discussion and book talk of their native English-speaking peers. These children can also demonstrate their storytelling abilities by drawing sequels or prequels to the story detailed in the illustrations alone. They might even be given the opportunity to share the story aloud in their native language or to comment on the illustrations in their native language.

Since many stories today are recorded in two or even three languages at once, discussing story events or analyzing pictures in a different language is a beneficial practice that can be accomplished in the 21st century classroom. Use of pictures and illustrations can also help the K–3 educator assess the capabilities of children who are struggling readers if the children's learning strength is spatial. Through targeted questions about how the pictures would change if different plot twists occurred or how the child might transform the story through changing the illustrations, the teacher can begin to assess struggling reader's deficits and strengths.

Children from ELL backgrounds can benefit from listening to a recorded version of a particular story with which they can read along. This gives them another opportunity to "hear" the story correctly pronounced and presented and to begin to internalize its language structures. In the absence of taped versions of some key stories or texts, teachers may want to make their own sound recordings.

Highly proficient readers can also be involved in creating these literature recordings for use with ELL peers or younger peers. This of course develops oral language proficiency and also introduces these skilled readers into the intricacies of supporting ELL reading instruction. When they actually see their tapes being used by children, they will be tremendously gratified.

See also Skills 13.2 and 13.3

COMPETENCY 14.0   UNDERSTAND HOW TO INTERPRET AND
                   COMMUNICATE THE RESULTS OF READING
                   ASSESSMENT

**Skill 14.1   Analyze the results of formal and informal reading
               assessments to determine whether a student is below, at, or
               above expected performance standards**

See Skill 13.2 and 13.3.

**Skill 14.2   Analyze the results of formal and informal reading
               assessments to determine specific areas of reading difficulty
               for individual students or groups of students**

See Skill 13.2 and 13.3.

**Skill 14.3   Demonstrate knowledge of strategies for collecting and
               organizing data from formal and informal classroom-reading
               assessments to show progress over time**

See Skill 13.2 and 13.3.

**Skill 14.4   Analyze miscues (e.g., syntactic, graphophonic, and semantic)
               to identify a reader's patterns of problem-solving, self-
               monitoring, and self-correction**

When using running records to informally assess the progress a student is
making with their reading skills, it is important to note the types of errors the child
is making. By examining the strategies and errors the student makes, the teacher
can plan instruction, monitor progress, and assess skill levels. Even if not using a
running record, teachers can use even more informal methods of using the errors
a student makes to find significant ways to help the student improve in their
reading.

Miscue analysis can be multi-faceted and provide both the teacher and reader
with a wealth of important information. First, examining the methods a student
uses to figure out unknown words helps the teacher understand which methods
require further instruction or fine tuning and which have already been mastered.
Typically, students use phonics skills (letter-sound correspondence), contextual
clues (the other words in the sentence/passage), semantic analysis, or structural-
analysis techniques to solve problems in reading. It is not through using only one
of these methods that a reader becomes more proficient, but rather by using a
combination of all of the approaches.

After collecting the running record, teachers can go back and look at which of the described strategies the students are successfully using. Tallying is one method to use. In this way, the educator can see the strategies used by the student and if one seems to be more dominant than others. This method will also help to point out specific strategies which are very weak for the student and would require more instruction. After this analysis, the teacher can develop an instructional plan to address weak areas and determine a more balanced problem-solving approach for the student.

Additionally, the teacher can look at the student's ability to monitor his/her own reading and comprehension. Noting these self-monitoring attempts allows the teacher to see if the student recognizes when they make a mistake. This is a very important skill for readers to develop. Once they realize something does not make sense, students should be able to go back and apply a correction strategy so as to not hinder comprehension. This becomes more important as the complexity of text increases.

Self-corrections by students begin to show a maturity of reading skills. However, students who make a tremendous amount of self-corrections lack fluency in reading and will eventually lose some comprehension. It is an important step for beginner readers, but as with any other learning process, we want students to pass through it rapidly, leaving in its place fluent, well-comprehended reading.

Skill 14.5 Analyze data and evidence from classroom reading assessments to identify students who may need additional support beyond the classroom to address reading weaknesses

Siegfried Engelmann, Dr. Wesley Becker, and several other researchers proposed what they call direct instruction, a teaching method that emphasizes well-developed and carefully-planned lessons with small learning increments. It assumes that clear instruction that eliminates misinterpretations will improve outcomes. Their approach is being used by thousands of schools. It recommends that the popular valuing of teacher creativity and autonomy be replaced by a willingness to follow certain carefully prescribed instructional practices. At the same time, it encourages the hard work, dedication, and commitment to students. It demands that teachers adopt and internalize the belief that all students, if properly taught, can learn.

There are many ways to evaluate a child's knowledge and assess his/her learning needs. In recent years, the emphasis has shifted from "mastery testing" of isolated skills to authentic assessments of what children know. Authentic assessments allow the teacher to know more precisely what each individual student knows, can do, and needs to do. Authentic assessments can work for both the student and the teacher in becoming more responsible for learning.

One of the simplest, most efficient ways for the teacher to get to know his/her students is to conduct an entry survey. This is a record that provides useful background information about the students as they enter a class or school. Information collected through an entry survey can give valuable insights into a student's background knowledge and experience. Teachers can customize entry surveys according to the type of information considered valuable. Some of the information that may be incorporated includes student's name, age, family members, health factors, special interests, strengths, needs, fears, parent expectations, languages spoken in the home, and what the child likes about school.

At the beginning of each school term the teacher will likely feel compelled to conduct some informal evaluations in order to obtain a general awareness of his/her students. These informal evaluations should be the result of a learning activity rather than a "test" and may include classroom observations, collections of reading and writing samples, and notations about the students' cognitive abilities as demonstrated by classroom discussions and participation including the students' command of language. The value of these informal evaluations cannot be underestimated. These evaluations, if utilized effectively, will drive instruction and facilitate learning.

After conducting initial informal evaluations and following up with appropriate instruction, teachers should fine tune individual evaluations to provide optimum learning experiences. Some of the same types of evaluations can be used on an ongoing basis to determine individual learning needs as were used to determine initial general learning needs. It is somewhat more difficult to choose an appropriate evaluation instrument for elementary-aged students than for older students. Therefore, teachers must be mindful of developmentally appropriate instruments. At the same time, teachers must be cognizant of the information they wish to obtain from a specific evaluation instrument. Ultimately, these two factors—students' developmental stage and the information to be derived—will determine which type of evaluation will be most appropriate and valuable. There are few commercially designed assessment tools that will prove to be as effective as the tool that is constructed by the teacher.

A simple-to-administer, information-rich evaluation of a child's reading strengths and weaknesses is the running reading record. "This technique for recording reading behavior is the most insightful, informative, and instructionally useful assessment procedure you can use for monitoring a child's progress in learning to read," (Traill, 1993). The teacher uses a simple coding system to record what a child does while reading text out loud. At a later time the teacher can go back to the record and assess what the child knows about reading and what the teacher needs to address in an effort to help the student become a better reader.

If the teacher is evaluating a child's writing, it is a good idea to discourage the child from erasing his/her errors and to train the child to cross out errors with a single line so that the teacher can actually see the process the student went through to complete a writing assignment. This writing not only becomes an important means of getting to know the students' writing process, it is also an effective and valuable writing evaluation.

One of the most valuable and effective assessment tools available to any teacher is classroom observation. As instructional decision makers, teachers must base their instructional strategies upon students' needs. An astute observer of student behaviors and performance is most capable of choosing instructional strategies that will best meet the needs of the learners. Classroom observations take place within the context of the learning environment, allowing the observer the opportunity to notice natural behaviors and performances.

To permit a constant awareness of student progress, classroom observations should be sensitive and systematic. One of the shortcomings of classroom observations is that they are often performed randomly and frequently are focused on those students whose behaviors are less than desirable. If the teacher establishes a focused observation process, the observations become more valuable. A good suggestion is to focus observations on five or six students at a time for a period of one to two weeks.

For observations to truly be useful, teachers must record the information obtained from observations. When doing a formal behavioral observation, the teacher writes what the child is doing for a designated time period. At times the teacher tallies the occurrences of specific behaviors within a designated time period. When making focused observations that are ongoing, the teacher may simply use a blank piece of paper with only the student's name and date written on it and space for the teacher to write anecdotal notes. Or a teacher might write on post-it notes and put the information in a student's file. If it is not possible to record the information as it occurs and is observed, it is critical that it be recorded as soon as possible in order to maintain accuracy.

Sometimes it is helpful to do an observation simply to watch for frequency of a specific behavior. An observation can answer questions such as: Is the student on-task during independent work time? Is the student interacting appropriately with peers? Is the student using materials appropriately? These behaviors can be tallied on a piece of paper with the student's name and date of observation.

Classroom observations can provide the teacher with one of the most comprehensive means of knowing their students. Teachers can observe students to see how they interact with their peers, which activities they choose, what they like to read, and how frequently they choose to work alone. "Everything you hear a child say and see a child do is a glimpse into a mind and a source of information to 'know' from." (Traill, 1993)

Skill 14.6   Demonstrate knowledge of effective methods for communicating results of reading assessments to students, parent(s)/guardian(s), administrators, support personnel, and other classroom teachers or specialists who work with given students

The effective teacher uses advanced communication skills such as clarification, reflection, perception, and summarization as a means to facilitate communication. Teachers who are effective communicators are also good listeners. Teacher when they consistently use behaviors such as eye contact, focusing on student body language, clarifying students' statements, and using "I" messages. In order to facilitate establishing and maintaining an optimum classroom learning environment, the teacher must communicate with students, listen effectively, identify relevant and non-relevant information, and summarize students' messages.

Any assessment done on students must be documented and samples kept so that the parents and other teachers can understand the results. Communicating the findings of assessments is not something that has to wait for parent-teacher interviews or the report card. It is something that teachers should report to parents on a regular basis, such as in monthly notes or telephone calls, arranged meetings or even simple chats.

Guidance and speech counselors should communicate the results of assessments to teachers and parents as soon possible after the testing is complete. In many districts this is called a debriefing and takes the form of an arranged meeting in which the counselor discusses the findings and suggests how best to meet the needs of the child.

Often in schools, parents, grandparents, and other people involved in children's lives, want to take a more active role in the educational process. They also all seem to have an opinion on the appropriate method for teaching students how to read. Sometimes this can lead to controversy and misunderstandings.

It is important to provide opportunities for the public to come into the school and participate in activities to encourage reading. During these fun programs, it is just as important to share tidbits of information about the methodologies and strategies being implemented. In this way, the public can begin to understand the differences in reading instruction today in comparison to what occurred when they attended school. This is often the biggest statement of concern made by adults concerning current educational trends.

Taking the time to educate parents and other family members not only helps to enhance understanding and open communication, it can also provide more support for students than the school alone would ever be able to provide.

Some strategies for educating parents and family members include:

- Bingo games where the correct answer on the Bingo board is a fact about reading instruction
- Small parent workshops offered on various topics
- Newsletter pieces or paragraphs
- Individual parent meetings
- Inviting parents to observe lessons
- Small pieces of information shared during other social times where parents are invited into the school

Communicating general information about reading and appropriate reading instruction is important. It is just as important to share specific information about students with parents, other school personnel, and the community. Once the teacher has gathered sufficient information on the students, he/she must find appropriate methods to share this information with those who need the data. Again, depending on the audience, the amount and type of information shared may vary.

Some ways to share information with parents/guardians include:

- Individual parent meetings
- Small group meetings
- Regular parent updates through phone calls
- Charts and graphs of progress sent home
- Notes home

Some ways to share information with school personnel include:

- Faculty meetings
- Power point or other presentations
- Email
- Conferences
- School board presentation
- Graphs and charts

COMPETENCY 15.0   UNDERSTAND THE USE OF ASSESSMENT DATA TO PLAN AND TAILOR INSTRUCTION FOR READERS AT ALL SKILL LEVELS

Skill 15.1   Demonstrate familiarity with assessments used to determine students' independent, instructional and frustration reading levels, and recognize the importance of using data from such assessments to select appropriate and readable materials for individuals and groups at all levels of reading proficiency

Adjustment of Reading Instruction Based on Ongoing Assessment

Running records of their students help teachers identify the cueing systems the children might be using. It is important for the teacher to adjust reading instruction based on the pattern of miscues gathered from several successive reading records. When the teacher carefully reviews a given student's substitutions and self-corrections, certain patterns begin to surface. For example, a child may use visual cues as he/she reads and adds meaning to self correct. To the alert teacher, this reliance on visual miscues indicates that the reader doesn't make sense of what is being read. This means that the teacher needs to check what cueing system the child uses when he/she is reading "just right" books. Children who use meaning and structure but not visual/graphophonic cues need to be reminded and facilitated to understand the importance of getting and reconstructing the author's message. They have to be able to share the author's story, not their own.

Materials in a child's ongoing assessment notebook can not only be used by the teacher to adjust the child's current instruction, they can document for the child his/her growth as a successful reader over time. In addition, if the same concerns surface over the use of a particular cueing system or high frequency word, the teacher can adjust the class wall chart and even devote a whole class lesson to the particular element.

Techniques for Determining Students' Independent, Instructional, and Frustration Reading Levels

Instructional reading is generally judged to be at the 95% accuracy level, although Taberski places it at between 92% and 97%. Taberski tries to enhance the independent reading levels by making sure that readers on the instructional reading levels read a variety of genres, and have a range of available and interesting books within a particular genre to read.

Taberski's availability for reading conferences helps her to both assess first hand her children's frustration levels and to model ongoing teacher/reader book conversations by scheduling child-initiated reading conferences when she personally replenishes their book bags.

To allay children's frustration levels while reading and to foster their independent reading, it is important to some children that the teacher personally take time out to hear them read aloud and to check for fluency and expression. After they have read aloud, children's frustration level can be immeasurably lessened if they are explicitly told by the teacher that they need to read without pointing and that they should try chunking words into phrases that mimic their natural speech.

Strategies for Selecting and Using Meaningful Reading Materials at Appropriate Levels of Difficulty

Matching young children with "just right" books fosters their independent reading, no matter what their age. The teacher needs to have an extensive classroom library. Emergent readers and early readers should be matched with books that are set in fairly large print and have appropriate spacing to allow the reader to easily see where a word begins and ends. These books should have few words per page so that the young reader can focus on the all-important concerns of top-to-bottom, left-to-right, directionality, and the one-to-one match of word to print.

Illustrations for young children should support the meaning of the text and language patterns and predictable text structures should make these texts appealing to young readers. Most important, the content of the story should relate to the children's interests and experiences as the teacher knows them. Only after all these considerations have been addressed, can the teacher select "just right" books from an already leveled bin or list. Similarly, when the teacher is selecting books for transitional and fluent readers, the following ideas need to be taken into account:

Book Length. The book should take at least two sittings to complete, allowing children to get used to reading longer books.

Character Complexity and Plot Intricacy. The fluent and transitional reader needs to deal with more complex characters and more intricate plotting. Look for books that set the stage for plot development with a compelling beginning. Age appropriateness of the concepts, plot, and themes are important so that the child will sustain interest in the book.

Advanced Book Features. Look for book features such as Table of Contents or Index to help children navigate through the book. Series books are wonderful to introduce at this point in the children's development.

Skill 15.2   Recognize the importance of using data from assessments to plan flexible groupings in instruction to address students' changing reading needs

When considering both formal and informal assessment data gathered on students, it is important to quantify the information into terms easily recognized by other teachers, administrators, and parents. In reading, general practice is to categorize the information into levels of reading. These levels go across both kinds of assessments, using the percentage of word accuracy and comprehension to determine the reading level.

Levels of Reading

Independent. This is the level at which the child can read text totally on their own. When reading books at the independent level, students will be able to decode between 95%–100% of the words and comprehend the text at a level of 90% accuracy or better. Many bodies of research indicate that about 98% accuracy makes for a good independent reader; however, there is other research that goes as low as 95% accuracy.

Instructional. This is the level at which the student should be taught because it provides enough difficulty to increase their reading skills without providing so much that it becomes too cumbersome to finish the selection. Typically, the acceptable range for accuracy is between 85%–94% with 75% or greater comprehension. Some standards rely on the number of errors made instead of the accuracy percentage with no more than one error out of twenty words read being the acceptable standard.

Frustrational. Books at a student's frustrational level are too difficult for that child and should not be used. The frustrational level is any text with less than 85% word accuracy and/or less than 75% comprehension.

The use of independent, instructional, and frustrational levels allow educators to provide children with texts of different ranges depending on the skills necessary to be completed. Typically, standardized or formal assessments test to the instructional level. Therefore, if reading a standardized assessment such as an Iowa Test of Basic Skills, the reported reading level would be the instructional level for that student.

Additionally, some formal and informal test results use alternate methods of reporting information. Some use the grade level and month equivalent, where a 3.2 reading level would indicate the child is reading at the third grade level second month (typically October). Still others use their own leveling system. The Developing Readers Assessment (DRA) has its own unique method of coding book levels based on the work of Fountas and Pinnell. Regardless of the levels listed, the work can easily be translated into independent, instructional, and frustrational levels, by examining the comprehension and the word reading accuracy portions of the assessment.

Skill 15.3   Recognize the importance of using data from assessments to plan and implement timely classroom interventions, differentiated instruction, and individualized instruction to address the needs of students at all proficiency levels

Awareness of Strategies and Resources for Supporting Individual Students

See Skill 1.1.

Skill 15.4   Recognize how to use diagnostic reading data to build on the strengths and address the needs of students with reading difficulties

See Skill 15.2.

One of the first things a teacher learns is how to obtain resources and help for his/her students. All schools have guidelines for receiving this assistance, especially since the implementation of the Americans with Disabilities Act. The first step the teacher takes in securing help is approaching the school's administration or exceptional education department for direction to attain special services or resources for qualifying students. Many schools have a committee designated for addressing these needs such as a Child Study Team (CST) or Core Team. These teams are made up of both regular and exceptional education teachers, school psychologists, guidance counselors, and administrators. The particular student's classroom teacher usually has to complete some initial paperwork and conduct some behavioral observations.

The teacher takes this information to the appropriate committee for discussion and consideration. The committee then recommends the next step to be taken. Often subsequent steps include a complete psychological evaluation along with certain physical examinations such as vision and hearing screening and a complete medical examination by a doctor. One plan of action is an Academic Intervention Plan (AIP). An AIP consists of additional instructional services provided to the student to help them achieve better academically if the student has met certain criteria (such as scoring below the state reference point on standardized tests or performing more than two levels below grade-level).

Another plan of action is a 504 plan. A 504 plan is a legal document based on the provisions of the Rehabilitation Act of 1973 (which preceded IDEA). A 504 plan is a plan for instructional services to assist students with special needs in a regular education classroom setting.

When a student's physical, emotional, or other impairment (such as Attention Deficit Disorder) impacts his/her ability to learn in a regular education classroom setting, that student can be referred for a 504 meeting. Typically, the CST and perhaps even the student's physician or therapist will participate in the 504 meeting to determine if a 504 plan will be written.

Finally, a child referred to CST may qualify for an Individualized Education Plan (IEP). An IEP is a legal document that outlines the specific, adapted services a student with disabilities will receive. An IEP differs from a 504 plan in that the child must be identified for special education services to qualify for an IEP, and *all* students who receive special education services must have an IEP. Each IEP must contain statements pertaining to the student's present performance level, annual goals, related services and supplementary aids, testing modifications, a projected date of services, and assessment methods for monitoring progress. Each year, the CST and guardians must meet to review and update a student's IEP.

At times, the teacher must go beyond the school system to meet the needs of some students. An awareness of special services and resources and how to obtain them is essential to all teachers and their students. When the school system is unable to address the needs of a student, the teacher often must take the initiative and contact agencies within the community. Frequently there is no special policy for finding resources. It is simply up to the individual teacher to be creative and resourceful and to find whatever services he/she can to help meet the students' needs. Meeting the needs of all students is certainly a team effort that is most often spearheaded by the classroom teacher.

Skill 15.5 **Recognize how to use diagnostic reading data to build on the strengths and address the needs of English Language Learners**

When considering students for whom English is not the primary language, it is critical to understand the natural progress of second language acquisition before applying the general knowledge of reading assessments to this subgroup of students.

In general, second language students can take up to seven years to become proficient in the second language. This estimate factors in the acculturation process with speaking, listening, reading, and writing. This group of students, attempting to learn in a second language, generally tends to lag behind their peers, particularly in vocabulary. The connection between words and their meanings is essential in understanding what is being read.

Students who are fluent and able to read in their primary language before starting the second language are more likely to become fluent in the second language and in a shorter time than those who are not fluent in the primary language. These students (i.e. those already fluent in their primary language) can make the transition easily between the two languages because they are able to see or hear a word, translate it in their mind to the same or a similar word in their native language, then make the connection, and access that information to help them understand the text. Though this is a slow and labor-intensive process in the end the students are able to understand.

In contrast, students who are unable to complete these numerous steps require additional support, particularly in vocabulary development. Helping to build background knowledge is critical when introducing texts to these students through as concrete a process as is possible. The more concrete the examples a teacher can provide, the better for the students.

In looking at the other areas of reading, phonics and phonemic awareness skills can also pose problems. Students will sometimes substitute the sounds from their native language in the middle of the process. Additionally, they may have no connection within their native language because there may be no letters or combinations of letters that make those sounds.

In the end, good reading assessment and instruction are essential when working with students acquiring a second language. However, it must be married well with the body of research of how one learns a second language. Remember that oral language will develop first (receptive before expressive). After oral language reaches a conversational level, one can begin reading instruction.

GLOSSARY

These definitions are critical for success on all multiple choice questions on the examinations. Proper use of these terms is crucial for success in tackling a constructed response involving balanced literacy.

Ability grouping—Grouping of children with similar needs for instructional purposes. Ability groups do not remain constant throughout the year, but change as the children's needs within them change.

Alliteration—Occurs when words begin with the same consonant sound, as in *Peter Piper picked a pair of pickled peppers.*

Alphabetic principle—The idea that written spellings represent spoken words.

Anchor book—A balanced literacy term for a book that is purposely read repeatedly and used as part of both the reading and writing workshop. It is a good idea to use certain books that become the children's familiar and cherished favorites for reading, which subsequently inspires children's writing.

Assonance—Occurs when words begin with the same vowel sound.

Authentic assessment—Assessment activities that reflect the actual workplace, family community, and school curriculum.

Balanced Literacy Lesson Format—The Balanced Literacy Approach has its own specific format for the delivery of the literacy lesson, whether it is a reading or writing workshop lesson. The format begins with a 10- to 15-minute mini-lesson which the teacher delivers to the whole class. This mini-lesson is then followed by a 30-minute small-group lesson (when the children break into small groups to work). It concludes with a 10-minute sharing session during which the whole class reconvenes to share what they have done in the small groups. One can refer to this format as the whole-small-whole group approach.

Benchmarks—School, state, or nationally mandated statements of the expectations for student learning and achievement in various content areas.

BICS—Basic Interpersonal Communication Skills (ELL term)—Learning second language skills and becoming proficient in a second language through face-to-face interaction and translation through speaking, listening, and viewing.

Blending—The process of hearing separate phonemes and being able to merge them together to read the word.

Book features—Children need to be familiar with the following book features: front and back cover, title and half- title page, dedication page, table of contents, prologue and epilogue, and foreword and after notes. For factual books, children need to be familiar with: labels, captions, glossary, index, headings and subheadings within chapters, charts and diagrams, and sidebars.

Checklist—An assessment form that lists targeted learning and social behaviors as indicators of achievement, knowledge, or skill. These lists can be prepared by teachers or other professionals.

Cinquain—A five-line poem that can be read and then used as a model for writing. Line 1 of this format is generally a single word; line 2 has two words which describe the title in line 1; line 3 is comprised of three "movement" words; line 4 has four words that express feeling; and line 5 has a single word which can be a synonym for line 1's single word.

Comprehension—This occurs when the reader correctly interprets the print on the page and constructs meaning from it. Comprehension depends on activating prior knowledge, cultural and social background of the reader, and the reader's ability to use comprehension monitoring strategies.

Concepts about print—Includes: how to handle a book, how to look at print, directionality, sequencing, locating skills, punctuation, and concepts of letters and words.

Consonant diagraphs—The "voiceless" combination of two consonants that represent one new speech sound. In the word "diagraph" the *ph,* which sounds like /f/, is a diagraph.

Constructed meaning— If there were two words synonymous with reading comprehension as far as the Balanced Literacy Approach is concerned, they would be *constructing meaning.* Cooper, Taberski, Strickland, and other key theorists and classroom teachers conceptualize the reader as interacting with the text and bringing his/her prior knowledge and experience to it.

Contexts—Sentences deliberately prepared by the teacher which include sufficient contextual clues for the children to decipher meaning.

Contextual redefinition—Using context to determine word meaning.

Cooperative reading—Children read with a partner or buddy. It can be silent or oral reading.

Crisscrossers—An ELL term for second-language learners who have a positive attitude toward both first language and second language learning. These second-language learners, children from ELL backgrounds, are comfortable navigating back and forth between the two languages as they learn.

Cues—As they self monitor their reading comprehension, readers have to integrate various sources of information or cues to help them construct meaning from text and graphic illustrations.

Decoding—"Sounding out" a printed sequence of letters based on knowledge of letter sound correspondences.

Diphthongs—Two vowels in one syllable where the sound of each letter is heard. For instance in the word *house* both the *o* and the *u* are heard.

Directionality—Children use their fingers to indicate left to right direction and return sweep to the next line.

Differentiated instruction—The need for the teacher, based on observation of individual student's work, progress, test results, fluency, and other reading/literacy behaviors, to provide modified instruction and alternative strategies or activities. These activities are specifically developed by the teacher to address the individual student's different needs.

Early readers—These readers recognize most high-frequency words and many simple words. They use pictures to confirm meaning. Using meaning, syntax, and phonics, they can figure out most simple words. They use spelling patterns to figure out new words. They are gaining control of reading strategies. They use their own experiences and background knowledge to predict meanings. They occasionally use story language in their writing. This stage follows emergent reading.

Emergent readers—The stage of reading in which the reader understands that print contains a consistent message. The reader can recognize some high frequency words, names, and simple words in context. Pictures can be used to predict meaning. The emergent reader begins to attend to left-to-right directionality and features of print and may identify some initial sounds and ending sounds in words.

Encode—To change a message into symbols. For example, readers encode oral language into writing.

English Language Development (ELD)—Refers to improving the English skills of students, especially those who are learning English as a second language

English Language Learner (ELL)—Individuals who are acquiring English as a second language.

English as a Second Language (ESL)—A way of teaching English to a person whose native or primary language is one other than English and using English as the language of instruction.

Expository text—Non-fiction that provides information and facts. This category of text is what newspapers, science, mathematics, and history texts use. Currently there is much focus—even in elementary schools—on teaching children how to comprehend and author expository texts. They must produce brochures, guides, recipes, and procedural accounts on most elementary grade levels. The teaching of reading of expository texts requires working with a particular vocabulary and concept structure that is very different from that of narrative text. Therefore time must be taken to teach the reading of expository texts and contrast it with the reading of narrative texts.

First language—An ELL term for the language any child acquires in the first few years of life. It is through this acquired language that the child acquires phonological and phonemic awareness.

Fluent readers—These readers identify most words automatically. They can read chapter books with good comprehension. They consistently monitor, cross-check, and self-correct reading. They can offer their own interpretations of text based on personal experiences and prior reading experiences. Fluent readers are capable of reading a variety of genres independently. Furthermore, they can respond to texts or stories by sharing pertinent examples from their lives. They can also readily make connections to other books that they have read. Finally, they are capable of beginning to create spoken and written writings which are in the style of a particular author.

Formal assessment—A test or an observation of a performance task done under controlled and regulated conditions.

Functional reading—The reading of instructions, recipes, coupons, classified ads, notices, signs, and other documents which we have to read and correctly interpret in school and in society.

Grade equivalent/grade score—A score transformed from a raw score on a standardized test into the equivalent score earned by an average student in the norming group.

Graphic organizers—Graphic organizers express relationships among various ideas in visual form including: sequence, timelines, character traits, fact and opinion, main idea and details, and differences and likenesses. Graphic organizers are particularly helpful for visual learners.

Graphophonemic knowledge— Graphophonemic knowledge is the recognition of the letters of the alphabet and the understanding of sound-symbol relationships.

Guided reading—This is one of the key modes of instruction in the Balanced Literacy Approach. During guided reading, the teacher "guides" the child through silent reading of a text by giving them prompts, target questions, and even helping the child start an answer to a specific prompt or question. At the end of each guided reading section or excerpt of the text, the child stops to talk with the teacher about the text. By definition, guided reading is an interactive discussion between the child and the teacher. This mode of reading instruction is generally used when children need extra support in constructing meaning because the text is complex or because their current independent reading capacities are still limited.

High frequency—This refers to frequently used words. These words appear many more times than do other words in ordinary reading material. Examples of such words include: *as, in, of,* and *the.* These words are also sometimes called service words. These words are also part of sight vocabulary words. A classic best-known high frequency word list was generated by Dolch (1936). http://literacyconnections.com/

Independent reading—This is a set period of time within the daily literacy block when children read books with 95%–100% accuracy on their own. This independent reading—where children can comprehend without teacher support—promotes lifelong literacy and love of learning, which enhances reading mileage, builds fluency, and helps children orchestrate integrated cue strategies.

Informal assessment—Observations of children made under informal conditions; these can include kid watching, checklists, and individual child/teacher conversations.

Informal Reading Inventory (IRI)—A series of reading excerpts that can be used to determine a child's reading strengths and needs in comprehension and decoding. Many published reading series have an IRI to go with their series.

Justified type—Inserting space between words to expand a line so that both left and right margins align.

Kid watching—Term used within the Balanced Literacy Approach for the teacher's deliberate, detailed, and recorded observations of individual student and class literacy behaviors, often done during small group work. The teacher then reconfigures lessons on experiences to meet the students' individual and group needs.

Kinesthetic—Learning is tactile, unlike activities where the learner sits still or attempts to sit still in one place. Cutting and moving syllables, creating word strips, or using sandpaper letters are all kinesthetic activities.

Language experience—Children giving dictation to the teacher who writes their words on a chart or their drawings. This shows children that words can be written down.

Learning logs—Daily records of what students have learned.

Listening post—Sets of headphones attached to a single tape or CD player. Children can go to centers where they listen to audio recordings of books while reading the print book. These posts are in many libraries as well.

Literature circles—A group discussion involving four to six children who have read the same work of literature (narrative or expository text). They talk about key parts of the work, relate it to their own experience, listen to the responses of others, and discuss how parts of the text relate to the whole.

Manipulation—Moving around or switching sounds within a word or words within a phrase or sentence.

Meaning vocabulary—Words whose meanings children understand and can use.

Miscue— An oral reading error made by a child, where the child's reading differs from the actual printed text.

Miscue analysis—The teacher keeps a detailed recording of the errors or inaccurate attempts of a child reader during a reading assessment. These are recorded within a running record. This helps the teacher see whether the cues—syntactic, semantic, or graphophonemic— that the child is using are accurate.

Monitoring reading—Various strategies that children use to monitor their readings. Some samples are: maintaining fluency by bringing prior knowledge to the story to make predictions, using these predictions to do further checking, searching and self-correcting as the story progresses, and using problem-solving word study skills to make links from known words to unknown words.

Morphemes—The smallest units of meaning in words. There are two types of morphemes: free morphemes, which can stand alone, such as *love,* and bound morphemes, which must be attached to another morpheme to carry meaning, such as *ed* in *loved.*

Narrative text—One of the two basic text structures. The narrative text tells or communicates a story, e.g., novels, short stories, and plays. Some poems are narratives as well. Narrative text needs to be taught differently than expository text because of its structure.

One-to-One Matching—Matching one spoken word with one written word.

Onset-rime blending—The blending of the onset (everything before the vowel) and rime (the vowel and everything after it). For example, the word "sleep" can be broken into /sl/ and /eep/. Word families are built using rimes. The /eep/ word family would include *jeep, keep,* and *weep.*

Orthography—A method of representing spoken language through letters and diacritics.

Percentile—A value on a scale of one hundred that indicates the percent of a distribution that is equal to or below it. If a child scores at the 56th percentile for his/grade level, his/her score is equal to or above that of 56 percent of the children taking that standardized test and below that of 46 percent of the children on whose scores the test was normed.

Performance assessment—Having children do a task that demonstrates their knowledge, skills, and competency. Having children author their own alphabet book on a particular topic would be a performance assessment for knowledge of the alphabet.

Phoneme—The speech sound units that make a difference in meaning. The word *rope* has three phonemes /r/, /o/, and /p/. Change one phoneme, e.g., /r/ to /n/, and it becomes different word: *nope.*

Phonemic awareness—The understanding that words are composed of sounds. Phonemic awareness is a specific type of phonological awareness dealing only with phonemes in a spoken word.

Phonics—The study of relationships between phonemes (speech sounds) and graphemes (letters) that represent the phonemes. It is also decoding or the sounding out of unknown words that are written.

Phonological awareness—The ability to recognize the sounds of spoken language and how they can be blended together, segmented, and switched/manipulated to form new combinations and words.

Phonological cues—Readers use their knowledge of letter/sound and sound/letter relationships to predict and confirm reading.

Phonology—The study of speech structure in language that includes both the patterns of basic speech units (phonemes) and the tacit rules of pronunciation.

Portfolios—Collections of a child's work over time. They include a cover letter, reflections from the child and teacher, and other supportive documents including standards, performance task examples, prompts, and sometimes peer comments.

Primary language (ELL term)—The language in which an individual is the most fluent and with which they are the most at ease. This is usually, but not always the individual's first language.

Prompts—When the teacher intervenes in the child's independent reading to help the child pronounce or comprehend a specific word or prompt. On a reading record, the teacher notes the prompt. When the teacher wants to match a child with a particular book or determine the child's stage of reading level, the teacher does not use prompts.

Question-generating strategy for an expository text—First the child previews the text by reading titles, subheads, looking at pictures or illustrations, and reading the first paragraph. Next the child asks a "think" question which he/she records. Then the child reads to find information that might answer the "think" question. The child may write down the information found or think about another question that is answered by what the child is reading. The child continues to read using this strategy.

Raw score— This is the actual number of points scored on a test.

Reading for information—Reading with the purpose of extracting facts and expert opinion from the text. Children should be introduced to the following information resources: web resources that are age- and grade-appropriate for children; the concept of the table of contents, chapter headings, glossaries, and indexes; and pictures, maps, charts, diagrams, and text structures in an information text. They should be taught to use notes, graphs, organizers, and mind maps to share information extracted from a text.

Recode—To change information from one code into another, such as recoding writing into oral speech.

Recognition vocabulary—The group of words which children are able to correctly pronounce, read orally, and understand on sight.

Record of reading behavior (*a.k.a., running record*)—An objective observation during which the teacher records, using a standard set of symbols, everything the child reader says as the child reads a book selected by the teacher. These oral reading records can be used by the K–3 teacher to assess how well children are using cueing systems.

Reflection—To analyze, discuss, and react to one's learning on any grade or age level.

Retelling—This can be written or oral. Children are expected and encouraged to tell as much of a story as they can remember. Retelling is far more extensive than just summarizing. Children should include the beginning, middle, and end plot lines and should be able to tell about the book's characters.

Rubric—A set of guidelines or acceptable responses for the completion of any task. Usually, a rubric ranges from 0 to 4 with 4 being the most detailed response and 0 indicating a response to the task which lacked detail or was in other ways insufficient.

Running record—An objective observation during which the teacher records, using a standard set of symbols, everything the child reader says as the child reads a book selected by the teacher. These oral reading records can be used by the K–3 teacher to assess how well children are using cueing systems.

Scaffolding—Refers to the teacher support necessary for the child to accomplish a task or to achieve a goal which the child could not accomplish on his/her own. Vygotsky termed this window of opportunity the "zone of proximal development." Ultimately as the child becomes more proficient or capable, the scaffold is withdrawn. The goal of scaffolding is to help the child to perform the reading task independently and internalize the behavior. During *shared reading,* the task is scaffolded by the teacher's reading to the children aloud. As the teacher reads, the teacher scaffolds the initial decoding and helps with the meaning making/construction.

Searching—Children pause to search in the picture, print, or their memory for known information. This can happen as the child tackles an unknown word or has just made an error.

Second language—(ELL term)—A language acquired or learned simultaneously with or after a child's acquisition of a first language.

Segmenting—The process of hearing a spoken word and identifying its separate phonemes or syllables.

Self-correction—Children begin to correct some of their own reading errors. Generally this behavior is accompanied by the rereading of the previous phrase or sentence.

Semantic cues—Children use their prior knowledge, sense of the story, and pictures to support their predicting and confirming the meaning of the text.

Semantic web—A visual graphic organizer that the teacher can use to introduce a reading on a specific topic. It visually represents many other words associated with a target word. The web can help activate the children's prior knowledge and extend or clarify it. It can also serve to check new learning after guided or independent reading.

Spatial learning—Using images, color, or layout to help readers whose learning style is spatial.

SQ3R (Survey, Question, Read, Recite, and Review Studying)—This is a technique that makes it possible and feasible to learn the content of even large amounts of text.

Standard score—How far a child's grade on a standardized test deviates from the average score (mean) on the test in terms of the standard deviation. If a child scores 70 on a standardized test and the standard deviation is 5 and the average (mean) score is 65, the child is one standard deviation above the average.

Standardized test—A test given under specified conditions allowing comparisons to be made. A set of norms or average scores on this test will be used for comparisons.

Stop and Think strategy—A balanced literacy strategy for constructing meaning. As the text is being read, the child reflects: *Does this make sense to me? If it does not make sense to me, I should then try to reread it or read ahead. I can also look up words that I don't know or ask for help.* Generally the teacher models this strategy with the whole class as a mini-lesson and posts it prominently in the classroom for continued reference by the children.

Strategic readers—As defined by researchers Marie Clay and Sharon Taberski, strategic readers are self improving and carry out the tasks listed below as they read:

(A lengthy glossary explanation of this term has been provided because it can appear in a variety of multiple choice questions on the examination as well as part of a constructed response question).

- Monitor their reading to see if it makes sense semantically, syntactically, and visually.
- Look for and use semantic, syntactic, and visual clues.
- Uncover and identify new things about the text.
- Cross check and use one cueing system against another.
- Self-correct their reading when what the first read does not match the semantic, syntactic, and visual clues
- Solve for and identify new words using multiple cueing systems

Beyond these behaviors, a strategic or self-improving reader uses many strategies to construct meaning. When their reading experience is going well— they know the words and understand the text or story—they are working continuously (even if they are not conscious of it) at maintaining meaning. If and when the strategic or self-improving reader runs into an unfamiliar word, then he/she has many strategies to identify that word. Becoming a successful strategic reader is a goal that can and should be shared with children as early as the middle of the first grade, although the term "self-improving reader" might be used at that point.

Text features—Children need to be alerted to the following text features which may initially appear strange to them. Text features include: a period marking the end of a "telling sentence," a question mark placed at the end of a sentence that asks a question; an exclamation mark used at the end of a sentence to express surprise or excitement; capital letters: first word of a sentence and the proper names of persons, places, and things; bold, italicized, or underlined text to highlight key ideas and create emphasis; quotation marks to indicate dialogue; a hyphen used to break a long word up into its syllables; a long dash used to show a break in an idea or to indicate a parenthetical element or an omission; an ellipse to indicate an deliberate omission of text or a break in the text; and new a paragraph in nonfiction which shows a new point being made.

Transitional readers—These readers recognize an increasing number of "hard" words that are content related. They can provide summaries of the stories that they read. They are more at ease with handling longer, more complex, connected text with short chapters. Transitional readers can read independent level texts with correct phrasing, expression, and fluency. When they encounter unfamiliar words, they have a variety of strategies to figure out the unfamiliar words. Their reading demonstrates that they are able to integrate meaning, syntax and phonics in a consistent manner so that they can understand the texts they are reading.

Venn diagram—A diagram consisting of two or three intersecting circles to visually represent similarities and differences for texts, characters, and topics. No author study is complete without Venn diagrams comparing different author's works. This is the most commonly used graphic organizer in elementary schools today. It can be used effectively as part of an answer to a constructed response question.

Visual cues—Readers use their knowledge of graphemes to predict and confirm text. The graphemes may be words, syllables or letters.

Word analysis—Employing letters, phonic structures, contextual clues, or dictionary skills to analyze.

Word identification—How the reader determines the pronunciation and meaning of an unknown word.

Word recognition—The process of determining the pronunciation and some degree of the meaning of an unknown word.

Word work—the term that the Balanced Literacy Approach uses for the study of vocabulary.

DIRECTORY OF THEORISTS AND RESEARCHERS

Introduction

Many questions on the teacher certification examinations can only be correctly answered if teachers know the theorist or the research that is referenced. The teaching of reading owes much to the work, principles, and guidelines of teacher/educators and university field researchers who have changed the style, methods, and practice of teaching reading. While those listed in this directory are by no means all the major researchers (page constraints would make a complete listing impossible), the individuals listed below are those whose contributions are frequently referenced on the certification tests and whose work is evident in today's elementary classroom teaching and learning of reading.

Phonics Centered Approach

In 1955 Rudolph Flesch gained national prominence when he published *Why Johnny Can't Read.* This book went on to become a best seller and has now become a classic which is readable and speaks to current concerns. Flesch became the spokesperson for a war that periodically resurfaces in the reading world.

Flesch, Chall (1967), Stahl (1992), Adams (1990), and Johnson and Bauman (1984) believe that a phonics-based approach is crucial for reading success. Flesch and others feel that the balanced literacy advocates are seriously undermining the crucial role that phonics plays in the children's development as successful decoding readers. However, it must be noted that while balanced literacy does emphasize the use of literature based reading programs, it in no way dismisses phonics from its reading program; indeed phonics is included in the crucial "word work" component of the reading and writing workshop.

The phonics advocates point to the fact that most research shows that early and systematic instruction in phonics skills results in superior reading achievement in elementary school and beyond.

Adams (1990) detailed what type of phonics instruction is needed:

> To learn to read skillfully, children need practice in seeing and understanding decodable words in real reading situations and with connected text. ... phonics instruction {needs to be} part of a reading program that provides ample practice in reading and writing. Encouraging children with connected text can also show them the importance of what they are learning and make the lessons in phonics relevant and sensible. Phonics centered advocates believe that children should begin to learn letter associations in kindergarten with most useful phonics skills being taught by first grade. These basic skills should then be reviewed in second grade and beyond. Consonant sounds should be taught first, since they are more reliable in their letter-sound associations. Short vowel sounds appear more frequently in beginning reading materials, so they should be introduced before long vowels.

MIDDLE GRADES READING 144

Phonics advocates believe that most beginning readers need to be taught letter-sound associations explicitly. Phonics advocates also believe that beginning readers need to read stories that have words to which phonics skills apply. This allows them to practice their phonics skills as they write and spell words. They should also play lots of letter-sound association games.

Phonics advocates claim that when phonics is abandoned reading scores drop and balanced literacy advocates counter with the fact that they have never advocated abandoning the teaching of phonics.

As Jeanne Chall, a professor at Harvard's Graduate School of Education notes: "a beginning reading program that does not give children knowledge and skill in recognizing and decoding words will have poor results."

Theorists and Researchers:

Adams, Marilyn Jager
Noted for her research on early reading, Adams lists five basic types of phonemic awareness tasks which should be covered by the end of first grade. These include: ability to hear rhymes and alliterations, ability to do oddity tasks, ability to orally blend words, ability to orally segment words, and ability to do phonemic manipulation tasks.

Clay, Marie M. Marie
Clay is a New Zealand-born researcher in the field of special needs emergent literacy and in the development of assessment tools for these children. Her research in this field is felt throughout the Reading Recovery movement. Her book, *Reading Recovery: A Guidebook for Teachers in Training,* is used in a majority of graduate courses on emergent literacy and in many classrooms in the U.S. including those that do not have a Reading Recovery teacher.

Her doctoral thesis focused on what was to become her life's work, emergent reading behavior. At the crux of her research for the dissertation, Clay reviewed and detailed the week-by-week progress of 100 children during their first year of school (1966). An important outcome of the dissertation was her development of reliable observation tools for the assessment and analysis of changes over time in children's literacy learning. These assessments are the crux of *An Observation Survey of Early Literacy Achievement* (1993) which is an essential work for the primary school educator. The assessments have been validated and reconstructed for learners from the Spanish, Maori, and French languages. A special appendix in this guide includes the *Record of Reading Behavior* tool she created with Kenneth Goodman.

Reading Recovery is a key Clay contribution to the field of "foundations of reading" teaching. The movement, which is discussed in detail in this section, was born out of the concerns of classroom educators who were upset that even with excellent programs and expert teaching, they were not able to positively influence the literacy progress of some of their young children. Clay posed the question of investigating what would happen if the design and delivery of traditional reading education were changed for these struggling young learners.

The whole thrust of the Reading Recovery movement has been to improve the early identification and instructional delivery for these struggling young readers. Her goal was to develop a system that would bring those children scoring the lowest in assessment measures to the level of the average readers within their classes.

With the support of Barbara Watson and others, the program was developed in three years. The first field tests of the program took place in the late 1970s in Auckland schools. To date, circa 2005, the program is operating in most English-speaking countries and has been reconstructed for use in Spanish and French.

Janet S. Gaffey and Billie Askew have said of Marie Clay (1991) that her contribution "has been to change what is possible for individual learners when teaching permits different routes to be taken for desired outcomes."

Reading Recovery has been identified by the International Reading Association as a program that not only teaches children how to read, but also reduces the number of children who are labeled as "learning disabled." It further lowers the number of children who are placed in remedial reading programs and classes.

Clay Reading Recovery lessons are designed to promote accelerated learning so that children can catch up to their peers and continue to learn independently.

The hallmark of the Reading Recovery program is that the Reading Recovery teacher works with one student at a time over a 12- to 20-week period. Each daily 30-minute lesson is tailored to address the needs of the individual student. Therefore Reading Recovery teachers generally teach no more than four or five students per day in individual lessons.

The Clay Observation of Early Childhood Achievement (1993) is used to assess children's strengths and weaknesses. Reading Recovery teachers devote the first 10 minutes of their sessions to assessment with individual children as they engage in reading and writing. A running record of the child's progress is taken every day and is used to plan future lessons.

The lessons themselves include the use of familiar stories. Children engage in assembling and in sequencing cut up stories. They work with letters or write a story. Teaching style involves the teacher demonstrating strategies and the child then developing effective strategies to continue reading independently. Key components of each lesson include: phonemic awareness, phonics, spelling, and comprehension study. Much time is devoted to problem solving so that the children's decoding is purposeful. Children are given time to practice and demonstrate fluency skills.

Ultimately what sets Reading Recovery apart is the fact that it is one-to-one tutoring. This is also what makes it effective for children. However, what raises issues about it are the additional costs incurred in the school systems wanting to adopt it. Obviously the districts and education systems have to decide whether they want to pay the costs of this and other individualized tutoring systems now in the primary school years or pay later as these children become adults whose literacy skills are not sufficient for proactive citizenship.

Fountas, Irene C. and Gay Su Pinnell
These two researchers have developed a leveling system for reading texts, which arranges them by level of difficulty. Beyond a specific analysis of set titles, the theorists have explained in several published works how to use their leveling system to meet and assess the progress of various readers. They also provide detailed explanations and support for reading teachers of young children K–3 in using reading records and benchmark texts.

They are the key articulators of the balanced literacy model that includes reading and writing workshop. Among their other contributions to the field are: guidelines for creating sets of leveled books, assessment rubrics, strategies for fostering "word solver" skills in child readers, and methods for teaching phonics and spelling in the literacy classroom.

Routman, Regie
Routman's contributions to Reading Foundations are the result of over three decades of experience as an elementary school teacher, a reading specialist, a learning disabilities tutor, a Reading Recovery teacher, a language arts teacher, a mentor, and a staff developer. Due to these various experiences, her insights into reading resonate with a broad spectrum of school community members.

Routman's works are conversational, teacher-to-teacher sharings of her daily experiences in classrooms. In her published books on the teaching of reading, i.e. *Reading Essentials* (Heinemann, 2002), Routman shows teachers how to teach consistent with the findings in reading research, yet also with highly practical "scripted lessons" and teaching tips that make the classroom come alive. She advocates literature-based teaching and meaning-centered approaches for learning.

In addition, she is a strong advocate of using poetry from grades one and beyond as an integral thread for a reading program. She is the author of series *Kids' Poems: Teaching Children to Love Writing Poetry* (Scholastic, 2000) which includes separate volumes of poetry for grades K–4.

Routman believes in teaching reading to meet specific children's needs regardless of the particular reading program in place. She is a strong advocate for the use of small guided-reading groups and reading for understanding. Phonics and other word-analysis strategies are part of her reading framework, but not at its core. Her focus for the reading classroom is on the development and use of the classroom library as the center for an independent reading program, shared reading, and reading aloud.

Routman has designed informal reading evaluations on books/texts her students are reading (her published works are known for their appendices, replete with templates for evaluations, projects, reports, book lists, suggested texts by topics, etc.). Her classroom model includes matching children with specific library books as well as linking assessment with instruction. Finally she is a researcher who sees reading as intimately linked to writing.

Routman is also involved with the politics of literacy. This vision of literacy involves the image of the teacher as an informed professional who regularly reads the latest professional books, collaborates with colleagues in school and beyond, and deals with the most recent research developments. Interestingly, Routman is one researcher who also feels that an informed professional can and should know when to question research. Other aspects of the politics of literacy as Routman conceptualizes them are: communicating effectively with parents and dealing with testing and standards mandates.

Two of her published works, *Conversations: Strategies for Teaching, Learning, and Evaluating* (Heinemann, 2000) and *Invitations: Changing as Teachers and Learners, K–12* (Heinemann, 1991 and 1994) are essential for the elementary reading teacher's bookshelf and can take the teacher through several years of work.

Taberski, Sharon

Taberski is an experienced elementary teacher/educator who is also a member of the Primary Literacy Standards Committee run by the National Center on Education and the Economy and the University of Pittsburgh. Her works in the field are served up as wonderfully accessible and necessary advice from "the veteran teacher across the hall" who loves her students and is delighted to help a new colleague.

Unlike many theorists in the field of reading, Taberski's work is not focused around a prescribed set of skills, but rather around a series of interconnected interactions with the learner.

Among these interactions, which are detailed and clearly communicated in her book *On Solid Ground: Strategies for Teaching Reading K–3* (Heinemann, 2000), are:

- Assessment—Procedures to assess children's reading, conduct informed teaching, schedule and manage reading conferences, take oral reading records, and use retellings as discussion tools.
- Demonstration—Taberski developed and field tested strategies for using shared reading and read aloud as platforms for figuring out words and comprehending texts. She is a strong advocate of small group work-guided reading, word-study groups, and teaching children one on one.
- Practice—In the Taberski framework, independent reading is used as a time for practice. Students play key roles in this practice and Taberski has a set of detailed and easily adaptable guidelines for matching children with books for independent reading. Her work includes booklists and ready to use information that is available for reproduction.
- Response—It's important for students to know that they are doing well and where they must focus their efforts to improve skills. Taberski explains how her students use writing and dialogue as tools for independent reading.

Vail, Priscilla

Noted for her research in the study of dyslexia and its myths, Vail has articulated ways in which children can develop their reading skills as they cope with this disorder. She also provides techniques parents and educators can use to support reading development. She has also worked on specific test taking skills for children coping with dyslexia and other special needs. Her strategies can be infused in the regular education program to enhance all students' reading achievement. She is a proponent of using phonics instruction and skills within the context of an integrated whole-language approach (once called integrated language arts).

Another focus of Vail's research is the link between language and thinking. She is concerned with how a child's receptive language, expressive language, and metacognition can be fostered. She has developed assessment methods for each of these capacities and activities to help strengthen them in children grades K–4.

BIBLIOGRAPHY OF PRINT RESOURCES

PROFESSIONAL BOOKS:

Adams, Marilyn Jager. (1990). *Beginning to Read: Thinking and Learning about Print.* Cambridge, MA: MIT Press.

Anders, P. and Bos, C. (1986). Semantic Feature Analysis: An Interactive Strategy for Vocabulary Development and Reading Comprehension, *Journal of Reading*, 29, 610–616.

Blevins, W. (1997). *Phonemic Awareness Activities for Early Reading Success.* New York: Scholastic.

Boyd-Bastone, P. (2004). Focused Anecdotal Record Assessment (ARA): A Tool for Standards-Based Authentic Assessment. *Reading Teacher, 58* (3), pp. 230–239.

Calkins, Lucy McCormick. (2000). *The Art of Teaching Reading.* New York: Longman.
   This is the woman who beautifully explains the reading workshop and its relationship to the writing workshop as she shares wonderful snapshots of mini-lessons, conferring, conferencing, independent reading, guided reading, book talks, prompts, coaching, and classroom library use. Exceedingly readable and direct.

Campbell, Robin. (2004). *Phonics, Naturally: Reading and Writing for Real Purposes.* Portsmouth, NH: Heinemann.
   This work focuses on how children who deftly absorb and interconnect symbols and sounds of their universes can be supported in K–1 classes to extend this ability into phonics learning. Campbell demonstrates how immersion in a highly literate classroom filled with print and language stimuli allows kids to build accurate letter-sound relationships. The book provides a framework for teaching phonics using proven field-tested Campbell strategies.

   Among these strategies are: early mark making, read alouds, playing with language in rhyme and song, writing and reading in a variety of genres, exploring environmental and classroom print, and using students' own names. Samples of student work are included.

Chancey, C. (1994). Language development, metalinguistic awareness, and emergent literacy skills of 3-year-old children in relation to social class. *Applied Psycholinguistics*, 15, 371–394.

Clay, Marie M. (2006). *An Observation Survey of Early Literacy Achievement,* (2nd Edition), Portsmouth, NH: Heinemann.
Clay, Marie M. (1993). *Reading Recovery: A Guidebook for Teachers in Training.* Portsmouth, NH: Heinemann.

Cooper, J. David. (2004). *Literacy: Helping Children Construct Meaning.* Boston, MA: Houghton Mifflin. (5th Edition).

This book explains with numerous charts, tables, templates, and excerpts from actual texts and what the Balanced Literacy Approach means to the teaching of reading and writing. It offers the new teacher: exact schedules, strategies, guidelines, assessment tools, bibliographies, research, and even scripts for conferring with children.

Cooper is a clear and crisp writer who does not overwhelm the reader, but rather engages the reader. Even veteran teachers would return again and again to this text for support and refreshing insights.

Cox, Carole. (2005). *Teaching Language Arts.* Boston, MA: Pearson.
A compendium of state-of-the-art lesson plans, web resources, online case studies, teaching ideas, and extensive templates. All of these materials are aligned to the balanced literacy reading and writing workshop model.

The book also includes teaching ideas for the ELL reader, children with learning disabilities, and speakers of non-standard dialects. The book also features snapshots of second language learners as well as bi-literacy web resources.

Cullinan, Bernice E., Scala, Marilyn C., and Schroder, Virginia C. (1995). *Three Voices: An Invitation to Poetry Across the Curriculum.* New York: Stenhouse. K–3.
Two classroom educators and a noted researcher in children's literature demonstrate how poetry can be used in the classroom to teach various aspects of reading and to nurture lifelong literacy. Thirty-three grade- and age-appropriate strategies are included which have been field tested in classrooms across the country.

Ezell, H. K. and Justice, L. M. (2000). Increasing the Print Focus of Adult-Child Shared Book Reading through Observational Learning. *American Journal of Speech Pathology*, 9, 36–37.

Flesch, Rudolf. (1998). *Why Johnny Can't Read,* Cutchogue, NY: Buccaneer Books.

Fountas, Irene C. and Gay Su Pinnell. (2001). *Guiding Readers and Writers, Grades 3–6, Teaching Comprehension, Genre, and Content Literacy.* Portsmouth, NH: Heinemann.
This work includes 1,000 leveled books with guidelines for using them as part of a reading and writing workshop. The book explains how to use various genres in the classroom and how to use visual graphic organizers for the teaching of reading and writing.

Fountas, Irene. C. and Gay Su Pinnell. (1999). *Matching Books to Readers: Using Leveled Books in Guided Reading, K–3*. Portsmouth, NH: Heinemann. This major contribution to the field has a list of 7,500 grade- and age-appropriate books. In addition the authors include word counts to be used for keeping running records, text characteristics, guidelines for leveling of additional books and suggestions for developing classroom library collections.

Other works by these researchers also published by Heinemann include: *Voices on Word Matters: Learning about Phonics and Spelling in the Literacy Classroom* (1999) and *Word Matters: Teaching Phonics and Spelling in the Reading/Writing Classroom* (1998).

Fry, Edward Bernard, Kress, Jacqueline, and Fountoukidis, Dona Lee. (2000). *The Reading Teacher's Book of Lists*. San Francisco, CA: Wiley Press. This book is an invaluable one for the working classroom educator. It includes ready-to-use lists that cover a multiplicity of teacher needs. Among them are: spelling demons, readability graphs, phonics, useful words, reading math, vowel lists, anagrams, portmanteaus (do you know what they are and how well they can work in word study?), web sites, classic children's literature, etc. Even a veteran teacher/educator will find useful and new resources. Also, this book is wonderful for developing independent word study investigations and literature explorations.

Ganske, Kathy. (2000). *Word Journeys: Assessment-Guided Phonics, Spelling, and Vocabulary Instruction*. New York, NY: Guilford Press. This book offers a practical approach for assessing children's spelling. The author has created a DSA (Development Spelling Analysis) tool that teachers can use to evaluate individual children's spelling progress and to differentiate instruction. The book includes snapshots of children at different levels of spelling development.

Hall, Susan. (2001–2008). *Using Picture Books to Teach Literary Devices: Recommended Books for Children and Adults*. (Four-Volume Series). Westport, CT: Greenwood Publishing Group.

How to Help Every Child Become a Reader. Just Publishing. K–6 and beyond. This accessible text draws on materials developed by the U.S. Department of Education to share research, resources, referrals, and suggestions for supporting all children to become lifelong and engaged readers. It offers specific suggestions and resources for assisting struggling readers including those with special needs and those from ELL backgrounds.

Labov, L. (2003). When Ordinary Children Fail to Read. *Reading Research Quarterly*, 38, 128–31.

Macmillan, B. M. (2002). Rhyme and Reading. A Critical Review of the Research Methodology. *Journal of Research in Reading,* 25(1), 4–42.

Makar, Barbara. *Primary Phonics Readers*. Short story books that K–2 can own and read independently.

> They feature phonetically controlled texts, sounds, and spellings that are grade and age appropriate and high interest child-centered themes. As children progress through the series of 20 titles, they review and enhance their mastery of phonetic elements, sight words, and sequences at a more rapid pace. This material is compatible with the majority of phonics programs.

Munro, J. (1998). Phonological and Phonemic Awareness: Their Impact on Learning to Read Prose and Spell. *Australian Journal of Learning Disabilities*, 3, 2, 15–21.

> Paperback Nursery Rhyme Sampler. Whispering Coyote Press.
> Essential for a Pre-K–1 classroom and useful even in grades 1 and 2; these classic nursery rhymes promote phonemic and phonological awareness and children's ownership of their reading through song and movement.

Routman, Regie. (2000). *Conversations: Strategies for Teaching, Learning, and Evaluating*. Portsmouth, NH: Heinemann.

Routman, Regie. (1994). *Invitations: Changing as Teachers and Learners K–12*. Portsmouth, NH. Heinemann.

Routman, Regie. (1996). *Literacy at the Crossroads: Crucial Talk about Reading, Writing, and Other Teaching Dilemmas*. Portsmouth, NH: Heinemann.

Routman, Regie. (2002). *Reading Essentials: The Specifics You Need to Teach*. Portsmouth, NH: Heinemann.

Staman, Ann L. *Handprints: A Comprehensive Leveled Reader Library*. Educators Publishing Service. Grades K–2.

> These fifty titles which come with five teacher's guides were leveled using the Fountas and Pinnell Guided Reading Leveling System. The stories reflect real world situations and people young readers know. They include: sentence structure, pictures and cues that focus strategic reading. Print size, sentence positioning, and word spacing is appropriate for the level of the particular storybook. The titles build a strong sight vocabulary through the use of high frequency words. Language used within the series progresses from natural to formal book language.

Schumm, Jeanne Shay. *The Reading Tutor's Handbook*. Free Spirit. K–6 and beyond.

> This guide offers step-by-step instructions, templates, and handouts for providing children with differentiated reading support. It is not only helpful for teachers, but also can be shared with paraprofessionals, teachers, interns, and parents as a support framework for the classroom reading program.

Taberski, Sharon. (2000). *On Solid Ground: Strategies for Teaching Reading K–3*. Portsmouth, NH: Heinemann.

Terban, Marvin. (1997). *Time to Rhyme: A Rhyming Dictionary*. Honesdale, PA. Boyds Mills Press. Grades 1–3.

This book is formatted easily enough so that it can be used to introduce children in the early elementary grades to the use of a rhyming dictionary as a reference tool. Its simple word groupings encourage writing which can also reinforce and reciprocally enhance reading skills through the reading and writing workshop.

Vail, Patricia. (1999) *Reading Comprehension: Students' Needs and Teachers' Tools*. Educators Publishers Service. K–6 and beyond.

This is a compendium of explanations of specific instructional practices, terms, student projects, learning games, and resources that are critical for successfully teaching reading.

ALPHABET BOOKS

A major genre of fiction and non-fiction for the teacher of reading is the alphabet book. These books' appeal, concepts, and efficiency as models for reading and writing merit them a special section in this bibliography. Even those books whose text is simple enough for Pre-K–2, can serve as anchor books and models for writing workshop in grades 3–6.

Aigner-Clark, Julie. (2002). *Baby Einstein: The ABCs of Art*. Illustrations by Nadeem Zaidi. New York: Hyperion Books.

Baby Einstein books are designed to captivate and stimulate the imagination of babies and young children. Unique combinations of fine art, beautiful photography, and bold illustrations with poetry, languages, and core developmental and learning concepts make these books invaluable teaching tools. Baby Einstein books will give babies gifts they will never outgrow: curiosity and a capacity for wonder. Young children will discover the world of fine art in Baby Einstein's The ABCs of Art. Each letter of the alphabet is introduced to children though photographs of famous works of art from Van Gogh to Warhol. In addition to learning the alphabet, children will develop a lifelong love of art through exploring the pages of this beautifully illustrated book.

Beaton, Clare. (2000). *Zoe and Her Zebra*. Cambridge, MA. Barefoot Books. Pre-K–1.

This board book features a character young children can identify with named Zoe. Her adventures are told in a simple, repetitive text with a soft, literally "touchy," felt art.

Bunting, Eve. *Girls A to Z*. Illustrated by Suzanne Bloom. Honesdale, PA. Boyds Mills Press.
Pre-K–1.
    This book uses the alphabetic format to promote the opportunity for girls to select various professions and careers ranging from astronaut to zookeeper. Bunting's text is breezy and rhymes.

Cheney, Lynne. (2002). *America: A Patriotic Primer*. New York: Simon and Schuster Books. Illustrated by Robin Priess Glasser.

Cheney, Lynne. (2003). *A Is for Abigail: An Almanac of Amazing American Women*. Illustrated by Robin Priess Glasser. New York: Simon and Schuster Books. Ages 4–8.

Glaser, Shirley. (2003). *The Alphazeds*. Illustrations by Milton Glaser. Miramax. Ages 4–8.

Grimes, Nikki. (2002) *C is for City*. Illustrated by Pat Cummings. Honesdale, PA. Boyds Mills Press. K–3.
    This alphabet rhyme book doubles as a guide to city activities. With its built in invitations to readers to search for alphabetical items, it is perfect for use as an informal assessment tool or an interactive/paired reading anchor text.

Inkpen, Mick. (2005). *Kipper's A to Z: An Alphabet Adventure*. San Diego: Harcourt Children's Books. Ages 3–7.

Isadora, Rachel. (1999). *ABC Pop!* (Picture Books). Viking Juvenile. Ages 4–8.

Johnson, Stephen. (2000). *Alphabet City*. Penguin Books.
    Pastels and watercolors capture objects in everyday surroundings that look like the letters of the alphabet in this 1996 Caldecott Honor-winning book for children of all ages.

Kelley, Marty. (2001). *Summer Stinks*. Zino Press Children's Books. Pre-K–1.
    This work is a rhyming litany of summertime woes describing the summer season in terms of things which "stink" about it, including ants, bugs, and sweat.

Martin, Mary Jane. (1996). *From Anne to Zach*. Illustrated by Michael Grejniec. Boyd Mills Press.
    In this captivating book, which can serve as a touchstone text to model collaborative authoring, children learn the letters of the alphabet through other children's names.

Melmed, Laura Krauss. (2003) *Capital! Washington D.C. from A to Z*. Illustrated by Frane Lessac. New York: Harper Collins.

Musgrove, Margaret. (1992). *Ashanti to Zulu: African Traditions*. Illustrated by Leo and Diane Dillon. New York: Penguin USA.

This Caldecott-winning book uses the alphabetic format for a richly detailed and researched study of 26 African peoples. It includes a map and pronunciation guide and illustrations that were researched in the Schomberg Center and the American Museum of Natural History. Even the frame design for each illustration reflects the African Kano knot which signifies endless searching.

Paratore, Colleen. (2004) *26 Big Things Hands Do*. Minneapolis, MN: Free Spirit.

What is delightful about this alphabet book is that it presents the alphabet letters as positive actions children can perform with their own small hands to help others. These actions include: applauding, giving gifts, planting, and volunteering. Of course, alphabet study can continue with adding other "helping actions" to the word wall or substituting them in the text.

Pelham, David, (2001). *A is for Animals*. New York: Simon and Schuster Children's Publishing.

Seeley, Laura L. (1994). *The Book of Shadow Boxes*. Atlanta, GA. Peachtree Publishers.

Within the shadow of each letter's shadow box lies a hidden treasure for the young reader to find. The book is intricately and exquisitely designed and conceptualized by Ms. Seeley. Its visual fascination extends well beyond the elementary grades as it fosters not only the alphabetic principle, but also reading comprehension and literacy response.

Sneed, Brad. (2002). *Picture a Letter*. New York: Dial.

Seuss, Dr. (renewed 1991). *Dr. Seuss's ABC*. New York: Random House. Ages 2 and up.

Thornhill, Jan. (2004). *The Wildlife ABC and 123: A Nature Alphabet and Counting Book*. Toronto, Ontario, Canada. Maple Tree Press. K–1 with additional nature notes on the species for the teacher/parent.

In addition to fostering the alphabetic principle, the book nicely mixes geographic, multicultural, and scientific knowledge into a beautifully designed text. It uses children's fascination with nature to foster reading and math literacy.

Zschock, Martha Day and Heather. (2002). *Journey Around New York from A to Z. Beverly*, Mass: Commonwealth Editions

Zschock, Martha. (2001). *Journey Around Boston from A to Z*. Beverly, Mass: Commonwealth Editions.

TRADE BOOKS

These books foster particular aspects of reading skills, fluencies, and competencies.

Blackstone, Stella. (1996) *Where's the Cat?* Illustrated by Debbie Harter. Abbeville. Pre-K–K.

> This book, which focuses its primary school readers on searching for a lost cat, provides excellent use of repetitive language and encourages interactive reading.

Campbell, Bebe Moore. (2003). *Sometimes My Mommy Gets Angry.* Illustrated by E. B. Lewis. New York, New York: G. P. Putnam's Sons.

> This is a moving story about a young girl whose mother suffers from mental illness. It is told in a way that is easy to read, along with beautiful illustrations. The main character is Annie. Sometimes her mother is very happy and other times very angry and sad. Annie has learned what to do when her mom is having a bad episode. She has books to read, a special stuffed animal, and some secret snacks. Annie also has a strong support system in place with friends, neighbors, her teacher, and grandmother.

> This book is a good introduction to the issue of mental illness. It is especially important in that students see how this young girl is able to cope with this difficult part of her life. "Sometimes by mommy has a dark cloud inside of her. I can't stop the rain from falling, but I can find sunshine in my mind." Teachers can introduce students to this issue with this poignant book. Students can brainstorm different scenarios and discuss how they can be resolved. They can discuss who their support network includes and what it takes for a person to be strong enough to weather such a storm.

> The book is a much needed resource for children in times where Annie's situation is far more common than is generally known. Annie's capacity to make effective, affirming social decisions makes the work an inspirational touchstone for other peers who need to confront their parents' emotional crises. Children might be inspired to author poetry or create deliberately fictionalized narrative accounts about how they have confronted various crises.

> In offering an upper elementary grade and age appropriate narrative of a peer dealing with an emotionally ill parent, this book provides readers confronting similar family and caregiver issues with an opening for discussion and for hopeful outreach. Just reading this account may well be the first step necessary to assist a youngster in acknowledging a "hidden problem" and getting crucial adult assistance in dealing with the crisis.

Garza, Carmen Lomas. (2005). *Family Pictures/Cuadros de Familia*. Children's Book Press.

> This book tells the story of the author's childhood growing up in a Hispanic community in Texas. The book is written in both Spanish and English, accompanied by the author's most incredible paintings. The paintings are unique, somewhat folksy, colorful, and totally entrancing. They bring you into Carmen's world. Once inside it, you don't want to leave.
>
> There is so much to explore in this book; it works well with the study of "myself and family," community, communities around the world, Mexico, family traditions, and customs. It emphasizes social and emotional learning and how a young girl can find her way in the world. The traditions followed by her community and family were not necessarily accepted or understood by white America. Yet these values gave her the strength to be her own person and to rely on both her relationships and rich inner life to express herself.
>
> There are so many activities which this book inspires. Children can study the origins of the piñata, and make one. They can make a cookbook of recipes from Mexico or from their own homes. Children can also be encouraged to design their own book of family pictures. They can emphasize special occasions that they celebrate or focus on family traditions which reflect their cultural backgrounds. The richness and lushness of the paintings invites the readers to construct meaning and to create their own narratives, procedural accounts, poetry, and dialogues inspired by one or more of the paintings.
>
> Picture walk through the illustrations. Given the Spanish/English text, this strategy can be an engaging spatial entry point for descriptive and narrative spoken and written presentations. The lushly detailed illustrations of family rites and celebrations can be springboards for children's literary and artistic renditions of equivalent family pictures and events which are prompted by Carmen's selections.
>
> Use of dual language text for the book validates children's and family member's responses in languages other than English. Obviously, this book and its format are inspirational for ELL/Bilingual learners and for special needs learners who can be captivated by the paintings.
>
> The power of this book lies in its accessing and modeling the magic of family rites and rituals for a broad spectrum of linguistics, intrapersonal, spatial, and kinesthetic learners from monolingual, bilingual, and special needs backgrounds. Common to all of its audience members are the social and emotionally celebratory components of Family Pictures.

Glaser, Shirley and Glaser, Milton. (2003). *The Alphazeds*. New York: Hyperion Books for Children.

This book is incredible in so many ways! It is an alphabet book that can be read by or to little ones and not so little ones. It starts with an empty room. One by one, each letter of the alphabet enters the room, each with its own distinct look, fantastic illustrations, and typography by the designer Milton Glaser. Each of these letters also has its own distinct personality. A is angry, B is bashful, J is jealous, and so on. The room gets quite crowded. How do all of these different personalities manage to get along and coexist? Not too well apparently, as there is shouting, pushing, hitting, and kicking. In the midst of all the chaos, the light in the room goes out and there is silence.

"When the light came back on, something extraordinary had happened. Four letters had gotten together to comfort one another.
    Together they had managed to create something larger and more important than themselves.
"They had made the first word."

This is a great lesson on how each of us can be an individual, yet when we work together, something wonderful can happen. This book illustrates an incredible lesson in social and emotional maturity, and helps the child realize that it isn't just about "me."

There are many different activities that a teacher can use with this book. The children can work in groups to make their own alphabet book of emotions. They can then present the book as a group, discussing the roles each of them played, and how they each used their unique talents to make the book.

Older children grades 3 and up, can research and present as a group some important discoveries that were made more special because they involved people working together. They can also work on a project about cooperative learning, perhaps surveying class and schoolmates on how they feel they learn the best.

Hest, Amy. (1985). *The Purple Coat*. Illustrated by Amy Schwartz. New York: Macmillan Publishing Co.

In the autumn of every year, Gabrielle travels with her mother to New York City to visit her Grandpa who owns a tailor shop. Once there, he always makes her a new coat, but this year Gabrielle decides the usual navy blue coat won't do. The Purple Coat follows Gabrielle in her attempt to establish her own identity.

Lionni, Leo. (1980). *Inch by Inch*. Astor-Honor Publishing Co. Inc.

In *Inch by Inch*, an inchworm (which is a caterpillar, or larval stage, of the fall cankerworm, which becomes a moth) keeps itself from being eaten by various birds by proving its worth as a measuring device.

Lupton, Hugh. (2005) *The Story Tree: Tales to Read Aloud*. Illustrated by Sophie Fatus. Cambridge, MA. Barefoot Books. K–3
> These seven multicultural stories are accessible enough to children to encourage their eventually taking over the read-aloud sharing on their own. This book is also a good one for family literacy sessions and for parent volunteers to read aloud in the classroom.

Martin Jr., Bill, and John Archambault. (1997). *Knots on a Counting Rope*. Illustrated by Ted Rand. New York, New York: Henry Holt and Company.
> This beautifully illustrated book reaches out in so many different directions, and we can all learn so much from it. Knots on a Counting Rope is the story of a Native-American boy, Boy-Strength-of-Blue-Horses, who is blind and is learning from his grandfather how to survive in this world. The boy insists on hearing the story of his birth over and over again.

> Every time his grandfather retells the story of the boy's birth, he adds a knot to his counting rope. Each time he hears the story, Boy-Strength-of-Blue-Horses gains more confidence in himself. The story emphasizes the Native-American tradition of storytelling, and there are numerous art, math, and social studies lessons that offshoot from this book.

> Of course, the telling and retelling of the story celebrate the young blind hero's strengths and weaknesses and ability to set goals with optimism. Stories of one's birth related by others are powerful demonstrations of social skills of the highest order.

> This book also deals extensively with social and emotional learning. Children learn that those with disabilities need to be treated with sensitivity while learning to find their place in the world. One way in which children's social and emotional learning is strengthened is by understanding themselves and those around them. In order to facilitate this, each child will interview at least one family member about when he/she was born. The accounts collected with appropriate photos or memorabilia can then be shared in class and perhaps even authored into a *Knots on a Counting Rope* style book format.

> Children can also retell the story of the boy using the counting system of cultures other than Native American. This literary response will incorporate cultural study, respect and empathy into ongoing reading and writing workshop efforts.

McCully, Emily Arnold. (1992). *Mirette on the High Wire*. G. P. Putnam's Sons.
> Mirette helps her mother run a boarding house for acrobats, jugglers, actors, and mimes. Her life changes when she discovers a boarder crossing the courtyard, seemingly on air. Actually, he is walking on a tightrope. She begs him to teach her how he does it. At first, he refuses to teach her, so she begins practicing on her own. As she improves, he begins to help her and in turn she gives her teacher a valuable lesson about faith and courage.

Rabe, Bernice and Hoban, Lillian (1981). *The Balancing Girl.* E. P. Dutton. Margaret, a girl in a wheel chair, is excellent at balancing all kinds of objects. Margaret shows her friend Tommy how good she is at balancing at the school carnival.

Ringgold, Faith. (1991). *Tar Beach.* New York, New York: Crown Publishers. This book is moving in its words, art, and the beautiful story it tells. This is an effective book to use for younger grades to connect with "myself, my family, and my community." It can also be used in connection with a mapmaking unit. The children can be encouraged to make a map of their neighborhood from an aerial view.

A starting point for a discussion would be why the author portrayed New York from such a vantage point. In this beautiful book, the narrator, Cassie Louise Lightfoot, lets her dreams and ambitions take her to places in New York City that she ordinarily would not be able to be part of because of her circumstances. As a result of her self-motivation and self-awareness, Cassie is able to go as far as her dreams will let her. In this book Cassie also shows strengths in the areas of emotional sensitivity, as well as inter- and intra-personal relationships.

Children can author their own *Tar Beach*-equivalent night fantasies and then share them with one another through an exhibit or big books. Although Cassie's family is obviously poor, since they have to picnic on their roof, Cassie's dreamlike, lushly-illustrated flight over Harlem validates the beauty of their family life and of the city landscape which is accessible to all. This is an invaluable lesson in the importance of the wealth inherent in the appreciation of family connections and the beauty of nature and public architectural designs—a song of family and of the city!

Schories, Pat. (2004) *Breakfast for Jack* and *Jack and the Missing Piece.* Honesdale, PA. Boyds Mills Press.
These wordless stories help preliterate children, ELL learners new to this country, and special needs children explore the basic elements of story, character, setting, and plot. The lack of words allows the children to "construct their own meaning," and create their own different stories which "fit" the illustrations.

Steinberg, Laya. (2005). *Thesaurus Rex.* Illustrated by Debbie Harter. Cambridge, MA. Barefoot Books.
This book introduces a dinosaur with an interest in words whose story is told through a wonderful rhyming text which can be used for fostering phonemic awareness and for choral readings.

Uhlberg, Myron. (2003). *The Printer*. Illustrated by Henri Sorensen. Atlanta, GA. Peachtree Publishers.

> This story celebrates the conventions of print in that the boy-narrator's father is a deaf man who speaks with his hands and as a job chooses to turn lead type letters into words and sentences. An excellent book to support family literacy and an appreciation for the conventions of print.

Van Allsburg, Chris. (1988). *Two Bad Ants*. Boston, MA. Houghton Mifflin Co.

> In *Two Bad Ants*, news comes to the ant world of a great discovery in a faraway place. A delicious crystal has been found. A group of ants set out to bring back this crystal to their queen. Two ants are overwhelmed by the treasure and stay behind in this dangerous alien world. It is a tale of choices, consequences, and the discovery of life's real treasures.

Walter, Mildred Pitts. (2004). *Alec's Primer* Illustrated by Larry Johnson. Lebanon, NH: University Press of New England.

> This is the true account of a Virginian slave who was taught to read by his owner's daughter. He later fought in the Civil War, on the Union side, and became a landowner himself in Vermont. The beautifully written narrative is complemented by the vibrant paintings of Larry Johnson which include authentic period details.

WEBLIOGRAPHY

Reading Online
http://www.readingonline.org
This online web resource, provided by the International Reading Association, is full of specific reading teaching ideas, lessons, and new research. It includes summaries of conference presentations and even tips on how to use technology to teach reading.

Balanced Literacy
http://www.thekcrew.net/balancedliteracy.html
Established in 1996, this site is organized according to the components of the Balanced Literacy Approach. It also has an excellent listing of professional books that can assist with various aspects of teaching reading.

Carol Hurst
http://www.carolhurst.com/index.html
This is a terrific resource for exploring the children's literature works which are at the crux of author and genre study. It can be used for material to supplement period studies and discussions of authors' lives. Older children will be able to explore it on their own.

ReadWriteThink
http://www.readwritethink.org/lessons/
This resource, established and maintained by the National Council of Teachers of English (NCTE) and the International Reading Association (IRA), has a growing database of age- and grade-specific literacy lesson plans. It also includes all the graphic organizers cited in this book and many more, ready to download.

Inspiration Software
http://www.inspiration.com
This is the home site for the *Inspiration* and *Kidspiration* mind mapping software that is focused on teaching thinking skills through visual learning tools. The software includes complete symbol palettes, templates, and activities to assist the reading teacher with customizing the various graphic organizers discussed throughout the book, and with gaining the ability to design customized graphic organizers for a particular theme, study, or student group. A free trial version of this child-friendly resource can be downloaded from http://www.inspiration.com/freetrial/index.cfm .

Visual Thesaurus
http://www.visualthesaurus.com/online/
This is really both an online dictionary and a thesaurus.

Resources for Read Aloud, Shared Reading, and Independent Reading available on the Internet include the following:

http:// www.mightybook.com/library_4to6.htm.
This is a library of books read aloud by the computer. Children can listen to these books or practice reading with a buddy as the computer broadcasts the text. Of course, this type of read-aloud would only be used *in addition to* the vibrant read aloud of the teacher.

http://www.enchantedlearning.com/Rhymes.html
These are online nursery rhymes ready for reading to the children and posting throughout for room or for literacy center display.

SEDL Framework of Reading
http://www.sedl.org/reading/framework/assessment.html
This is an excellent resource for readings in the theories and methods of foundations of reading. There are topic-aligned links to specific theorists which can be included at the close of the teacher's lesson planning and may be reviewed before certification tests.

APPENDIX
TOOLS TO HELP TEACHERS TEACH
THE FOUNDATIONS OF READING AND SUCCEED IN
CONSTRUCTED RESPONSE CERTIFICATION EXAMINATIONS

The Record of Reading Behavior—A close up look at a key assessment tool

Often, constructed-response questions on the *foundations of education certification tests* or *general elementary certification tests* ask the educator to analyze a record of reading behavior or to construct an appropriate one from data given in an anecdote. Furthermore with the current climate of accountability, it is a good idea for new teachers and for career changers to examine closely the basic elements of recording reading behavior.

While there are various acceptable formats for emergent literacy assessment used throughout the country, the one selected for use here is based on the work of Marie Clay and Kenneth Goodman. These are two key researchers in the close observation and documentation of children's early reading miscues (reading mistakes).

It is important to emphasize that the teacher should not just "take the Record of Reading Behavior" and begin filling it out as the child reads from a random book. There are specific steps for taking the record and analyzing its results.

1. Select a text. If teachers want to see if the child is reading on instructional level, choose a book that the child has already read. If the purpose of the test is to see whether the child is ready to advance to the next level, choose a book from that level which the child has not yet seen.

2. Introduce the text. If the book is one that was read previously, teachers does need to introduce the text, other than by saying the title. However, if the book is new to the child, teachers should briefly share the title and tell the child a bit about the plot and style of the book.

3. Take the record. Generally with emergent readers' in grades 1–2, there are only 100–150 words in a passage used to take a record. Make certain that the child is seated beside you, so that you can see the text as the child reads it.

If desired, the teacher may photocopy the text in advance to make direct notations on the text while the child reads from the book.

After introducing the text, the teacher makes certain that the child has the chance to read the text independently without "teaching" or helping the child, other than to supply an unknown word that the child requests. The purpose of the record is to see what the child does on his/her own.

As the child reads the text, the teacher must use the following guidelines to record the child's reading behaviors (the notation for filling out the Record of Reading Behavior involves noting the child's response on the top with the actual text below it):

First and foremost, enough time must be allowed for the child to work independently on a problem before the teacher tells or supplies the word with which the child is struggling. At the same time, if the teacher waits too long before helping, he/she runs the risk of having the child lose the meaning of and interest in the story. The teacher must be aware of this delicate balance between holding off and helping.

If the child is way off track, it is recommended that the teacher tell him or her to "try that again" (TTA). If a whole phrase is troubling, put it into square brackets and score it as only one error.

Comprehension Check

This can and should be done by inviting the child to retell the story. This retelling can then be used to ask further questions about characters, plot, setting, and purpose which allow the teacher to observe and record the child's level of comprehension.

Calculating the Reading Level and the Self-Correction Rate

Calculating the reading level lets the teacher know whether the book is at the level on which the child can read it independently, or comfortably with guidance, or whether the book is at a level where reading it frustrates the child.

Generally, an accuracy score of 95%–100% suggests that the child can read the text and other books or texts on the same level.

An accuracy score of 90%–94% indicates that the text and texts likely will present challenges to the child, but with guidance from the teacher, a tutor or parent, the child will be able to master these texts and enjoy them. This is instructional level.

However, an accuracy score of less than 89% tells the teacher that the material selected for the child is too hard for the child to control alone. Such material must either be read to the child or shared with him/her in a shared reading situation.

Keeping Score on the Record

Insertions, omissions, substitutions, and teacher-told responses, all count as errors. Repetitions are not scored as errors. Corrected responses are scored as self-corrections.

Multiple unsuccessful attempts at a word score as one error only. No penalty is given for a child's multiple attempts at self-correction that results in a finally incorrect response but the attempts should be noted.

The lowest score for any page is zero. If a child omits a line or lines, each word omitted is counted as an error. If the child omits a page, deduct the number of words omitted from the total number of words used for the record.

Calculating the Reading Level

Note the number of errors made on each line on the Record of Reading Behavior in the column marked E (for Error).

Total the number of errors in the text and divide this number into the number of words that the child has read. This will give the teacher the error rate.

If a child read a passage of 100 words and made 10 errors, the error rate would be 1 in 10. Convert this to an accuracy percentage, or 90%.

Calculating the Self-Correction Rate

Total all the self-corrections.

Next, add the number of errors to the number of self-corrections and divide by the number of self-corrections.

A self-correction rate of 1-in-3 to 1-in-5 is considered good. This rate indicates that the child is able to help himself or herself as problems are encountered in reading.

Analyzing the Record

This record should assist the educator in developing a detailed date-specific picture of the child's progress in reading behavior. It should be used to help the educator individualize instruction for the specific child.

As the errors are reviewed, consider whether the child made the error because of semantics (cues from meaning), syntactic (language structure), or visual information difficulties.

As self-corrections are analyzed, consider what led the child to make that self-correction. Check out and consider what cues the child does use effectively and which the child does not use well.

Consider the ways in which the child tackles a word which is unknown to characterize that behavior and consider how the teacher can assist the child with this issue.

If a child can retell at least three quarters of a story, this is considered adequate for retelling.

Analysis of reading behavior records can and should support the educator in designing appropriate mini-lessons and strategies to help the child with his/her recorded errors and miscues.

SAMPLE TEST

1) **The major difference between phonemic and phonological awareness is:**

    A) One deals with a series of discrete sounds and the other with sound-spelling relationships.

    B) One is involved with teaching and learning alliteration and rhymes.

    C) Phonemic awareness is a specific type of phonological awareness that deals with separate phonemes within a given word.

    D) Phonological awareness is associated with printed words.

2) **The theorist in early reading (emergent reading) who has identified five tasks for phonemic awareness is:**

    A) John Munro

    B) Brian Cambourne

    C) Marilyn Jager Adams

    D) Lucy Calkins

3) **An oddity task is one in which children:**

    A) Identify the odd number in a mathematical series and talk about how they did it

    B) Perform a creative exercise designed for differentiated learning styles

    C) Recognize which sound is odd in a series of like sounds

    D) Design a different activity for themselves

4) **All of the following are true about phonological awareness EXCEPT:**

    A) It may involve print.

    B) It is a prerequisite for spelling and phonics.

    C) Activities can be done by the children with their eyes closed.

    D) It starts before letter recognition is taught.

5) Ms. James is seated with a child by her side. The child is reading aloud from an open book. Ms. James is teaching in a school that has embraced the Balanced Literacy Approach. Therefore, it is most likely that Ms. James is writing and recording:

A) The child's use of expression in reading aloud

B) The child's errors and miscues

C) Her observations of the child's attitude toward reading

D) The child's feelings about the particular passage being read

6) Most of the children in first-year teacher Ms. James's class are really doing well in their phonemic-awareness assessments. However, Ms. James is very concerned about three children who do not seem to be able to distinguish between spoken words that "sound alike" but are different. Since she is a first-year teacher, she feels her inexperience may be to blame. In truth, the reason these three children have not yet demonstrated phonemic awareness is most likely that:

A) They are not capable of becoming good readers.

B) They are bored in class.

C) They may be from an ELL background.

D) Ms. James does not pronounce the different phonemes clearly enough.

7) **Ms. Ramsey has forgotten her credit cards and has limited cash in her wallet. She is buying supplies for her reading classroom that she wants to have annotated with the children's names by the first day of school. She should buy all of the following with her cash EXCEPT:**

A) Folders

B) Markers

C) Rulers

D) Index cards

8) **Ms. Rivers is preparing for a parent-teacher conference. She does all of the following EXCEPT:**

A) Collects individual child running records

B) Puts away all the book bags and leveled pots so the classroom will be more spacious

C) Puts out, by each child's seat, the child's weekly log and spelling folder

D) Sets up work samples by each child's place

9) **In terms of a balanced literacy classroom, a "leveled bin" indicates:**

A) A plant set at child's eye level for descriptive writing purposes

B) A bin with books the child has selected

C) A bin with books leveled by the teacher

D) A bin with all kinds of reading materials, including magazines and packaging, on a child's level

10) **Mark Garner has been told that he will have to support some special-needs readers in his classroom in addition to the rest of the students. He can expect to have:**

A) Gifted children who are accelerated in reading skills for their grade and age

B) Children who have disabilities and will need special support in accessing the content and methods he uses with the rest of the class

C) Children who come from native language backgrounds other than English

D) Children who display the capacities and needs detailed in A, B, and C

11) Julia has been hired to work in a school that serves a local public housing project. She is working with kindergarten children and has been asked to focus on shared reading. She selects:

A) Chapter books

B) Riddle books

C) Alphabet books

D) Wordless picture books

12) It is 4 PM, yet Francine is still in her classroom. The seats in her classroom are filled with adults of various ages who are holding books. They are seated in pairs with each person holding a copy of the same book. Francine probably is:

A) Explaining to parents how she will teach a particular story

B) Demonstrating shared reading with a buddy for volunteer parents

C) Hosting a parents organization meeting for her grade level

D) Distributing old books from the class library to parents

13) The work of Chard and Osborn (1999) in establishing guidelines for children with reading disabilities has shown that it is essential for them to:

A) Read wordless picture books

B) Learn at least 10 sight words

C) Work intensely on the alphabetic principle

D) Focus on using syntactic clues

14) A key theorist whose work has helped teacher's document children's oral reading progress throughout the school year is:

A) Jerome Bruner

B) Daniel J. Chard

C) J. David Cooper

D) Marie Clay

15) The first grade class is on a neighborhood walk. As the children approach the neighborhood Kentucky Fried Chicken chain, Danny reads from the store window: "Kentucky Fried Chicken Hot and Crunchy." Danny has never read or been taught to read this before. The most likely explanation for Danny's being able to read this is that he is:

A) An advanced reader who is self improving

B) His parents have taught him to read the signs and materials at the Kentucky Fried Chicken store

C) He is in the logographic phase of phonics learning

D) This was just a lucky guess on his part

16) An observer enters Julia's first grade classroom. Children are working with oak tag strips and placing the word letters on these strips on a sentence strip holder. Then they seem to be involved in some kind of counting. The observer is confused. This activity is taking place during the reading block. Julia explains:

A) The children are counting letters.

B) This is word sorting and the children are grouping words by length, common letters, and sound.

C) The children are combining mathematics counting and word study.

D) The children are doing a strategy sheet based on a particular word family.

17) As he walks up and down the hallway, Mr. Adams, the new Assistant Principal, continually hears Ms. Brown telling her children to go to the wall. Mr. Adams looks briefly at the literacy block schedule and continues on his walk through the building. He realizes that Ms. Brown's children are at work on:

A) A new hall display

B) Taking down an old display and then redoing it for a new theme

C) Adding words to their spelling word wall

D) Measuring the height of plants for a mathematics lesson

18) Randy is proud of how many new vocabulary words he has learned. He enjoys playing with a device his teacher has because it helps him to show all the words he can create from various letters. The device is a:

A) Word strip

B) Letter holder for making words

C) Word mask

D) None of the above

19) Ability grouping means:

A) Grouping of children according to the results of an IQ test

B) Grouping of children with similar test results for instructional purposes

C) Grouping of children according to their oral reading accuracy rate

D) Grouping of children with similar needs for instructional purposes

20) Tim is not in the same ability group as his best friend Alex. He starts to cry even though he is a second grader. The teacher comforts him by telling him the truth that:

A) He is just as smart as Alex.

B) He can play with Alex during recess.

C) Ability groups change as the children's needs change during the year.

D) Tim is smarter than his best friend Alex.

21) "Beautiful Beth is the Best Girl in the Bradley Bay Area." This sentence could be used to help children learn about:

A) Assonance

B) Alliteration

C) Rhyming pairs

D) None of the above

22) Greg Ball went to an author signing where Faith Ringgold gave a talk about one of her many books. He was so inspired by her presence and by his reading of her book *Tar Beach* that he used the book for his reading and writing workshop activities. His supervisor wrote in his plan book that he was pleased that Greg had used the book as an/a _____ book.

A) Basic book

B) Feature book

C) Anchor book

D) Focus book

23) A delegation from the United Kingdom has come to the United States and since they are considering adapting the balanced literacy approach, they are very interested in seeing the small group demonstrated. Mr. Adams knows that he should bring them into Greg's room when Greg is doing which activity?

A) A mini-lesson

B) A conference with individual students

C) A time when children are divided into small and independent study groups

D) A read-aloud

24) As the visitors from the United Kingdom tour the school, they are pleased to hear a sing-song chant: "Don't fall asleep at the page, don't forget the _____." Mr. Adams explains to them that the first graders are learning about pointing at words and moving from the left to the right; this is called:

A) Directionality

B) Return sweep

C) Top to bottom

D) Line for line reading

25) Andrew is just starting school, but it looks like he will be successful in reading because:

A) He comes from a family that cares about his progress.

B) He is phonemically aware and knows his alphabet.

C) He has been in preschool.

D) He is well behaved.

26) Gracie seems to be struggling with her reading, even in first grade, although her mother works at a publishing firm and her dad is an editor. Her speech is also full of mispronunciations, although her parents were born in the school neighborhood. Gracie should be checked by:

A) A reading specialist

B) A speech therapist or an audiologist

C) A pediatrician

D) A psychologist

27) Ronald's parents are hearing impaired. He probably will need:

A) Extensive work with the use of picture cues

B) Work with songs, rhymes, and read-alouds to promote phonemic awareness

C) No extra work or support

D) None of the above

28) Maria was an outstanding student in her elementary school in Brazil. Now she is nervous about starting fourth grade in the U.S., although she learned English as a second language in Brazil. She and her parents should be relieved to know that:

A) She will get extra help in the United States with her English.

B) There is a positive and strong correlation between a child's proficiency in his/her native language and his/her learning of English.

C) Her classmates will help her.

D) She will have a few months to study for the reading test.

29) Paul is a new teacher. He has just started his logs and assessments for his children's phonemic awareness. He asks a reading teacher to look over his log, but the log is returned to him:

A) Paul gave the log to the wrong colleague

B) The colleague would not help him out by reviewing it

C) The log did not have the dates the child's behavior was observed and had no stated performance standards

D) The log didn't have a cover letter from Paul

30) The term graphophonemic knowledge refers to:

A) Handwriting skills

B) Letter to sound recognition

C) Both the alphabetic principle and sound-symbol relationships

D) Phonemic awareness

31) A stationery store owner in the neighborhood of the school is amused by the fact that the children, who are on a school walk, are rushing up to various store signs and street signs. The children are probably exploring:

A) The alphabetic principle

B) The principle that print carries meaning

C) Letter sound recognition

D) Phonemic awareness

32) As Ms. Maxwell enters a first grade class, the teacher is busily writing down what the children are saying. The teacher is probably doing this to:

A) Demonstrate how to copy down speech

B) Make a connection and promote awareness of the relationship between spoken and written language

C) Authenticate the children's comments

D) Raise the children's self esteem

33) A district observer notes that fifth graders are showing younger peers in the third grade how to hold a book and walk around with it. The observer assumes:

A) That the fifth graders are particularly theatrical

B) That the fifth graders are proud of how they read stories aloud

C) That the fifth graders are training the younger children in book holding

D) That this has nothing to do with instruction

34) Environmental print is available for all of the following EXCEPT:

A) A newspaper

B) The page of a library book

C) A supermarket circular

D) A commercial flyer

35) Book handling skills include ALL of the following EXCEPT:

A) Putting a cellophane or plastic cover on a book

B) Identifying the back cover of the book

C) Reading the book jacket

D) Reading dedication page and the title page of the book

36) The best way for a primary grade teacher to model directionality and one-to-one word-matching would be:

A) Using a regular library or classroom text book

B) Using her own reading book

C) Using a big book

D) Using a book dummy

37) As far as the balanced literacy movement is concerned, the "WHOLE" is:

A) All the reading themes to be covered that day

B) The whole class meeting for the mini-lesson

C) The complete unit to be covered over the month

D) All of the reading and writing work to be done in connection with one book

38) **The "TO, WITH, BY" continuum means:**

A) The teacher works with the children.

B) The children work Independently.

C) Everything is led by the teacher and taught to the children.

D) The teacher first teaches to the children and then works with them, and ultimately the children learn by themselves.

39) **Factual book features children should learn include:**

A) Captions.

B) Glossaries

C) Diagrams

D) All of the above

40) **When they are in sixth grade, children should be able to independently go through an unfamiliar collection and:**

A) Use only the table of contents

B) Use the first line indices and find a poem by author and subject

C) Use only the glossary

D) None of the above.

41) **At a faculty meeting, Ms. Riley found out that she might have crisscrossers in her class and that Mr. Brown had them and he was happy about it:**

A) Crisscrossers are students who have skipped a grade.

B) Crisscrossers are students with excellent skills in reading and in math.

C) Crisscrossers are second-language learners who have a positive attitude toward first- and second-language learning.

D) Crisscrossers are second-language learners who are only positive about English Language Learning.

42) **Cues in reading are:**

A) Vowel sounds

B) Digraphs

C) Sources of information used by readers to help them construct meaning

D) None of the above

43) As part of a study for a unit on the history of Massachusetts, Mr. Gentry is using the early childhood book *26 Letters and 99 Cents* by Tana Hoban. He wants his readers to study it and create a more detailed guide to their state using its concept. This is a technique frequently used in:

A) Reading and writing workshops

B) Writing process instruction

C) Readers workshop

D) Technical writing

44) A key theorist who supports a phonics centered approach is:

A) Marie Clay

B) Sharon Taberski

C) Shelley Harwayne

D) Rudolf Flesch

45) To decode is to:

A) Construct meaning

B) Sound out a printed sequence of letters

C) Use a special code to decipher a message

D) None of the above

46) To encode means that you:

A) Decode a second time.

B) To change a message into symbols.

C) Tell someone a message.

D) None of the above.

47) There are two basic types of text structure:

A) Fiction and nonfiction

B) Primary and pre-k

C) Expository and narrative

D) Wordless and text rich

48) While the supervisor is pleased overall with Barbara's first year of teaching, he feels that given the fact that two of her students are transfers from Mexico and one student has a hearing impairment, she has to plan for:

A) Extra homework for all of them

B) Extra time for the hearing-impaired child

C) A buddy to work with the two students from Mexico

D) Differentiated instruction to meet these students varied special needs

49) The district is emphasizing that all students in grades 3–6 must focus this month on the reading of functional documents. Ms. Ramirez just smiles and scoops up a handful of free newspapers which she gets on subscription. This is Wednesday and there is a food section. She plans to use:

A) The main news stories

B) The sports pages

C) The recipe pages

D) The comics

50) Ms. Ramirez also wants the children to share their functional reading skills with their families, so she asks that they take the newspapers home to focus on the:

A) Advice columns

B) Fill-in coupons

C) Metropolitan news briefs

D) Weather section

51) Mr. Adams was pleased with Ms. Ramirez's reading lesson, but he realized that she would have better visually represented the comparisons she was trying to get the children to make, if she had used:

A) a big book.

B) More expressive language.

C) A better literary example.

D) A graphic organizer.

52) Margaret is the winning PS 123 orator. She loves reciting poetry by Shel Silverstein. Who would guess that she is also a poet in her first language? Margaret's first language is definitely:

A) English

B) French

C) Spanish

D) NOT English

53) A teacher is asking children to look at the beginning letters of words. She then asks the child to connect the beginning letter to the text and story and to think about what word would make sense there. This is an example of:

A) A balanced literacy approach

B) A phonemic approach

C) A phonics approach

D) AN ELL differentiated approach

54) The teacher is watching the children go from oral speech to writing. The teacher says, "Great job. This is ..."

A) A good decoding

B) A good recoding

C) A good encoding

D) All of the above

55) By November, the first graders have a vocabulary of words they can correctly pronounce and read aloud. These words are their:

A) Sight vocabulary

B) Recognition vocabulary

C) Personal vocabulary

D) Working vocabulary

56) If a child makes an incorrect attempt while reading, the teacher must prompt:

A) That is a mistake, do it again.

B) No, you are stupid. Why can't you get it?

C) Does that make sense to you?

D) Forget it, this is too hard for you.

57) Asking a child if what he or she has read makes sense to him or her, is prompting the child to use:

A) Phonics cues

B) Syntactic cues

C) Semantic cues

D) Prior knowledge

58) When you ask a child if what he or she has just read "sounds right" to him or her, you are trying to get that child to use:

A) Phonics cues

B) Syntactic cues

C) Semantic cues

D) Prior knowledge

59) **By definition, which children in a classroom will have trouble with syntactic cues?**

A) Those from families who do not have household libraries

B) Those not in a top reading group

C) Those from ELL backgrounds

D) All of the above

60) **"Self correct" in reading means:**

A) The teacher corrects on the record the errors the child makes.

B) The child goes back and corrects errors made in a running record.

C) The reading specialist teaches this to the child.

D) A and B.

61) **A natural role for a highly proficient reader would be:**

A) To assist the teacher with cleaning the classroom and organizing the student folders

B) To develop charts for the teacher by copying needed poems for full class study

C) To tutor and support struggling readers

D) To work on his/her own interests while the teacher works with the rest of the class

62) **A theorist who believes that there is a finite body of approved literature children should be taught on various grade levels and has produced books about what everyone needs to know to be literate on various grade levels is:**

A) Rudolf Flesch

B) J. David Cooper

C) John Dewey

D) E. D. Hirsch

63) Children "own" words when all of the following happen EXCEPT:

A) They find these words on their own.

B) The teacher provides a mandated word list.

C) They use the words in their own writings.

D) The words appear in literature that interests them.

64) A discussion circle can convene:

A) After the children have finished reading a text as a group

B) Before the children read a text as a group

C) While the reading of the text is going on

D) All of the above

65) To promote word study, children can:

A) Be required to go to the dictionary at least once or twice a day

B) Collect and share words of interest they find in their readings

C) Do vocabulary work sheets from a basal reader or commercial vocabulary book

D) Do all of the above

66) In order to get children to compile specialized vocabulary, they can use:

A) Newspapers

B) Internet resources and approved websites that focus on the special interest

C) Experts they can interview

D) All of the above

67) If children are engaged in creating a museum with a classroom project to exhibit their work, they are:

A) Not doing any reading or writing

B) Doing many authentic reading, writing, and researching tasks

C) Not likely to visit a real museum

D) All of the above

68) Teachers should select at least ___words for a prereading vocabulary discussion:

A) 12

B) 15

C) 2–3

D) 8–10

69) The teacher should choose words for pre-story discussion and exploration based on:

A) The teacher's interest

B) Whether the teacher feels the children have prior knowledge of or experience with the words

C) A pre-existing grade-level required vocabulary list

D) Words that will impress his or her supervisor

70) Two steps a teacher might take before selecting words for study are:

A) Reading the story and story mapping

B) Asking advice from a veteran teacher and the grade leader

C) Looking in a teacher's guide and copying out the words listed there

D) All of the above are correct

71) A teacher discovers after considering his class's prior knowledge of the story material that he would need to teach at least 12 words before he starts teaching the story to the whole group. This indicates:

A) The children will need a read-aloud.

B) The children will need independent reading.

C) The children will need guided reading.

D) The children will need shared reading.

72) **The teacher is very concerned about identifying a book that is "just right" for Jay to read independently. This means that Jay should be able to read this book with:**

A) Below 92% accuracy

B) 100% accuracy

C) 95%–100% accuracy

D) 92%–97% accuracy

73) **Jay really wants to read a book that he can only read with 94% accuracy. He could get to read this book as:**

A) An independent reading

B) A guided reading

C) A shared reading

D) All of the above

74) **When taking a child's running record, the kinds of self corrections the child makes:**

A) Are not important, but the percentage of accuracy is important

B) May show something about which cueing systems the child relies on

C) Can be meaningful if analyzed over several records

D) Both B and C

75) **A "decodable text" is:**

A) A text that a child can read aloud with correct pronunciations

B) A text that a child can answer comprehension questions about with a high percentage of accuracy

C) Text written to match the sequence of letter-sound relationships that have been taught

D) None of the above

76) **Once a teacher has carefully recorded and documented a running record:**

A) There is nothing further to do as long as the teacher keeps the running record for conferences and documentation of grades.

B) The teacher should review the running record and other subsequent ones taken for growth over time.

C) The teacher should differentiate instruction for that particular student as indicated by growth over time and evidence of other needs.

D) Both B and C

77) The reliability of a test is measured by:

A) The number of children who can pass it

B) The number of children who fail it

C) The degree to which it measures what it is supposed to measure over time

D) None of the above

78) A quartile on a test is:

A) A quarter of the grades grouped

B) The division of the percentiles into four segments, each of which is called a quartile

C) 25 of the tests scored

D) B and C

79) Validity in assessment means:

A) The test went off without any previewing of the questions or leaks on its contents.

B) The majority of test takers passed.

C) The correct time was allowed for the children to complete the test.

D) The test assessed what it was supposed to assess and measure.

80) Vocabulary should be introduced after reading if:

A) The children have identified words from their reading which were difficult and which they need explained.

B) The text is appropriate for vocabulary building.

C) The teacher would like to teach vocabulary after the reading.

D) A and B

81) The teacher is working on a life science unit in grade five and using many print and electronic sources for information. Some of these words have a linear and some of them a hierarchical relationship to one another. The teacher has spent much time explaining how the words connect with one another. At this point, it would be a good idea to:

A) Use a root family diagram or tree

B) Work with the base words

C) Use hierarchical and linear arrays

D) Start semantic mapping for a particular concept

82) **Direct teaching of a concept or strategy means:**

A) The teacher teaches the concept or strategy as part of a genre lesson.

B) The teacher teaches the concept as part of the writing workshop.

C) The teacher explicitly announces to the class that this strategy will be taught.

D) The teacher teaches the strategy to a small group of children or to an individual child.

83) **The word "bat" is a ___word for "batter-up":**

A) Suffix

B) Prefix

C) Root word

D) Inflectional ending

84) **"Ballgame" is a _____word. Its meaning is derived from the combination of "ball" and "game."**

A) Contraction

B) Compound

C) Portmanteau

D) Palindrome

85) **In a balanced literacy classroom, new vocabulary would most likely appear on:**

A) An experiential chart

B) A class newspaper

C) The word wall

D) Outside the room on a bulletin board

86) **An effective way to build vocabulary and to make connections with mandated science and mathematics material is to teach Greek and Latin roots using:**

A) Semantic maps.

B) Hierarchical arrays.

C) Linear arrays.

D) Word webs.

87) **As a parent walked through the first grade floor of her school, she kept hearing repeated clapping. Most likely the children were:**

A) Clapping to show respect for one another

B) Rehearsing for how they would clap at a play

C) Clapping out syllables of multisyllabic words

D) All of the above

TEACHER CERTIFICATION STUDY GUIDE

88) As part of studying about the agricultural products of their state, children have identified 22 different types of apples produced in the state. They can use a _____ to compare and contrast these different types of apples:

A) Word web

B) Semantic map

C) Semantic features analysis grid

D) All of the above

89) **Based on individual conferences with many children, the teacher realizes that although they are all self-improving readers, they need help in better use of the context to define words. The teacher decided to try the use of:**

A) A dictionary to look up words

B) A thesaurus to use with the dictionary

C) Contextual redefinition training

D) Instruction in how to effectively use a dictionary

90) The parents of Ramon, a child who has grown up in Puerto Rico and studied English there as a second language, ask that the teacher provide him with individual support in context redefinition. Ramon is scoring above grade level in reading. His mother, who is also a teacher of reading, argues that:

A) He should get extra help because he has just transferred from another country

B) Being walked through the process of using contexts is helpful for an ELL student

C) He needs to work with a peer on this skill

D) None of the above

91) **A bound morpheme is:**

A) A prefix

B) A contraction

C) An inflectional ending that can be added to a base word to change its case, gender, number, tense or form

D) A root word

MIDDLE GRADES READING   189

92) **A second grader is writing his first book review. He has conferred with his teacher several times while writing the book review. Now he is rehearsing it with the teacher before he reads it aloud to the class. The child's learning of how to compose and deliver a book review has been:**

A) Done independently

B) Assisted by family support

C) Done in a cooperative group setting

D) Scaffolded by the teacher

93) **One of the many ways in which a child can demonstrate comprehension of a story is by:**

A) Filling in a strategy sheet

B) Retelling the story orally

C) Retelling the story in writing

D) All of the above

94) **A strategy is:**

A) A practice or routine the teacher can continually refer to

B) A practice or routine a child can continually refer to or use

C) A sheet or template for a practice the child can continually fill out

D) All of the above

95) **The Stop and Think Strategy means that the child reader will:**

A) Read through until the end of the story or text

B) Ask himself or herself if what he or she has read makes sense to him or her

C) Stop after reading some text and write down his/her concerns

D) All of the above

96) Taking responsibility for a child's own learning will usually involve the child in:

A) Reading and writing on his/her own

B) Developing a personal literacy project, which will later be shared with the teacher and peers and family

C) Putting away books and materials when directed

D) A and B

97) "Sounds right" can sound wrong to:

A) Any reader who is not a fluent or early reader

B) AN ELL reader

C) A struggling reader

D) None of the above

98) "Bias" in testing occurs when:

A) The assessment instrument is not an objective, fair, and impartial one for a given cultural, ethnic, or special needs participant.

B) The testing administrator is biased.

C) The same test is given with no time considerations or provisions for those in need of more time or those who have handicapping conditions.

D) All of the above.

99) Norm-referenced tests:

A) Give information only about the local samples' results

B) Provide information about what the local test takers did compared to a representative sampling of national test takers

C) Make no comparisons to national test takers

D) None of the above

100) If you get your raw score on a test, you will get:

A) The actual number of points you scored on the test

B) The percentage score of the number of questions you answered correctly

C) A letter grade for your work on the test

D) An aggregated score for your performance on the text

101) The data coordinator of the district who is concerned with federal funding for reading will probably want to start aggregating scores immediately because:

A) It is interesting to crunch more data.

B) By aggregating, the individual scores can be combined to view performance trends across groups.

C) This will help the district determine which groups need more remedial instruction.

D) B and C

102) A standardized test:

A) Will be given out with the same predetermined questions and format to all

B) Will not be given to certain children

C) May be taken over a lengthier test period (i.e., four hours versus three or two), if given out in exactly the same format with the same content,

D) All of the above

103) Mr. Mandrake is subbing for Ms. Matley. He sees by the schedule that he is supposed to start the day after the morning meeting with a Read-Aloud. He notes a large picture book on the easel and grabs it just two minutes before the Read-Aloud is to start. He shouldn't heave a sigh of relief because:

A) He needs to be familiar with the book so that he can plan the read-aloud.

B) He does not know if the class has already heard this book.

C) He has not planned vocabulary, themes, or activities to go with the book.

D) All of the above.

104) The science fair is coming up and Ms. Gardner is trying to find time in her busy schedule to work on her class's earth worm diary project. With all of the mandated tests and assemblies, she has not found time to start her students on their earth worm research. Within the context of reading instruction, she can:

A) Begin a thematic study unit

B) Start with a read-aloud of the *Diary of an Earth Worm* by Doreen Cronin

C) Scaffold the research process by going online with her children using an approved search engine to find matches for earthworm sites

D) All of the above

105) Annie's mother has been invited to class to serve as a guest reader. She scoops up her favorite books from her family bookshelf and rushes off to school. When she gets to Annie's classroom, she is greeted and ushered into a rocking chair and given a special hat to wear. The explanation is:

A) The children are excited to have a volunteer and are bored with their teacher day in and day out

B) This is a class-designated author's chair and an author's hat has been worked on by the whole class for anyone who comes to read to them or who reads his/her own writings

C) Both A and B

D) None of the above

106) **Four of Ms. Wolmark's students have lived in other countries. She is particularly pleased to be studying Sumerian proverbs with them as part of the sixth-grade unit in analyzing the sayings of other cultures because:**

A) This gives her a break from teaching and the children can share sayings from other cultures they and their families have experienced

B) This validates the experiences and expertise of ELL learners in her classroom

C) This provides her children from the US with a lens on other cultural values

D) All of the above

107) **As Ms. Wolmark looks at the mandated vocabulary curriculum for the sixth grade, she notes that she can opt to teach foreign words and abbreviations which have become part of the English language. She decides:**

A) To forego that since she is not a teacher of foreign language

B) To teach only foreign words from the native language of her four ELL students

C) To use the ELL students' native languages as a start for an extensive study of foreign language words

D) To teach 2–3 foreign-language words that are now in English and let it go at that

108) As Mr. Adams exits his school building, he notices that Mr. Mark, a new teacher, is leading a group of happy looking fifth graders back into the building. They are carrying all kinds of free pamphlets and circulars from a local coffee house. Mr. Adams immediately asks Mr. Mark why the class went to that coffee house during the lunch break. When he hears Mr. Mark's answer, he is delighted:

A) Mr. Mark says they went looking for environmental print and words with a café and latte root.

B) Mr. Mark says they didn't spend any money and got free hot chocolate.

C) The children will have to summarize a pamphlet as homework.

D) All of the above.

109) Mr. Adams has complained to Mr. Mark that there are too many newspapers piled up in his classroom. Mr. Mark has responded that he does not want to throw away these piled up newspapers because:

A) They can be used for letter-sound correspondence.

B) They represent environmental print.

C) They can be used to create print-meaning signs.

D) All of the above.

110) In Ms. Francine's class, dictionary use is a punishment. Mr. Adams is:

A) Pleased with the way that Ms. Francine approaches dictionary use

B) Unconcerned with this approach to the use of the dictionary

C) Convinced that the teacher should model her own fascination and pleasure in using the dictionary for the children

D) Delighted by the fact that children are being forced to use the dictionary

111) **Dictionary study:**

A) Can begin in grades 1 or 2.

B) Can begin in pre-K using lush picture dictionaries

C) Should start on grade three level

D) A and B

112) **An excellent research project that can combine dictionary study with science research would be:**

A) A student-authored dictionary with terms and phrases about earthworms

B) A teacher-developed, specialized dictionary of words and phrases about earthworms

C) A collection of articles on earthworms put together by the school librarian

D) B and C

113) **A veteran teacher waited for her adult daughter outside of her daughter's first class in the Teaching of Reading. As she and her daughter talked about the first session of the course, the teacher never heard an explicit mention of reading comprehension. All she heard about was:**

A) Learning about narratives

B) Dealing with text structures

C) Constructing meaning

D) All of the above

114) **Making inferences from the text means that the reader:**

A) Is making informed judgments based on available evidence

B) Is making a guess based on prior experiences

C) Is making a guess based on what the reader would like to be true of the text

D) All of the above

115) **Sometimes, children can be asked to demonstrate their understanding of a text in a *non-written* format. This might include all of the following EXCEPT:**

A) A story map

B) A Venn diagram

C) Storyboarding a part of the story with dialogue bubbles

D) Retelling or paraphrasing

116) **A very bright child, in a first-grade class, comes from a family which does not a have a strong oral story telling or story reading tradition in its native language. This child would need support in developing:**

A) Letter-sound correspondence skills

B) Schemata for generic concepts most children have in their memories and from experiences based on family oral traditions and read-alouds

C) Oral expressiveness

D) B and C

117) **The concerned parent whose child had a visual impairment wanted as much help for him as the teacher and the school district could give. She begged: "Please, he didn't attend preschool. He has no prior knowledge." Strictly speaking, this is:**

A) Correct, since he didn't get preschool experiences

B) Incorrect, since prior knowledge covers everyone's experiences

C) Incorrect, since he did have prior knowledge experiences but these didn't match those of many of his peers, so he would need to enhance his prior knowledge

D) B and C

118) **Mr. Mark is a brand new teacher who is not from the neighborhood where his school is located. He is a bit nervous as this is his first teaching assignment. He does not yet know how to relax enough to get his students to activate prior experience. He should:**

A) Try a free recall statement: "Tell us what you know about ..."

B) Try an unstructured statement: "Let's talk about ..."

C) Use a word association question: "What do you associate X with ...?"

D) All of the above

119) **Among the literary strategies that teachers can use to activate prior knowledge are:**

A) Predicting and previewing a story

B) Story mapping

C) Venn diagramming

D) Linear arrays

120) **Ms. Angel has to be certain that her fourth graders know the characteristics of the historical fiction genre. She can best support them in becoming comfortable with this genre by:**

A) Providing sequel and prequel writing opportunities using that genre

B) Reading them many different works from that genre

C) A and B

D) Having them look up the definition of that genre in a literary encyclopedia

121) **"Author's viewpoint" questions stump Gary. His teacher can help him by asking him during their reading conferences:**

A) If Gary feels the book he is reading is just right for him

B) What the author would say about what the character is doing in the story

C) How the story can be changed to another genre

D) If Gary wants to read more books by this author

122) **Ms. Clark is seen by outside observers from her district, seated in front of her class of sixth graders with a notebook in her lap and an easel. She reads aloud from a book and then writes down a series of questions. As she reads along, she sometimes writes down the answers to her own questions. This is most likely:**

A) A sign that Ms. Clark is uncertain of her own comprehension capacity

B) She is modeling self questioning for the children

C) She is aware that she is being watched and wants to make a good impression

D) All of the above

123) **Bill has been called up to the teacher for an individual conference. She asks him to retell one of the books he has listed on his weekly log. He begins and is still talking seven minutes later. Most probably, Bill:**

A) Told the entire story with all its details and minor characters

B) May or may not have really gotten the main points and perspectives of the story

C) May have really liked the Story

D) None of the above

124) **Ms. Ancess used to take time to have her children memorize major poems and even had an assembly for parents and school staff where the children dramatically recited various poems. Now that she is worried about the children's reading scores, she doesn't want to waste time with this memorization. Actually if she would still include this high-interest, child-centered experience:**

A) The children could use their oral fluency and her modeling as a bridge for enhanced comprehension.

B) The children could get a sense of "ownership" of the words.

C) Children and parents would have a "break" from worrying about the test.

D) None of the above.

125) **To help children with "main idea" questions, the teacher should:**

A) Give out a strategy sheet on the main idea for children to place in their reader's notebooks

B) Model responding to such a question as part of guided reading

C) Have children create "main idea" questions to go with their writings

D) All of the above.

ANSWER KEY

1.	C	34.	B	67.	B	100.	A
2.	C	35.	A	68.	C	101.	D
3.	C	36.	C	69.	B	102.	D
4.	A	37.	B	70.	D	103.	D
5.	B	38.	D	71.	C	104.	D
6.	C	39.	D	72.	D	105.	B
7.	B	40.	B	73.	A	106.	D
8.	B	41.	C	74.	D	107.	C
9.	C	42.	C	75.	A	108.	D
10.	D	43.	A	76.	C	109.	D
11.	D	44.	D	77.	C	110.	C
12.	B	45.	B	78.	B	111.	D
13.	C	46.	B	79.	D	112.	A
14.	D	47.	C	80.	D	113.	C
15.	C	48.	D	81.	C	114.	A
16.	B	49.	C	82.	C	115.	D
17.	C	50.	B	83.	C	116.	B
18.	B	51.	A	84.	B	117.	D
19.	D	52.	D	85.	C	118.	D
20.	C	53.	C	86.	D	119.	A
21.	B	54.	B	87.	C	120.	C
22.	C	55.	B	88.	D	121.	B
23.	C	56.	C	89.	C	122.	B
24.	A	57.	C	90.	B	123.	A
25.	B	58.	B	91.	C	124.	A
26.	B	59.	C	92.	D	125.	D
27.	B	60.	B	93.	D		
28.	B	61.	C	94.	D		
29.	C	62.	D	95.	B		
30.	C	63.	B	96.	D		
31.	B	64.	A	97.	B		
32.	B	65.	D	98.	D		
33.	C	66.	D	99.	B		

RATIONALES FOR SAMPLE QUESTIONS

1) **The major difference between phonemic and phonological awareness is:**

   A) One deals with a series of discrete sounds and the other with sound-spelling relationships.

   B) **One is involved with teaching and learning alliteration and rhymes.**

   C) Phonemic awareness is a specific type of phonological awareness that deals with separate phonemes within a given word.

   D) Phonological awareness is associated with printed words.

The answer is "C." This is a sheer memorization question. By definition, phonemic awareness falls under the phonological awareness umbrella. All of the other choices do not deal with the *difference* between the two types of awareness.

2) **The theorist in early reading (emergent reading) who has identified five tasks for phonemic awareness is:**

   A) John Munro

   B) Brian Cambourne

   C) Marilyn Jager Adams

   D) Lucy Calkins

The answer is "C" and is another memorization question which can only be answered by either knowing Adams's theory or by knowing that the other theorists listed did not present that theory. Anywhere from 10%–15% of the questions on the certification tests are based on knowledge of the theorists and key terms associated with their theories.

3) An oddity task is one in which children:

A) Identify the odd number in a mathematical series and talk about how they did it

B) Perform a creative exercise designed for differentiated learning styles

C) Recognize which sound is odd in a series of like sounds

D) Design a different activity for themselves

This question involves the test taker's knowing that in reading the term "oddity task" involves identification of an odd sound within a series of like sounds. Choice "A," dealing with mathematics, plays on that discipline's definition of odd, which would not be tested on a "foundations of reading" exam. The other choices are "common sense definitions" of oddity which are not appropriate answers for a test in reading.

4) All of the following are true about phonological awareness EXCEPT:

A) It may involve print.

B) It is a prerequisite for spelling and phonics.

C) Activities can be done by the children with their eyes closed.

D) It starts before letter recognition is taught.

The key word here is "EXCEPT" which will be emphasized by employing upper case on the test as well. All of the options are correct aspects of phonological awareness except the first one, "A," because phonological awareness *does not* involve print.

5) **Ms. James is seated with a child by her side. The child is reading aloud from an open book. Ms. James is teaching in a school that has embraced the Balanced Literacy Approach. Therefore, it is most likely that Ms. James is writing and recording:**

A) The child's use of expression in reading aloud

B) The child's errors and miscues

C) Her observations of the child's attitude toward reading

D) The child's feelings about the particular passage being read

This question requires knowledge of running records and familiarity with error recording and miscues. The test taker has to know that this is the standard format for a running record of reading behaviors and that choices "C" and "D" deal with attitudes and feelings which are not part of the running records used as part of the Balanced Literacy Approach.   B is the correct answer.

6) **Most of the children in first-year teacher Ms. James's class are really doing well in their phonemic-awareness assessments. However, Ms. James is very concerned about three children who do not seem to be able to distinguish between spoken words that "sound alike" but are different. Since she is a first-year teacher, she feels her inexperience may be to blame. In truth, the reason these three children have not yet demonstrated phonemic awareness is most likely that:**

A) They are not capable of becoming good readers.

B) They are bored in class.

C) They may be from an ELL background.

D) Ms. James does not pronounce the different phonemes clearly enough.

Choice "A" is not correct. All children are capable of becoming good readers and the other choices, given Ms. James's dedication, are not the most likely reason these three children (a minority of the class) are struggling.   C is the correct answer.

7) **Ms. Ramsey has forgotten her credit cards and has limited cash in her wallet. She is buying supplies for her reading classroom that she wants to have annotated with the children's names by the first day of school. She should buy all of the following with her cash EXCEPT:**

A) Folders

B) Markers

C) Rulers

D) Index cards

The answer is "B" because all of the other options are essential for record keeping. The key word here is "EXCEPT."

8) **Ms. Rivers is preparing for a parent-teacher conference. She does all of the following EXCEPT:**

A) Collects individual child running records

B) Puts away all the book bags and leveled pots so the classroom will be more spacious

C) Puts out, by each child's seat, the child's weekly log and spelling folder

D) Sets up work samples by each child's place

The answer is "B" because the teacher does not want the room to appear more spacious, but wants parents to have a feel for the book bags which indicate the primacy of reading.

9) **In terms of a balanced literacy classroom, a "leveled bin" indicates:**

A) A plant set at child's eye level for descriptive writing purposes

B) A bin with books the child has selected

C) A bin with books leveled by the teacher

D) A bin with all kinds of reading materials, including magazines and packaging, on a child's level

The answer is "C" and this is a memorization question.

10) **Mark Garner has been told that he will have to support some special-needs readers in his classroom in addition to the rest of the students. He can expect to have:**

   A) Gifted children who are accelerated in reading skills for their grade and age

   B) Children who have disabilities and will need special support in accessing the content and methods he uses with the rest of the class

   C) Children who come from native language backgrounds other than English

   D) Children who display the capacities and needs detailed in A, B, and C

All the answers are correct. "D"

11) **Julia has been hired to work in a school that serves a local public housing project. She is working with kindergarten children and has been asked to focus on shared reading. She selects:**

   A) Chapter books

   B) Riddle books

   C) Alphabet books

   D) Wordless picture books

Given the fact that this is a kindergarten in a public housing project, she will be most successful with wordless picture books, since there is no guarantee that the children have had prior exposure to the other types of books listed. Answer "D" will allow them to construct a story from the pictures.

12) It is 4 PM, yet Francine is still in her classroom. The seats in her classroom are filled with adults of various ages who are holding books. They are seated in pairs with each person holding a copy of the same book. Francine probably is:

A) Explaining to parents how she will teach a particular story

B) Demonstrating shared reading with a buddy for volunteer parents

C) Hosting a parents organization meeting for her grade level

D) Distributing old books from the class library to parents

The answer is "B" because the question details that the adults are seated in pairs holding copies of the same book. This is the buddy reading style.

13) **The work of Chard and Osborn (1999) in establishing guidelines for children with reading disabilities has shown that it is essential for them to:**

A) Read wordless picture books

B) Learn at least 10 sight words

C) Work intensely on the alphabetic principle

D) Focus on using syntactic clues

The answer is "C" and this is a memorization question.

14) **A key theorist whose work has helped teacher's document children's oral reading progress throughout the school year is:**

A) Jerome Bruner

B) Daniel J. Chard

C) J. David Cooper

D) Marie Clay

The answer is "D," Marie Clay, and this is a name you "have to know" from this guide or your courses.

15) **The first grade class is on a neighborhood walk. As the children approach the neighborhood Kentucky Fried Chicken chain, Danny reads from the store window: "Kentucky Fried Chicken Hot and Crunchy." Danny has never read or been taught to read this before. The most likely explanation for Danny's being able to read this is that he is:**

A) An advanced reader who is self improving

B) His parents have taught him to read the signs and materials at the Kentucky Fried Chicken store

C) He is in the logographic phase of phonics learning

D) This was just a lucky guess on his part

This is a classic manifestation of "C," the logographic phrase of phonics learning.

16) **An observer enters Julia's first grade classroom. Children are working with oak tag strips and placing the word letters on these strips on a sentence strip holder. Then they seem to be involved in some kind of counting. The observer is confused. This activity is taking place during the reading block. Julia explains:**

A) The children are counting letters.

B) This is word sorting and the children are grouping words by length, common letters, and sound.

C) The children are combining mathematics counting and word study.

D) The children are doing a strategy sheet based on a particular word family.

The answer is "B". Again this answer would grow out of teaching experience and familiarity with manipulatives or reading this guide.

17) As he walks up and down the hallway, Mr. Adams, the new Assistant Principal, continually hears Ms. Brown telling her children to go to the wall. Mr. Adams looks briefly at the literacy block schedule and continues on his walk through the building. He realizes that Ms. Brown's children are at work on:

A) A new hall display

B) Taking down an old display and then redoing it for a new theme

C) Adding words to their spelling word wall

D) Measuring the height of plants for a mathematics lesson

The answer is "C" because in today's balanced literacy classroom, a wall is a "word wall."

18) Randy is proud of how many new vocabulary words he has learned. He enjoys playing with a device his teacher has because it helps him to show all the words he can create from various letters. The device is a:

A) Word strip

B) Letter holder for making words

C) Word mask

D) None of the above

The answer is "B" and this is a familiar device in today's reading classroom.

19) Ability grouping means:

A) Grouping of children according to the results of an IQ test

B) Grouping of children with similar test results for instructional purposes

C) Grouping of children according to their oral reading accuracy rate

D) Grouping of children with similar needs for instructional purposes

The answer is "D" and this is a key definition which should be memorized.

20) **Tim is not in the same ability group as his best friend Alex. He starts to cry even though he is a second grader. The teacher comforts him by telling him the truth that:**

   A) He is just as smart as Alex.

   B) He can play with Alex during recess.

   C) Ability groups change as the children's needs change during the year.

   D) Tim is smarter than his best friend Alex.

The answer is "C" by definition. Also, a teacher would never get into the other personal comments offered as choices with a second grader.

21) **"Beautiful Beth is the Best Girl in the Bradley Bay Area." This sentence could be used to help children learn about:**

   A) Assonance

   B) Alliteration

   C) Rhyming pairs

   D) None of the above

This is a question that any English literature or Reading major can answer. The answer is "B."

22) Greg Ball went to an author signing where Faith Ringgold gave a talk about one of her many books. He was so inspired by her presence and by his reading of her book *Tar Beach* that he used the book for his reading and writing workshop activities. His supervisor wrote in his plan book that he was pleased that Greg had used the book as an/a _____ book.

A) Basic book

B) Feature book

C) Anchor book

D) Focus book

This is another question using current terminology. While all the other choices make sense, "C" is correct because a book that is used to teach reading and writing is called an Anchor book.

23) A delegation from the United Kingdom has come to the United States and since they are considering adapting the balanced literacy approach, they are very interested in seeing the small group demonstrated. Mr. Adams knows that he should bring them into Greg's room when Greg is doing which activity?

A) A mini-lesson

B) A conference with individual students

C) A time when children are divided into small and independent study groups

D) A read-aloud

"C" is the only correct answer choice because small refers to group size.

24) **As the visitors from the United Kingdom tour the school, they are pleased to hear a sing-song chant: "Don't fall asleep at the page, don't forget the _____." Mr. Adams explains to them that the first graders are learning about pointing at words and moving from the left to the right; this is called:**

   A) Directionality

   B) Return sweep

   C) Top to bottom

   D) Line for line reading

The answer is "A" and this term is in the glossary.

25) **Andrew is just starting school, but it looks like he will be successful in reading because:**

   A) He comes from a family that cares about his progress.

   B) He is phonemically aware and knows his alphabet.

   C) He has been in preschool.

   D) He is well behaved.

This IS a deliberately tricky question. Each of the choices has merit. The best choice is "B" because that one is confirmed by current research.

26) **Gracie seems to be struggling with her reading, even in first grade, although her mother works at a publishing firm and her dad is an editor. Her speech is also full of mispronunciations, although her parents were born in the school neighborhood. Gracie should be checked by:**

A) A reading specialist

B) A speech therapist or an audiologist

C) A pediatrician

D) A psychologist

This one is "B" because Gracie is a neighborhood child and shouldn't be having these difficulties with pronunciation.

27) **Ronald's parents are hearing impaired. He probably will need:**

A) Extensive work with the use of picture cues

B) Work with songs, rhymes, and read-alouds to promote phonemic awareness

C) No extra work or support

D) None of the above

This is one you can work out. The answer is "B" because obviously Ronald's parents will not be singing with him and doing lots of read-alouds.

28) **Maria was an outstanding student in her elementary school in Brazil. Now she is nervous about starting fourth grade in the U.S., although she learned English as a second language in Brazil. She and her parents should be relieved to know that:**

A) She will get extra help in the United States with her English.

B) There is a positive and strong correlation between a child's proficiency in his/her native language and his/her learning of English.

C) Her classmates will help her.

D) She will have a few months to study for the reading test.

All of these choices have an element of truth in them, but go with "B" which reflects research results.

29) **Paul is a new teacher. He has just started his logs and assessments for his children's phonemic awareness. He asks a reading teacher to look over his log, but the log is returned to him:**

A) Paul gave the log to the wrong colleague

B) The colleague would not help him out by reviewing it

C) The log did not have the dates the child's behavior was observed and had no stated performance standards

D) The log didn't have a cover letter from Paul

The answer is "C" because all logs need to have dates and standards.

30) **The term graphophonemic knowledge refers to:**

A) Handwriting skills

B) Letter to sound recognition

C) Both the alphabetic principle and sound-symbol relationships

D) Phonemic awareness

The answer is "C" and it is a definition question. If you missed it, reread through the glossary.

31) **A stationery store owner in the neighborhood of the school is amused by the fact that the children, who are on a school walk, are rushing up to various store signs and street signs. The children are probably exploring:**

A) The alphabetic principle

B) The principle that print
carries meaning

C) Letter sound recognition

D) Phonemic awareness

The behavior described here only matches one reading activity, "B."

32) **As Ms. Maxwell enters a first grade class, the teacher is busily writing down what the children are saying. The teacher is probably doing this to:**

A) Demonstrate how to copy down speech

B) Make a connection and promote awareness of the relationship between spoken and written language

C) Authenticate the children's comments

D) Raise the children's self esteem

This is another deliberately tricky question. All of the answers may appeal to you, but, choice "B" is the theoretical way to describe what the teacher is doing when he/she writes down what the children are saying.

33) **A district observer notes that fifth graders are showing younger peers in the third grade how to hold a book and walk around with it. The observer assumes:**

A) That the fifth graders are particularly theatrical

B) That the fifth graders are proud of how they read stories aloud

C) That the fifth graders are training the younger children in book holding

D) That this has nothing to do with instruction

This is a standard part of "book holding," so the answer is "C."

34) **Environmental print is available for all of the following EXCEPT:**

   A) A newspaper

   B) The page of a library book

   C) A supermarket circular

   D) A commercial flyer

The key word here is "EXCEPT" and environmental print is not defined as print in a library book, so choice "B" is the right one.

35) **Book handling skills include**
    ALL of the following EXCEPT:

   A) Putting a cellophane or plastic cover on a book

   B) Identifying the back cover of the book

   C) Reading the book jacket

   D) Reading dedication page and the title page of the book

Ironically "A" is correct because book handling as defined in reading, does not include putting covers on books.

36) **The best way for a primary grade teacher to model directionality and**
    one-to-one word-matching would be:

   A) Using a regular library or classroom text book

   B) Using her own reading book

   C) Using a big book

   D) Using a book dummy

Key word in this question is "best" and the answer is "C" because this type of a book is best for teaching and display.

37) As far as the balanced literacy movement is concerned, the "WHOLE" is:

A) All the reading themes to be covered that day

B) The whole class meeting for the mini-lesson

C) The complete unit to be covered over the month

D) All of the reading and writing work to be done in connection with one book

This is another deliberately tricky question, since all of the answers make sense. But only "B" is correct because that is the definition of "WHOLE" in balanced literacy.

38) The "TO, WITH, BY" continuum means:

A) The teacher works with the children.

B) The children work Independently.

C) Everything is led by the teacher and taught to the children.

D) The teacher first teaches to the children and then works with them, and ultimately the children learn by themselves.

The answer is "D" and is another definition question.

39) Factual book features children should learn include:

A) Captions.

B) Glossaries

C) Diagrams

D) All of the above

The answer is "D." *All of the above* is the correct answer because captions, glossaries, and diagrams are but three of the text features that students need to be able to identify in a text. Other text features include headings, charts, maps, indexes, and tables

40) **When they are in sixth grade, children should be able to independently go through an unfamiliar collection and:**

A) Use only the table of contents

B) Use the first line indices and find a poem by author and subject

C) Use only the glossary

D) None of the above.

This is a question, you can reason out. The most complex task described here is "B."

41) **At a faculty meeting, Ms. Riley found out that she might have crisscrossers in her class and that Mr. Brown had them and he was happy about it:**

A) Crisscrossers are students who have skipped a grade.

B) Crisscrossers are students with excellent skills in reading and in math.

C) Crisscrossers are second-language learners who have a positive attitude toward first- and second-language learning.

D) Crisscrossers are second-language learners who are only positive about English Language Learning.

This is a definition question and the answer is "C."

42) **Cues in reading are:**

A) Vowel sounds

B) Digraphs

C) Sources of information used by readers to help them construct meaning

D) None of the above

This too is a definition question and the answer is "C."

43) **As part of a study for a unit on the history of Massachusetts, Mr. Gentry is using the early childhood book *26 Letters and 99 Cents* by Tana Hoban. He wants his readers to study it and create a more detailed guide to their state using its concept. This is a technique frequently used in:**

A) Reading and writing workshops

B) Writing process instruction

C) Readers workshop

D) Technical writing

The answer is "A." The fact that Mr. Gentry wants his class to use this for both reading and writing, should help you pick the right choice even if you don't know the answer.

44) **A key theorist who supports a phonics centered approach is:**

A) Marie Clay

B) Sharon Taberski

C) Shelley Harwayne

D) Rudolf Flesch

The answer is "D." Flesch was a proponent of the phonics approach to reading in his book *Why Johnny Can't Read* which was essentially a critique of the American educational system. None of the other three choices proposes explicit teaching of phonics to help children master reading.

45) **To decode is to:**

A) Construct meaning

B) Sound out a printed sequence of letters

C) Use a special code to decipher a message

D) None of the above

The answer is "B" and a definition question.

46) To encode means that you:

A) Decode a second time.

B) To change a message into symbols.

C) Tell someone a message.

D) None of the above.

The answer is "B" and is a definition question. If you are missing many definitions, perhaps make flash cards of the glossary words and study them intensively.

47) There are two basic types of text structure:

A) Fiction and nonfiction

B) Primary and pre-k

C) Expository and narrative

D) Wordless and text rich

The answer is "C," Expository and Narrative. Fiction and non-fiction are genres, Primary and pre-K are grade levels, and "wordless" and "text rich" are types of books for young children.

48) **While the supervisor is pleased overall with Barbara's first year of teaching, he feels that given the fact that two of her students are transfers from Mexico and one student has a hearing impairment, she has to plan for:**

A) Extra homework for all of them

B) Extra time for the hearing-impaired child

C) A buddy to work with the two students from Mexico

D) Differentiated instruction to meet these students varied special needs

This is a tricky question because all of the choices have an element of truth in them. But the best choice is "D" because it includes the special approaches Barbara will have to take with her ELL and special needs students.

49) **The district is emphasizing that all students in grades 3–6 must focus this month on the reading of functional documents. Ms. Ramirez just smiles and scoops up a handful of free newspapers which she gets on subscription. This is Wednesday and there is a food section. She plans to use:**

A) The main news stories

B) The sports pages

C) The recipe pages

D) The comics

Functional literacy refers to knowing things that students have to do on a day-to-day basis. Reading a recipe is classified as functional literacy because students learn how to read directions to perform a task. The answer is "C."

50) **Ms. Ramirez also wants the children to share their functional reading skills with their families, so she asks that they take the newspapers home to focus on the:**

A) Advice columns

B) Fill-in coupons

C) Metropolitan news briefs

D) Weather section

Coupons, like want ads, are functional. The families can fill them in or act on them. The answer is "B."

51) **Mr. Adams was pleased with Ms. Ramirez's reading lesson, but he realized that she would have better visually represented the comparisons she was trying to get the children to make, if she had used:**

A) a big book.

B) More expressive language.

C) A better literary example.

D) A graphic organizer.

The answer is "A" because the BIG BOOK is a good visual display tool.

52) **Margaret is the winning PS 123 orator. She loves reciting poetry by Shel Silverstein. Who would guess that she is also a poet in her first language? Margaret's first language is definitely:**

A) English

B) French

C) Spanish

D) NOT English

This is a deliberately misleading question; all the test taker can know for certain is that Margaret's first language is NOT English. You know she is an ELL student because the question talks about her "first language." The answer is "D."

53) **A teacher is asking children to look at the beginning letters of words. She then asks the child to connect the beginning letter to the text and story and to think about what word would make sense there. This is an example of:**

A) A balanced literacy approach

B) A phonemic approach

C) A phonics approach

D) AN ELL differentiated approach

The focus on letters and sounds is "C" a phonics approach.

54) **The teacher is watching the children go from oral speech to writing. The teacher says, "Great job. This is …"**

A) A good decoding

B) A good recoding

C) A good encoding

D) All of the above

This is another definition question; read the definition section carefully before the exam. The answer has to be "B."

55) **By November, the first graders have a vocabulary of words they can correctly pronounce and read aloud. These words are their:**

A) Sight vocabulary

B) Recognition vocabulary

C) Personal vocabulary

D) Working vocabulary

The term is "B" recognition vocabulary. This is a definition you have to know.

56) If a child makes an incorrect attempt while reading, the teacher must prompt:

A) That is a mistake, do it again.

B) No, you are stupid. Why can't you get it?

C) Does that make sense to you?

D) Forget it, this is too hard for you.

Obviously, "B" cannot be right. Generally, a caring teacher would not say "D," but "C" is the preferred wording in use now in reading classrooms.

57) Asking a child if what he or she has read makes sense to him or her, is prompting the child to use:

A) Phonics cues

B) Syntactic cues

C) Semantic cues

D) Prior knowledge

Semantic cues are the hints that students can discern from the reading to help them make sense of the text. In some cases, the message of the text depends on the other words around them, so students learn how to determine the meaning from context clues. The answer must be "C."

58) When you ask a child if what he or she has just read "sounds right" to him or her, you are trying to get that child to use:

A) Phonics cues

B) Syntactic cues

C) Semantic cues

D) Prior knowledge

This is another one of those answers using the language of linguistics in reading. The answer has to be "B," syntactic clues.

59) By definition, which children in a classroom will have trouble with syntactic cues?

A) Those from families who do not have household libraries

B) Those not in a top reading group

C) Those from ELL backgrounds

D) All of the above

This question can actually have only one correct answer. It is "C" because by definition a child from an ELL background does not have a strong accurate sense of what "sounds right" in English.

60) "Self correct" in reading means:

A) The teacher corrects on the record the errors the child makes.

B) The child goes back and corrects errors made in a running record.

C) The reading specialist teaches this to the child.

D) a and b.

There is only one correct answer here and it is "B." This is a key principle of the running record.

61) A natural role for a highly proficient reader would be:

A) To assist the teacher with cleaning the classroom and organizing the student folders

B) To develop charts for the teacher by copying needed poems for full class study

C) To tutor and support struggling readers

D) To work on his/her own interests while the teacher works with the rest of the class

While all of the choices are possibilities, the concept of the highly proficient reader tutoring leads to answer "C."

62) **A theorist who believes that there is a finite body of approved literature children should be taught on various grade levels and has produced books about what everyone needs to know to be literate on various grade levels is:**

A) Rudolf Flesch

B) J. David Cooper

C) John Dewey

D) E. D. Hirsch

The answer is "D" and this has to be memorized and known.

63) **Children "own" words when all of the following happen EXCEPT:**

A) They find these words on their own.

B) The teacher provides a mandated word list.

C) They use the words in their own writings.

D) The words appear in literature that interests them.

Again the test taker has to find the choice that is incorrect and it is choice "B," when the teacher puts up a mandated word list.

64) **A discussion circle can convene:**

A) After the children have finished reading a text as a group

B) Before the children read a text as a group

C) While the reading of the text is going on

D) All of the above

By definition, a discussion group can convene only after the children have read a work. So, "A" is the answer.

65) **To promote word study, children can:**

A) Be required to go to the dictionary at least once or twice a day

B) Collect and share words of interest they find in their readings

C) Do vocabulary work sheets from a basal reader or commercial vocabulary book

D) Do all of the above

All of the answers will promote vocabulary, so the answer is "D."

66) **In order to get children to compile specialized vocabulary, they can use:**

A) Newspapers

B) Internet resources and approved websites that focus on the special interest

C) Experts they can interview

D) All of the above

The answer is "D" because all of the responses are correct.

67) **If children are engaged in creating a museum with a classroom project to exhibit their work, they are:**

A) Not doing any reading or writing

B) Doing many authentic reading, writing, and researching tasks

C) Not likely to visit a real museum

D) All of the above

There is only one correct answer here and it is logical, "B."

68) Teachers should select at least ___words for a prereading vocabulary discussion:

A) 12

B) 15

C) 2–3

D) 8–10

The correct answer is "C," 2–3 words. Teachers should select a small number of words for pre-teaching to allow the students time to comprehend the text and achieve the objectives related to the reading. For example, in a non-fiction text, these words could be key terms related to the main topic. Even students with an extensive oral vocabulary may not be able to recognize words in print because they are not words that they normally encounter in their reading. The activities the teacher plans in relation to the words will help the students internalize the strategies more readily when only a few words are selected each time.

69) The teacher should choose words for pre-story discussion and exploration based on:

A) The teacher's interest

B) Whether the teacher feels the children have prior knowledge of or experience with the words

C) A pre-existing grade-level required vocabulary list

D) Words that will impress his or her supervisor

This is another one where the only correct answer is "B." "D" is an unlikely choice.

70) Two steps a teacher might take before selecting words for study are:

A) Reading the story and story mapping

B) Asking advice from a   veteran teacher and the grade leader

C) Looking in a teacher's guide and copying out the words listed there

D) All of the above are correct

This is one you can reason through and choose "D" easily.

71) A teacher discovers after considering his class's prior knowledge of the story material that he would need to teach at least 12 words before he starts teaching the story to the whole group. This indicates:

A) The children will need a read-aloud.

B) The children will need independent reading.

C) The children will need guided reading.

D) The children will need shared reading.

This is one you can reason through, if you know that generally during Read-Aloud you do not stop to explain many words. You would not want to give material for independent or shared reading where so many words had to be explained. Hence the correct choice is "C," guided reading.

72) **The teacher is very concerned about identifying a book that is "just right" for Jay to read independently. This means that Jay should be able to read this book with:**

A) Below 92% accuracy

B) 100% accuracy

C) 95%–100% accuracy

D) 92%–97% accuracy

The answer is "D" because those are the "just right percentages."

73) **Jay really wants to read a book that he can only read with 94% accuracy. He could get to read this book as:**

A) An independent reading

B) A guided reading

C) A shared reading

D) All of the above

The answer by definition is "A" because "just right" (i.e. 92%–97% accuracy) is synonymous with the independent reading level.

74) **When taking a child's running record, the kinds of self corrections the child makes:**

A) Are not important, but the percentage of accuracy is important

B) May show something about which cueing systems the child relies on

C) Can be meaningful if analyzed over several records

D) Both B and C

The answer is "D" and related to taking a child's running record.

75) **A "decodable text" is:**

A) A text that a child can read aloud with correct pronunciations

B) A text that a child can answer comprehension questions about with a high percentage of accuracy

C) Text written to match the sequence of letter-sound relationships that have been taught

D) None of the above

This is choice "A" which is the definition of decodable.

76) **Once a teacher has carefully recorded and documented a running record:**

A) There is nothing further to do as long as the teacher keeps the running record for conferences and documentation of grades.

B) The teacher should review the running record and other subsequent ones taken for growth over time.

C) The teacher should differentiate instruction for that particular student as indicated by growth over time and evidence of other needs.

D) Both B and C

Students learn at different rates, therefore students in any class will be at varying levels of learning. By differentiating instruction and incorporating assessment *for* learning rather than assessment *of* learning, teachers can help students succeed. When teachers assess student growth over time and monitor the areas in which they are experiencing difficulty, they can alter the instruction and the activities to match student needs. The answer is "C."

77) The reliability of a test is measured by:

A) The number of children who can pass it

B) The number of children who fail it

C) The degree to which it measures what it is supposed to measure over time

D) None of the above

This is a definition question and the answer is "C."

78) A quartile on a test is:

A) A quarter of the grades grouped

B) The division of the percentiles into four segments, each of which is called a quartile

C) 25 of the tests scored

D) B and C

While this is also a definition question, choice "B" is one that a linguist would choose.

79) Validity in assessment means:

A) The test went off without any previewing of the questions or leaks on its contents.

B) The majority of test takers passed.

C) The correct time was allowed for the children to complete the test.

D) The test assessed what it was supposed to assess and measure.

"D" is the answer here and it also makes good sense to the test taker.

80) **Vocabulary should be introduced after reading if:**

   A) The children have identified words from their reading which were difficult and which they need explained.

   B) The text is appropriate for vocabulary building.

   C) The teacher would like to teach vocabulary after the reading.

   D) A and B

This is a question the literate test taker should be able to "reason" through. Vocabulary introduced by children and a good text with opportunities to expand vocabulary are needed. Answer "D" which includes both "A" and "B" is the right choice.

81) **The teacher is working on a life science unit in grade five and using many print and electronic sources for information. Some of these words have a linear and some of them a hierarchical relationship to one another. The teacher has spent much time explaining how the words connect with one another. At this point, it would be a good idea to:**

   A) Use a root family diagram or tree

   B) Work with the base words

   C) Use hierarchical and linear arrays

   D) Start semantic mapping for a particular concept

The astute test taker should get this right whether he/she actually knows these materials or not. "Hierarchical" appears in both the question and in the correct choice "C."

82) **Direct teaching of a concept or strategy means:**

A) The teacher teaches the concept or strategy as part of a genre lesson.

B) The teacher teaches the concept as part of the writing workshop.

C) The teacher explicitly announces to the class that this strategy will be taught.

D) The teacher teaches the strategy to a small group of children or to an individual child.

The answer is "C" and this is a definition question.

83) **The word "bat" is a ___word for "batter-up":**

A) Suffix

B) Prefix

C) Root word

D) Inflectional ending

The answer is "C."

84) **"Ballgame" is a _____word. Its meaning is derived from the combination of "ball" and "game."**

A) Contraction

B) Compound

C) Portmanteau

D) Palindrome

Answer "B."

85) **In a balanced literacy classroom, new vocabulary would most likely appear on:**

A) An experiential chart

B) A class newspaper

C) The word wall

D) Outside the room on a bulletin board

The answer can only be "C" and should be part of the test taker's theoretical background.

86) **An effective way to build vocabulary and to make connections with mandated science and mathematics material is to teach Greek and Latin roots using:**

A) Semantic maps.

B) Hierarchical arrays.

C) Linear arrays.

D) Word webs.

The answer is "D" and historically these have been used to teach Greek and Latin roots.

87) **As a parent walked through the first grade floor of her school, she kept hearing repeated clapping. Most likely the children were:**

A) Clapping to show respect for one another

B) Rehearsing for how they would clap at a play

C) Clapping out syllables of multisyllabic words

D) All of the above

This is related to phonics and the answer is "C."

88) **As part of studying about the agricultural products of their state, children have identified 22 different types of apples produced in the state. They can use a _____ to compare and contrast these different types of apples:**

A) Word web

B) Semantic map

C) Semantic features analysis grid

D) All of the above

The answer here is "D" and all of these graphic organizers would work with the topic of apples.

89) **Based on individual conferences with many children, the teacher realizes that although they are all self-improving readers, they need help in better use of the context to define words. The teacher decided to try the use of:**

A) A dictionary to look up words

B) A thesaurus to use with the dictionary

C) Contextual redefinition training

D) Instruction in how to effectively use a dictionary

The answer is "C" and the trick is to notice the "better use of context" in the question and match it up with "C," contextual redefinition training.

90) **The parents of Ramon, a child who has grown up in Puerto Rico and studied English there as a second language, ask that the teacher provide him with individual support in context redefinition. Ramon is scoring above grade level in reading. His mother, who is also a teacher of reading, argues that:**

A) He should get extra help because he has just transferred from another country

B) Being walked through the process of using contexts is helpful for an ELL student

C) He needs to work with a peer on this skill

D) None of the above

The answer is "B" and it is one that is confirmed in theory and is referenced in this guide.

91) **A bound morpheme is:**

A) A prefix

B) A contraction

C) An inflectional ending that can be added to a base word to change its case, gender, number, tense or form

D) A root word

The answer is "C," a definition question.

92) **A second grader is writing his first book review. He has conferred with his teacher several times while writing the book review. Now he is rehearsing it with the teacher before he reads it aloud to the class. The child's learning of how to compose and deliver a book review has been:**

A) Done independently

B) Assisted by family support

C) Done in a cooperative
   group setting

D) Scaffolded by the teacher

This is easy to see that it is "D," scaffolded by the teacher. The child has been assisted by the teacher as he prepared the book review.

93) **One of the many ways in which a child can demonstrate comprehension of a story is by:**

A) Filling in a strategy sheet

B) Retelling the story orally

C) Retelling the story in
   writing

D) All of the above

The answer is "D" since all the options are good ones.

94) A strategy is:

A) A practice or routine the teacher can continually refer to

B) A practice or routine a child can continually refer to or use

C) A sheet or template for a practice the child can continually fill out

D) All of the above

The answer is again "D" since all the options work.

95) The Stop and Think Strategy means that the child reader will:

A) Read through until the end of the story or text

B) Ask himself or herself if what he or she has read makes sense to him or her

C) Stop after reading some text and write down his/her concerns

D) All of the above

This is a tricky question and requires that the test taker know the very specific definition of the STOP and THINK strategy to know that the only correct answer is "B."

96) Taking responsibility for a child's own learning will usually involve the child in:

A) Reading and writing on his/her own

B) Developing a personal literacy project, which will later be shared with the teacher and peers and family

C) Putting away books and materials when directed

D) A and B

Again this has to do with the way "responsibility for your own learning" is now defined. The correct answer is "D."

97) "Sounds right" can sound wrong to:

A) Any reader who is not a fluent or early reader

B) AN ELL reader

C) A struggling reader

D) None of the above

This is a truism of ELL education and the answer is "B."

98) "Bias" in testing occurs when:

A) The assessment instrument is not an objective, fair, and impartial one for a given cultural, ethnic, or special needs participant.

B) The testing administrator is biased.

C) The same test is given with no time considerations or provisions for those in need of more time or those who have handicapping conditions.

D) All of the above.

This is one where the correct answer of "D" is also the commonsense response that a literate test taker would select.

99) Norm-referenced tests:

A) Give information only about the local samples' results

B) Provide information about what the local test takers did compared to a representative sampling of national test takers

C) Make no comparisons to national test takers

D) None of the above

There is only one correct answer here by definition and "B" is it.

100) If you get your raw score on a test, you will get:

A) The actual number of points you scored on the test

B) The percentage score of the number of questions you answered correctly

C) A letter grade for your work on the test

D) An aggregated score for your performance on the text

Again these are all definitions that the test taker should memorize before the test (see the glossary in this guide). The correct answer is "A."

101) The data coordinator of the district who is concerned with federal funding for reading will probably want to start aggregating scores immediately because:

A) It is interesting to crunch more data.

B) By aggregating, the individual scores can be combined to view performance trends across groups.

C) This will help the district determine which groups need more remedial instruction.

D) B and C

Again this is a definition answer and the correct choice is "D."

102) A standardized test:

D) Will be given out with the same predetermined questions and format to all

B) Will not be given to certain children

C) May be taken over a lengthier test period (i.e., four hours versus three or two), if given out in exactly the same format with the same content,

D) All of the above

This is all about what a standardized test means and answer is "D."

103) **Mr. Mandrake is subbing for Ms. Matley. He sees by the schedule that he is supposed to start the day after the morning meeting with a Read-Aloud. He notes a large picture book on the easel and grabs it just two minutes before the Read-Aloud is to start. He shouldn't heave a sigh of relief because:**

A) He needs to be familiar with the book so that he can plan the read-aloud.

B) He does not know if the class has already heard this book.

C) He has not planned vocabulary, themes, or activities to go with the book.

D) All of the above.

The answer is "D," but this is a question with which anyone who has gotten through the coursework or has taught, should have no problem.

104) **The science fair is coming up and Ms. Gardner is trying to find time in her busy schedule to work on her class's earth worm diary project. With all of the mandated tests and assemblies, she has not found time to start her students on their earth worm research. Within the context of reading instruction, she can:**

A) Begin a thematic study unit

B) Start with a read-aloud of the *Diary of an Earth Worm* by Doreen Cronin

C) Scaffold the research process by going online with her children using an approved search engine to find matches for earthworm sites

D) All of the above

This is a question someone who has taught or gone through course work should ace to get "D." Remember going online with children and using approved search engines is fine.

105) **Annie's mother has been invited to class to serve as a guest reader. She scoops up her favorite books from her family bookshelf and rushes off to school. When she gets to Annie's classroom, she is greeted and ushered into a rocking chair and given a special hat to wear. The explanation is:**

A) The children are excited to have a volunteer and are bored with their teacher day in and day out

B) This is a class-designated author's chair and an author's hat has been worked on by the whole class for anyone who comes to read to them or who reads his/her own writings

C) Both A and B

D) None of the above

The best answer is "B" and involves knowing about the "author's chair" concept.

106) **Four of Ms. Wolmark's students have lived in other countries. She is particularly pleased to be studying Sumerian proverbs with them as part of the sixth-gradeunit in analyzing the sayings of other cultures because:**

A) This gives her a break from teaching and the children can share sayings from other cultures they and their families have experienced

B) This validates the experiences and expertise of ELL learners in her classroom

C) This provides her children from the US with a lens on other cultural values

D) All of the above

This a question where the correct answer "D" makes good common and educational sense.

107) **As Ms. Wolmark looks at the mandated vocabulary curriculum for the sixth grade, she notes that she can opt to teach foreign words and abbreviations which have become part of the English language. She decides:**

A) To forego that since she is not a teacher of foreign language

B) To teach only foreign words from the native language of her four ELL students

C) To use the ELL students' native languages as a start for an extensive study of foreign language words

D) To teach 2–3 foreign-language words that are now in English and let it go at that

This is a question where you can reason your way to the correct answer, "C." "A" sounds chauvinistic and unrealistic and "B" is limiting and teaching only 2–3 words is not a good use of instructional time.

108) **As Mr. Adams exits his school building, he notices that Mr. Mark, a new teacher, is leading a group of happy looking fifth graders back into the building. They are carrying all kinds of free pamphlets and circulars from a local coffee house. Mr. Adams immediately asks Mr. Mark why the class went to that coffee house during the lunch break. When he hears Mr. Mark's answer, he is delighted:**

A) Mr. Mark says they went looking for environmental print and words with a café and latte root.

B) Mr. Mark says they didn't spend any money and got free hot chocolate.

C) The children will have to summarize a pamphlet as homework.

D) All of the above.

This is a question where the correct choice is "D" and makes good teaching and learning sense.

109) **Mr. Adams has complained to Mr. Mark that there are too many newspapers piled up in his classroom. Mr. Mark has responded that he does not want to throw away these piled up newspapers because:**

E) They can be used for letter-sound correspondence.

B) They represent environmental print.

C) They can be used to create print-meaning signs.

D) All of the above.

This is a question where choice "D" makes good sense to a teacher who knows the value of having newspapers for class projects.

110) **In Ms. Francine's class, dictionary use is a punishment. Mr. Adams is:**

A) Pleased with the way that Ms. Francine approaches dictionary use

B) Unconcerned with this approach to the use of the dictionary

C) Convinced that the teacher should model her own fascination and pleasure in using the dictionary for the children

D) Delighted by the fact that children are being forced to use the dictionary

The word "punishment" in the question should alert the test taker to the answer. Only "C" can be right.

111) **Dictionary study:**

A) Can begin in grades 1 or 2.

B) Can begin in pre-K using lush picture dictionaries

C) Should start on grade three level

D) A and B

This is a question that any literate test taker who has been in a children's book section recently can answer. Choice "D" is correct.

TEACHER CERTIFICATION STUDY GUIDE

112) **An excellent research project that can combine dictionary study with science research would be:**

A) A student-authored dictionary with terms and phrases about earthworms

B) A teacher-developed, specialized dictionary of words and phrases about earthworms

C) A collection of articles on earthworms put together by the school librarian

D) B and C

This question is tricky in that only choice "A," which deals with a student product, is correct. The others are all adult centered.

113) **A veteran teacher waited for her adult daughter outside of her daughter's first class in the Teaching of Reading. As she and her daughter talked about the first session of the course, the teacher never heard an explicit mention of reading comprehension. All she heard about was:**

A) Learning about narratives

B) Dealing with text structures

C) Constructing meaning

D) All of the above

The only answer here is "C" which emphasizes "constructing meaning," the current phrase for "reading comprehension."

114) **Making inferences from the text means that the reader:**

A) Is making informed judgments based on available evidence

B) Is making a guess based on prior experiences

C) Is making a guess based on what the reader would like to be true of the text

D) All of the above

This is a definition question that a literate test taker can answer based on the general definition of inferences. The answer is "A."

115) **Sometimes, children can be asked to demonstrate their understanding of a text in a *non-written* format. This might include all of the following EXCEPT:**

A) A story map

B) A Venn diagram

C) Storyboarding a part of the story with dialogue bubbles

D) Retelling or paraphrasing

Answer "D" is correct. Retelling and paraphrasing is usually done in oral form whereas the other choices all involve writing or the use of pencil and paper. By asking students to retell a story, the teacher can determine the level of comprehension. Of course, this has to be modeled for the student, especially paraphrasing, so that the student relates the important facts or events and does not include any information that is not necessary.

116) **A very bright child, in a first-grade class, comes from a family which does not a have a strong oral story telling or story reading tradition in its native language. This child would need support in developing:**

A) Letter-sound correspondence skills

B) Schemata for generic concepts most children have in their memories and from experiences   based on family oral traditions and read-alouds

C) Oral expressiveness

D) B and C

Although the question appears to be a very technical one, it actually can be easily and correctly answered by seeing how choice "B" echoes the fact that most children would have schemata based on family oral traditions.

117) **The concerned parent whose child had a visual impairment wanted as much help for him as the teacher and the school district could give. She begged: "Please, he didn't attend preschool. He has no prior knowledge." Strictly speaking, this is:**

A) Correct, since he didn't get preschool experiences

B) Incorrect, since prior knowledge covers everyone's experiences

C) Incorrect, since he did have prior knowledge experiences but these didn't match those of many of his peers, so he would need to enhance his prior knowledge

D) B and C

This is a question that a caring and literate test taker could correctly answer and get "D" as a response. Everyone has prior knowledge of some sort.

118) **Mr. Mark is a brand new teacher who is not from the neighborhood where his school is located. He is a bit nervous as this is his first teaching assignment. He does not yet know how to relax enough to get his students to activate prior experience. He should:**

A) Try a free recall statement: "Tell us what you know about ..."

B) Try an unstructured statement: "Let's talk about ..."

F) Use a word association question: "What do you associate X with ...?"

D) All of the above

Again this is a common sense question and "D" is the correct choice.

119) **Among the literary strategies that teachers can use to activate prior knowledge are:**

A) Predicting and previewing a story

B) Story mapping

C) Venn diagramming

D) Linear arrays

This is a question that a literate test taker could answer and the best choice is "A" because children evidence prior knowledge in their predictions.

120) **Ms. Angel has to be certain that her fourth graders know the characteristics of the historical fiction genre. She can best support them in becoming comfortable with this genre by:**

A) Providing sequel and prequel writing opportunities using that genre

B) Reading them many different works from that genre

C) A and B

D) Having them look up the definition of that genre in a literary encyclopedia

The answer is "C."

121) **"Author's viewpoint" questions stump Gary. His teacher can help him by asking him during their reading conferences:**

A) If Gary feels the book he is reading is just right for him

B) What the author would say about what the character is doing in the story

C) How the story can be changed to another genre

D) If Gary wants to read more books by this author

This is a question where the correct choice "B" is the only one that mentions an author.

122) **Ms. Clark is seen by outside observers from her district, seated in front of her class of sixth graders with a notebook in her lap and an easel. She reads aloud from a book and then writes down a series of questions. As she reads along, she sometimes writes down the answers to her own questions. This is most likely:**

A) A sign that Ms. Clark is uncertain of her own comprehension capacity

B) She is modeling self questioning for the children

C) She is aware that she is being watched and wants to make a good impression

D) All of the above

The only answer here is "B" because this is a technique children are taught and Ms. Clark is modeling it. Choices "A" and "C" are insulting to Ms. Clark.

123) Bill has been called up to the teacher for an individual conference. She asks him to retell one of the books he has listed on his weekly log. He begins and is still talking seven minutes later. Most probably, Bill:

A) Told the entire story with all its details and minor characters

B) May or may not have really gotten the main points and perspectives of the story

C) May have really liked the Story

D) None of the above

The only obvious choice after seven minutes of talk is "A."

124) Ms. Ancess used to take time to have her children memorize major poems and even had an assembly for parents and school staff where the children dramatically recited various poems. Now that she is worried about the children's reading scores, she doesn't want to waste time with this memorization. Actually if she would still include this high-interest, child-centered experience:

A) The children could use their oral fluency and her modeling as a bridge for enhanced comprehension.

B) The children could get a sense of "ownership" of the words.

C) Children and parents would have a "break" from worrying about the test.

D) None of the above.

Choice "A" is the best theory answer here.

125) To help children with "main idea" questions, the teacher should:

A) Give out a strategy sheet on the main idea for children to place in their reader's notebooks

B) Model responding to such a question as part of guided reading

C) Have children create "main idea" questions to go with their writings

D) All of the above.

This is one where all the options are right. The answer is "D."

CONSTRUCTED RESPONSE PROBLEMS

Constructed Response Problem One

Jean is a first-year teacher who is taking over the classroom of a thirty-year veteran teacher who is retiring. Jean goes in to meet with the teacher. The teacher, Ms. Banks, talks about the importance of teaching the young first graders the *concepts of print.*

She gives Jean a list of these concepts and suggests that Jean create some assessment format so that she can be certain that all of her first graders learn these concepts. She also tells Jean that she will be volunteering her time in a neighborhood preschool program close to her home and so she will be taking her private books and materials with her. She suggests that Jean go over the list of *concepts of print* and consider the needs of her class as she prepares for teaching this crucial set of skills. Before Jean leaves the classroom, Ms. Banks tells her that the kindergarten teacher has let her know that three children who will be in her class next year are from ELL backgrounds where their families are not involved in oral story telling or reading from native language texts.

Ms. Banks' list of *concepts of print* includes:

- STARTS ON LEFT

- GOES FROM LEFT TO RIGHT

- RETURN SWEEP

- MATCHES WORDS BY POINTING

- POINTS TO JUST ONE WORD

- POINTS TO FIRST AND LAST WORD

- POINTS TO ONE LETTER

- POINTS TO FIRST AND LAST LETTER

- PARTS of the BOOK: Cover, Title Page, Dedication Page, Author, and Illustrator

Jean thanks Ms. Banks for all of this help and asks if she can send Ms. Banks some of her teaching ideas for *Concepts of Print* and the ways she plans to differentiate instruction for her ELL students before the end of the year. Ms. Banks smiles and says she feels good to know that her classroom will be taken over by Jean. She promises to review Jean's response.

Constructed Response Problem One: Answer

First, as far as assessment for the key skills of *concepts of print,* I have decided that it is very important that I have a record of when and how well each of my students masters these concepts. After much thought, I realized that I will be keeping assessment notebooks for all of my students as part of my general reading and teaching. Therefore, I plan to print out all the key *concepts of print* on an 8" x 11" piece of paper in a grid format. This sheet will be included with other assessment grids for each individual child.

After I conference with the child and determine the child has demonstrated mastery of a particular concept, I will check it off on the grid and date that mastery. If I have other comments to make about the child's level of mastery or fluency, I will make an anecdotal notation about the child as well. I think that this will guarantee that I have a detailed checklist record and anecdotal record of individual progress on *concepts of print* for the children in my class.

I plan to use big books and many of the latest picture books, including Caldecott award winners in demonstrating and sharing with children many of the *concepts of print.* I will do much of my instruction mini-lessons. In fact I intend to use some of my own favorite alphabet books to introduce these conventions. With a book like Clare Beaton's *Zoe and Her Zebra*, I can easily and naturally cover the title page, cover, illustrator, and also manage to engage the children in the use of repetitive language.

Once I have shared that delightful book with the children as a read-aloud, we will be able to return to it again and use the repetitive language in it in its big-book format to demonstrate for the children how they can point under each word as if there is a button to push. I can also demonstrate for the children how they should start at the top of the text and move from left to right. I will model going back to the left and under the previous line in a return sweep.

After modeling this as part of the mini-lesson, the children can be divided in small groups or pairs to take other big books and practice the "point under each word" and the "return sweep" as part of "shared reading" or buddy reading. I should be able to identify some highly proficient readers who will be happy to serve as "buddy" reader/tutors for the ELL children. I will ask that these "buddies" take time in small groups to work on another book from the alphabet book collection to share with the class as a whole. The use of the alphabet books also helps me to get some time in on the alphabetic principle.

I will also do a classroom writing workshop using the original alphabet book I use for the read-aloud, say *Zoe and Her Zebra* as a model for creating our own story. Perhaps we will call it *Barry and His Boxer*. In this way, we will have a concrete literary product that demonstrates the children's mastery of and fluency in the *concepts of print* as they create an "in-the-style-of" story about a peer using illustrations, title page, dedication page, numbering of pages, back and front cover, and other *concepts of print.*

I think that using individualized assessments, a group/class collaborative writing project, and an anchor alphabet book, will help me successfully teach the *concepts of print* and address the needs of my ELL learners as well.

Constructed Response Problem Two

Marianne has been selected as one of a team of teachers who will start teaching in a brand new school building that has been under construction for several years. While Marianne, a grade three teacher, is thrilled to be moving into new facilities, she is a bit overwhelmed to have to "set up her room" all over again at the new site. Her administrator, Mr. Adams, tells her that there are five new teachers, with no previous experience teaching primary school-age children, who will be on staff. He tells her that these educators could really use help setting up their classrooms.

Marianne smiles and decides that she would very much like to use her set-up of her own grade three classroom as a workshop and demonstration for setting up a literacy teaching environment for these new staff members. Mr. Adams thinks that is a great idea and asks Marianne for an agenda and for a general description of what she will cover in her three-hour workshop so that he can give it to the district office.

Marianne is happy to comply because she realizes that she will be assisting new colleagues and getting 10 helping hands to help her set up all the materials she has accumulated over a 20-year career.

Constructed Response Problem Two: Answer

The concept of sharing with new colleagues how to set up a classroom is very exciting to me. I know, based on my experiences, how crucial a well-planned and conceptualized space is for young learners' literacy learning. Therefore, this is an agenda for what I will cover in my three-hour in-service session with my new colleagues.

First, I will discuss how whatever the size of the classroom space, it must be sectioned off into the following areas: a meeting area, with a sofa or "soft" setting; a chair, easel, and basket to store book bags; a conference table; children's tables; a bin/basket main area for trade books; and another space for computers.

I may even give out a diagram of my classroom from my old school and some pictures. We will discuss collaboratively how I will set up my own new space as well as how they will want to set up their own spaces to allow for different uses of space within their own classrooms.

I will get into the issue of whether or not they want to have a traditional desk for each student or use small tables for everyone. I think that they will need time to consider their own teaching styles in this regard. All teachers need to set up a space where they can easily confer with children and have access to individual assessment notebooks; reading folders; and poetry/spelling, reading response, and handwriting notebooks for all their students. I intend to show them how to prepare these folders for each child and how to store them so they can get to them when they need to make additional annotations for each child. Given the fact that I am working with new colleagues, I suspect that this will take at least an hour and a half of our time. I am also going to model for them a weekly reading log.

Most important of all, I am going to spend the major amount of time talking to them about the book bins as I place mine around the classroom. I will show them how to label the books using the Fountas and Pinnell levels and how to arrange the book bins with the spines out so that the children can see the books.

Together we will examine how the bookcases should be close to the walls and the expository books should be separated from the narrative texts. I will also get together my audio-cassettes and book sets so that they can see how I set up my read-along center for all my children. I will share some dual language tapes I use with ELL students as well. I have some extra "author's hats" and author's chair slipcovers I will share with them.

I also intend to show them how to select big books for the easel display and anchor books to be shown there as well. By the way, I will also coach them how to write away for supplies and how to store supplies in common areas so that some children are not missing necessary materials for class activities.

Even though we are focusing on literacy, I am going to show them where to store mathematics materials, other texts, and art supplies. I will end the session by making sure that they know where to place their *chart wall* and the *word wall*. If I have time, I will sit down with each of them and start them on the *word wall* and some key charts for their first day. They will leave my room with an actual experience of setting up a literacy environment, plus viable teaching and reading suggestions for the first day. Most importantly, I will be available for an in-school classroom consultation, if necessary.

Tips and Reflections for Answering the Constructed Response Problems:

- Use as many phrases and words from the problem as possible in your response.

- Be specific. Mention specific books, authors, theorists, and strategies you have studied. Even though this is a test about the teaching of reading, make specific use of children's trade books and literature if appropriate.

- Use as many details as you are given in the problem to make your response. Write no more than five to seven moderately brief paragraphs. The more you write, the larger the margin for error. Check your spelling and grammar. Also, check to see that you answered everything that was asked, but no more than what was asked. Be positive and proactive about your ability to respond to whichever situation is presented.

- Stick with strategies, teaching ideas, and methods that are tried and true.

- Reread your writing at least twice for spelling and grammatical errors.

ADDITIONAL PROFESSIONAL CITATIONS

Block, Cathy Collins. (2002). *Comprehension Instruction: Research-Based Practices.* New York: The Guilford Press.

Calkins, Lucy McCormick. (2000). *The Art of Teaching Reading.* New York: Longman.

Cambourne, Brian. (2002). "Conditions for Literacy Learning." *The Reading Teacher*, 55, (8): 758-62.

Cambourne, Brian. (1993). *The Whole Story: Natural Learning and the Acquisition of Literacy in the Classroom.* Auckland, NZ: Ashton, Scholastic.

Cunningham, Patricia M. (2000). *Phonics They Use: Words for Reading and Writing.* 3rd Edition. New York: Addison-Wesley Longman.

Evidence Based Reading Instruction. (2002) Articles from International Reading Association. Newark, Delaware: *International Reading Association.*

Hoyt, Linda. (2002). *Make it Real: Strategies for Success with Informational Texts.* Portsmouth, NH: Heinemann.

Kimball-Lopez, Kimberley. (1999). *Connecting with Traditional Literature.* Boston: Allyn and Bacon.

Moustafa, Margaret. (1997). *Beyond Traditional Phonics: Research Discoveries and Reading Instruction.* Portsmouth, NH: Heinemann.

Owocki, Gretchen. (2003). *Comprehension: Strategic Instructions for K–3 Students.* Portsmouth, NH: Heinemann.

Owocki, Gretchen and Goodman, Yetta. (2002*). Kidwatching: Documenting Children's Literacy Development.* Portsmouth, NH: Heinemann.

Quindlen, Anna. (1998). *How Reading Changed My Life.* New York: Ballantine Books.

Routman, Regie. (2000). *Conversations: Strategies for Teaching Learning, and Evaluating.* Portsmouth, NH: Heinemann.

Schultz, C. (2000). *How Partner Reading Fosters Literacy Development in First Grade Students.* Action Research project, Saginaw Valley State University, University Center, Michigan.

Short, Kathy G., Harste, Jerome C., and Burke, Carolyn L.. (1996). *Creating Classrooms for Authors and Inquirers.* 2nd Ed. Portsmouth, NH: Heinemann.

Trelease, Jim. (2001). *The Read-Aloud Handbook.* 4th Ed. New York: Penguin.

Wilde, Sandra. (2000). *Miscue Analysis Made Easy: Building on Student Strengths.* Portsmouth, NH: Heinemann.

Wilde, Sandra. (2000). *Reading Made Easy.* Portsmouth, NH: Heinemann.